D0884013

G-3366

HYMNAL
FOR THE HOURS

GIA PUBLICATIONS, INC.
CHICAGO

Copyright © 1989 by G.I.A. Publications, Inc.,
7404 South Mason Avenue, Chicago, Illinois
60638. International copyright secured. All rights
reserved. Printed in the U.S.A.

The English translation of the invitatory psalm and
antiphons from the *Liturgy of the Hours* © 1974,
International Committee on English in the Liturgy,
Inc. (ICEL); English translation of Psalm 95: from
the ICEL Liturgical Psalter Project, © 1987, ICEL.
All rights reserved.

Published with ecclesiastical approval: Archdiocese
of Chicago.

ISBN 0-941050-20-3

1 2 3 4 5 6 7 8 9 10

FOREWORD

This hymnal is intended primarily for communities which throughout the Church Year daily celebrate the Liturgy of the Hours, especially Morning and Evening Prayer. Hymnals for these celebrations compiled since the publication of the revised Divine Office of the Roman Rite (1971) provided for an immediate need and they served well. Repeated use of these resources, however, and a growing sensitivity to ongoing liturgical reform have made many communities aware of the shortcomings of available collections. This awareness is a necessary part of the ongoing process of building a worthy tradition of liturgical music in English. The present collection is, we hope, a significant step in this process.

Several years ago a number of liturgists and musicians from various religious communities began this collaborative effort. The inspiration towards collaboration came at a meeting of the North American Academy of Liturgy where many of us were members of the study group on Liturgy in Religious Communities. Each of us had some experience in collecting hymns for our communities' daily celebration of the Liturgy of the Hours. Some had completed such hymnals and were working on second editions; others were just beginning this work and were dissatisfied with the available resources. By articulating the specific reasons for our dissatisfaction we established the following brief for our work.

1. The reformed Roman Catholic Liturgy of the Hours is based on the Church's centuries-old tradition that the daily Office is a liturgy bound to certain times of the day and night.

> Since the Liturgy of the Hours is the means of sanctifying the day, the order of the prayer has been revised so that the canonical hours could be more easily related to the chronological hours of the day in the circumstances of contemporary life. (Apostolic Constitution, LAUDIS CANTICUM, no.2)

As its title suggests, the Liturgy of the Hours is a Christian celebration in which time itself becomes a symbol of the Paschal Mystery which is at the heart of our life. The rising and setting of the sun, dawn and dusk, the beginning and the closing of the day, the sun's light and the lights we kindle at the onset of darkness — these time-events become sacramental for Christians who celebrate these experiences in word, gesture and symbol. We celebrate Christ's Passover in the daily rhythms of our lives. Thus dusk:Cross/dawn:Resurrection imagery has guided our selection of hymns for the hinge Hours of Morning and Evening Prayer. This imagery is lacking in much of the hymnody assigned for these Hours in hymn collections now serving religious communities which celebrate the daily Office throughout the Church Year. We believe that it is important that the hymns for the celebration of the Hours be selected with care. It is not the case that "any old hymn" will do.

2. Our renewed sense of the Church Year makes us aware of the dearth of hymnody suitable for the daily celebration of the Hours during the liturgical seasons, especially Lent. Symptomatic of the situation is the fact that there are many more suitable hymns for the Solemnity of the Epiphany than for the entire Lenten season. Our retrieved understanding of Lent as the Church's annual retreat in preparation for the Sacraments of Initiation led us to see as generally unsuitable the bulk of Lenten hymnody centering on ascetic practice as the principle means of becoming united in Christ's Paschal Mystery. Much of this particularly penitential hymnody seems to make little reference to the Lenten season.

We do not intend to negate this aspect of our spiritual heritage. We have attempted, however, to select for the Lenten season hymns which make some reference to its baptismal focus.

3. If suitable Office hymnody for the liturgical seasons is sparse, that for the sanctoral celebrations is like a desert. It is our conviction that the Office, like all liturgical prayer, begins and ends as a sacrifice of praise to the God and Father of our Lord Jesus Christ and is not properly addressed to a particular saint.

> In the Liturgy of the Hours the Church exercises the priestly office of its head and offers to God 'unceasingly' a sacrifice of praise, that is, a tribute of lips acknowledging his name. This prayer is the 'voice of the bride herself as she addresses the bridegroom; indeed, it is also the prayer of Christ and his body to the Father.'
> (GENERAL INSTRUCTION ON THE LITURGY OF THE HOURS, no.15)

Devotional prayer, on the other hand, is sometimes addressed directly to one of the saints. The existing sanctoral material seems more often than not to fall into the devotional category. The poetry is often weak and the sentiments expressed are rarely grounded in Scripture and are often alien to the insights of contemporary liturgical theology. To fill this gap we have combed hymnals assembled by various communities but have found that there are few hymns which meet the criterion of being addressed to God for the celebration of the saints. We have commissioned new hymns from one of our members, Ralph Wright, O.S.B. This is a beginning; more work of quality is needed.

4. Virtually all the Churches of the English-speaking world share the often painful blessing of a new sensitivity to the often exclusive language of our liturgical prayers and hymns. We are also aware that the same Churches and/or members within a particular tradition do not yet enjoy unanimity with regard to the principles to be employed in revising these texts or writing new ones. We reflect that lack of agreement. An appendix to this collection includes the hymn text revisions of Ralph Wright, O.S.B. Though taking a different position on this question from other members of our group, Ralph has been willing to revise his texts for this collection. His appendix contains the original versions.

We have tried to be consistent in rejecting any hymn which could not be revised to modify horizontal exclusive language (generic man) or vertical pronominal usage (God as ''he''). If the copyright holders of hymn texts would not allow such revision their texts have been omitted from this collection. Our concern for language also focuses upon the archaic English of many hymns, especially those written or translated in the nineteenth century. In some instances ''old favorites'' were abandoned because we could not arrive at acceptable revisions.

5. Our attention has been centered on music as well as text. We have tried to provide singable hymn tunes while also offering resources to expand a community's musical repertoire. We have provided chant melodies in addition to classical hymn tunes. While chant may quite authentically be sung without accompaniment, the same holds for a number of familiar metrical tunes. Small communities should find this a useful feature. Where possible, we have also included a number of early American hymn tunes. Finally, several new tunes appear here. They have been commissioned for some of the new texts of Ralph Wright, O.S.B. When unfamiliar

music is given for a hymn, we try to provide alternatives for those who might wish to sing a text to a more familiar tune. Thus, wherever a chant tune appears a metrical tune is ordinarily provided immediately after as an option. Whenever an unfamiliar tune is encountered, the metrical index may be consulted to provide an alternative. Thus we expect that almost all of the texts here should be musically accessible to most communities.

We want to thank Peter Finn of ICEL for his constant support, encouragement and advice. This project would never have gone beyond our first few meetings were it not for the openness and cooperation of Robert J. Batastini of GIA. The North American Academy of Liturgy gave us an annual forum for meeting and sharing our work with other liturgists and musicians. We thank our own respective communities for their patience and support.

> If the prayer of the Divine Office becomes genuine personal prayer, the relation between liturgy and the whole Christian life also becomes clearer. The whole life of the faithful, hour by hour during night and day, is a kind of **leitourgia** or public service, in which the faithful give themselves over to the ministry of love toward God and humanity, identifying themselves with the action of Christ, who by his life and self-offering sanctified the life of all.
> (Apostolic Constitution, LAUDIS CANTICUM, no.18)

Andrew D. Ciferni, O.Praem.
Daylesford Abbey
Paoli, Pennsylvania

Jennifer Glen, C.C.V.I.
Sisters of Charity of the Incarnate Word
Houston, Texas

Mary E. McGann, R.S.C.J.
Loyola University
Chicago, Illinois

Kevin D. McGrath, O.S.B.
St. Bernard Abbey
Cullman, Alabama

Laurence Mayer, O.Praem.
St. Norbert Abbey
DePere, Wisconsin

Frank C. Quinn, O.P.
Aquinas Institute of Theology
St. Louis, Missouri

Samuel F. Weber, O.S.B.
St. Meinrad Archabbey
St. Meinrad, Indiana

David F. Wright, O.P.
St. Dominic - St. Thomas Priory
River Forest, Illinois

Ralph Wright, O.S.B.
St. Louis Abbey
St. Louis, Missouri

September 14, 1989
Feast of the Triumph of the Cross

Contents

Ordinary Time

Solemnities of the Lord/Ordinary Time

Proper of Saints

Commons

Office for the Dead

Appendix

Indexes

INVITATORY

Settings by
Howard Hughes, SM

Lord, o - pen my lips.

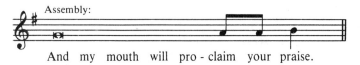

And my mouth will pro - claim your praise.

PSALM 95 AND INVITATORY ANTIPHONS

The proper antiphon is sung before the psalm and again after each strophe.

ICEL, 1970

Come, let us sing to the Lord /
   and shout with joy to the Rock who saves us. /
Let us approach him with praise and thanksgiving /
   and sing joyful songs to the Lord.

The Lord is God, the mighty God,*
   the great king over all the gods. /
He holds in his hands the depths of the earth *
   and the highest mountains as well. /
He made the sea; it belongs to him, /
   the dry land, too, for it was formed by his hands.

Come, then, let us bow down and worship, /
   bending the knee before the Lord, our maker, /
For he is our God and we are his people, /
   the flock he shepherds.

Today, listen to the voice of the Lord: /
   Do not grow stubborn, as your fathers did in the wilderness, /
when at Meriba and Massah*
   they challenged me and provoked me, /
Although they had seen all of my works.

Forty years I endured that generation. /
    I said, "They are a people whose hearts go astray *
and they do not know my ways." /
    So I swore in my anger, /
"They shall not enter into my rest."

Glory to the Father, and to the Son, /
    and to the Holy Spirit: /
as it was in the beginning, /
    is now, and will be for ever. Amen.

Tones for Psalm 95:

Tone (A)

Tone (B)

ICEL, 1987

Come, sing with joy to God, /
  shout to our Savior, our Rock. /
Enter God's presence with praise, /
  enter with shouting and song. /

God the Lord is great,*
  over the gods like a king. /
God cradles the depths of the earth,*
  holds fast the mountain peaks. /
God shaped the ocean and owns it, /
  formed the earth by hand. /

Come, bow down and worship, /
  kneel to the Lord, our maker, /
to our saving God, who shepherds, /
  who guides and tends this flock. /

Listen today to God's voice: /
  "Harden no heart as at Meribah, /
as the day in the desert at Massah. /
  There your forebears tried me,*
though they had seen my work. /

Forty years with that lot. /
  I said: They are perverse,*
They do not accept my ways. /
  So I swore in my anger: /
They shall not enter my rest."

Glory to the Father, and to the Son, /
  and to the Holy Spirit: /
as it was in the beginning, /
  is now, and will be for ever. Amen.

Tones for Psalm 95:

Tone (A)

Tone (B)

PROPER OF SEASONS

1. First Sunday of Advent until December 16:

Come, let us wor-ship the Lord, the King who is to come.

2. From December 17 to 23:

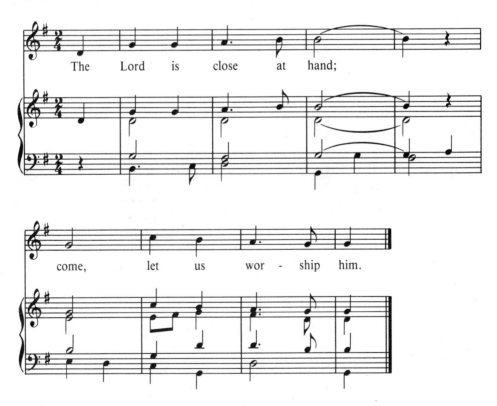

The Lord is close at hand;

come, let us wor - ship him.

3. December 24:

To - day you will know the Lord is com - ing, and in the morn - ing you will see his glo - ry.

4. Sunday and weekday offices during Christmas until the Epiphany:

Christ is born for us; come, let us a - dore him.

5. Holy Family:

Come, let us wor-ship Christ, the Son of God,

who was o - be - dient to Mar - y and Jo - seph.

6. January 1 (Solemnity) - Mary, Mother of God:

Let us cel - e - brate the moth-er-hood of the Vir-gin Mar-y; let us

wor - ship her Son, Christ the Lord.

7. Epiphany until the Feast of the Baptism of the Lord:

Christ has ap - peared to us; come, let us a - dore him.

8. Baptism of the Lord:

Come, let us wor-ship Christ, the be-lov-ed Son in whom the Fa - ther is well pleased.

9. Ash Wednesday to Saturday of the Fifth Week of Lent:

To - day if you hear the voice of the Lord,

hard - en not your hearts.

Or, the antiphon for Holy Week, from Passion Sunday until Thursday:

Come, let us wor - ship Christ the Lord, who for

our sake en - dured temp - ta - tion and suf - fer - ing.

10. Good Friday:

Come, let us wor-ship Christ, the Son of God, who re-

deemed us with his blood.

11. Holy Saturday:

Come, let us wor-ship Christ, who for our sake suf-fered

death and was bur-ied.

17

12. Easter Sunday until Wednesday before Ascension:

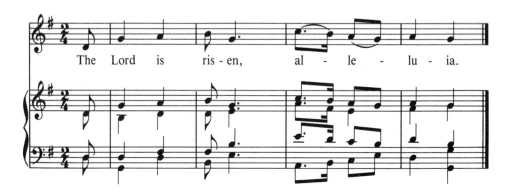

The Lord is ris-en, al - le - lu - ia.

13. Ascension:

Al - le - lu - ia, come, let us wor-ship Christ the Lord as he as-cends in-to heav-en, al - le - lu - ia.

14. From Ascension until Pentecost Sunday:

Come, let us a - dore Christ the Lord who prom-ised to send the Ho-ly Spir-it on his peo - ple, al - le-lu - ia, al - le - lu - ia.

15. Pentecost Sunday:

Al-le-lu - ia, the Spir-it of the Lord has filled the whole world; come let us wor-ship, al - le - lu - ia.

16. Trinity Sunday:

Come, let us wor-ship the true God: One in Trin-i-ty, Trin-i-ty in One.

17. Body and Blood of Christ:

Come, let us a-dore Christ the Lord, the bread of life.

18. Sacred Heart:

Come, let us wor - ship Je-sus, whose heart was wound-ed for love of us.

19. Christ the King:

Come, let us wor -ship Je - sus Christ, the King of kings.

20. Sunday:

Come, let us sing to the Lord, and shout with joy to the Rock who saves us, al - le - lu - ia.

21. Monday:

Let us ap - proach the Lord with praise and thanks - giv - ing.

22. Tuesday:

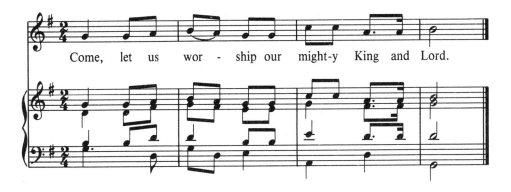

Come, let us wor - ship our might-y King and Lord.

23. Wednesday:

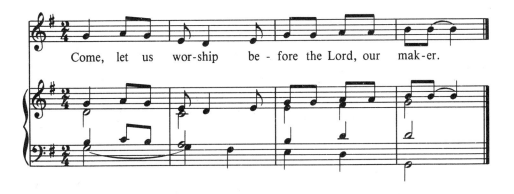

Come, let us wor-ship be - fore the Lord, our mak-er.

24. Thursday:

Come, let us wor-ship the Lord; the Lord is our God.

25. Friday:

Come, let us give thanks to the Lord, for God's great love is with-out end.

26. Saturday:

Come, let us wor - ship God, who brings the world and its

won - ders from dark - ness in - to light.

ORDINARY TIME, WEEKS II AND IV

27. Sunday:

Come, wor-ship the Lord, for we are the peo-ple that God gent-ly shep-herds, al - le - lu - ia.

28. Monday:

Come, let us sing joy-ful songs to the Lord.

29. Tuesday:

Come, let us wor-ship the Lord, our might-y God.

30. Wednesday:

Cry out with joy to the Lord, all the earth; serve the

Lord with glad-ness.

31. Thursday:

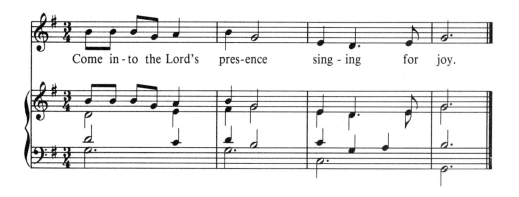

Come in-to the Lord's pres-ence sing-ing for joy.

32. Friday:

Come, let us praise the Lord, in whom is

all our de - light.

33. Saturday:

Let us lis-ten to the voice of the Lord; let us en-ter in - to God's rest.

PROPER OF SAINTS

34. January 25 (Feast) - Conversion of Paul, Apostle:

Come, let us wor - ship God, on the feast of the con- ver-sion of Saint Paul.

35. February 2 (Feast) - Presentation of the Lord:

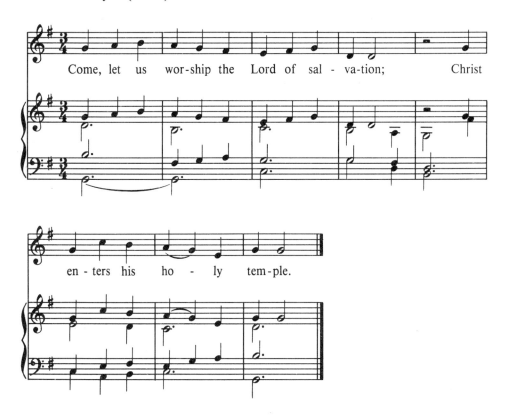

Come, let us wor-ship the Lord of sal - va-tion; Christ en - ters his ho - ly tem-ple.

36. February 22 (Feast) - Chair of Peter, Apostle:
(Common of Apostles #65)

37. March 19 (Solemnity) - Joseph, Husband of Mary:

Let us praise Christ the Lord as we cel - e - brate the feast of Saint Jo - seph (al - le - lu - ia).

38. March 25 (Solemnity) - Annunciation:

The Word was made flesh; come, let us wor - ship him (al - le - lu - ia).

39. April 25 (Feast) - Mark, Evangelist:

Come, let us wor-ship the Lord who speaks to us through the gos-pel (al - le - lu - ia).

40. May 1 (Optional Memorial) - Joseph the Worker:

Come, let us wor-ship Christ the Lord who was hon-ored to be known as the son of a car-pen-ter, al - le - lu - ia.

41. May 31 (Feast) - Visitation:

Let us sing to the Lord as we cel-e-brate the Vis-it - a - tion of the Bless-ed Vir - gin Mar-y (al-le-lu - ia).

42. June 11 (Memorial) - Barnabas, Apostle:

Come, let us a-dore the Ho-ly Spir-it, who has spo-ken to us through the proph-ets and teach-ers of the Church (al-le - lu - ia).

43. June 24 (Solemnity) - Birth of John the Baptist:

Come, let us wor-ship the Lord, the Lamb of God, pro-claimed by John.

44. June 29 (Solemnity) - Peter and Paul, Apostles:
(Common of Apostles #65)

45. August 6 (Feast) - Transfiguration:

Come, let us wor-ship the King of glo-ry, ex - alt - ed on high.

46. August 15 (Solemnity) - Assumption:

Come, let us wor-ship the King of kings; on this day his Vir-gin Moth - er was tak-en up to heav - en.

47. August 22 (Memorial) - Queenship of Mary:

Come, let us wor-ship Christ who crowned his moth-er as Queen of heav'n and earth.

48. August 29 (Memorial) - Beheading of John the Baptist:

Come, let us wor-ship the Lamb of God on the feast of Saint John who went be-fore Christ in life and death.

49. September 8 (Feast) - Birth of Mary:

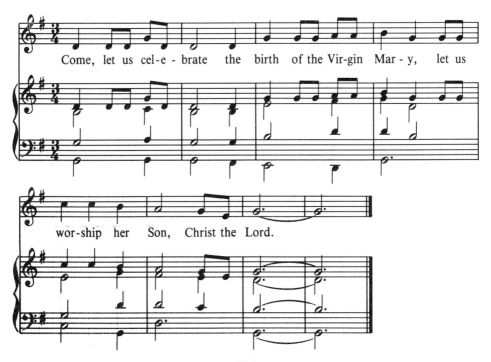

Come, let us cel-e-brate the birth of the Vir-gin Mar-y, let us wor-ship her Son, Christ the Lord.

50. September 14 (Feast) - Triumph of the Cross:

Come, let us wor-ship Christ the King who was lift-ed up on the cross for our sake.

51. September 15 (Memorial) - Our Lady of Sorrows:

Let us a-dore Christ, the Sav-ior of the world, who called his moth-er to share in his pas-sion.

52. September 29 (Feast) - Michael, Gabriel and Raphael, Archangels:

Come, let us wor-ship the Lord in the com-pa-ny

of the an-gels.

53. October 2 (Memorial) - Guardian Angels:

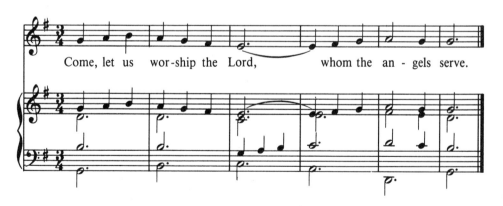

Come, let us wor-ship the Lord, whom the an-gels serve.

54. October 18 (Feast) - Luke, Evangelist:
(Same as Mark #39)

55. November 1 (Solemnity) - All Saints:

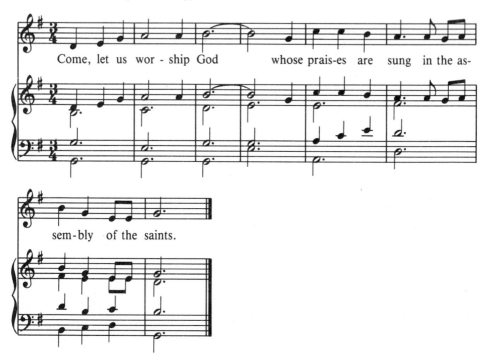

Come, let us wor-ship God whose prais-es are sung in the as-

sem-bly of the saints.

56. November 11 (Memorial) - Martin of Tours, Bishop:

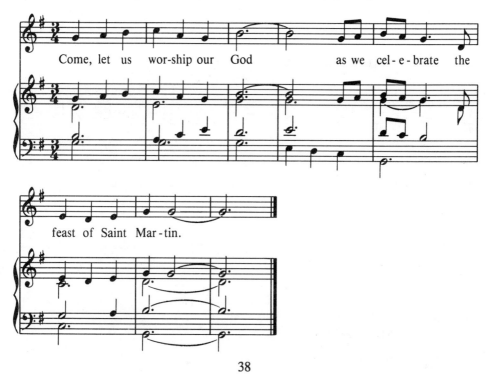

Come, let us wor-ship our God as we cel-e-brate the

feast of Saint Mar-tin.

57. December 8 (Solemnity) - Immaculate Conception:

Come, let us cel-e-brate the Im-mac-u-late Con - cep-tion of the Vir - gin Mar - y; let us wor-ship her Son, Christ the Lord.

58. December 12 (Feast) - Our Lady of Guadalupe:

Come, let us a - dore Christ, the Son of the ev-er Vir-gin Mar - y.

59. December 26 (Feast) - Stephen, Martyr:

Come, let us wor-ship the new - born Christ who has giv-en the glo - ri - ous crown to Saint Ste-phen.

60. December 27 (Feast) - John, Apostle and Evangelist:
(Common of Apostles #65)

61. December 28 (Feast) - Holy Innocents:

Come, let us wor - ship the new-born Christ who crowns with joy these chil - dren who died for him.

COMMONS

62. Dedication of a Church:

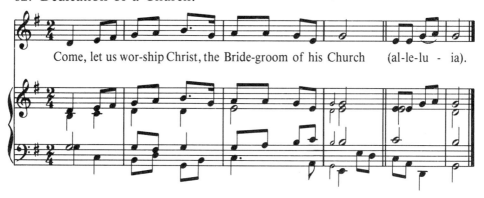

Come, let us wor-ship Christ, the Bride-groom of his Church (al-le-lu - ia).

OR

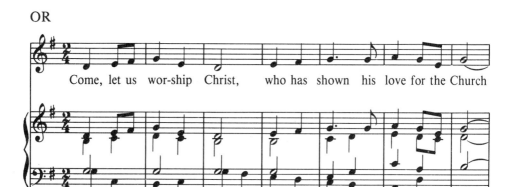

Come, let us wor-ship Christ, who has shown his love for the Church

(al-le-lu - ia).

63. Blessed Virgin Mary:

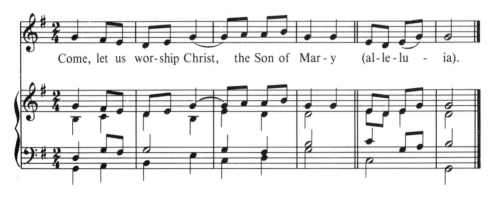

Come, let us wor-ship Christ, the Son of Mar-y (al-le-lu - ia).

OR

Come, let us sing to the Lord as we cel-e-brate this feast of the

Bless-ed Vir-gin Mar-y (al - le - lu - ia).

64. Memorial of the Blessed Virgin Mary on Saturdays of Ordinary Time:

Come, let us wor-ship Christ, the Son of Mar - y.

OR

Let us sing to the Lord as we keep this day in mem-o-ry of the

Bless-ed Vir-gin Mar - y.

65. Apostles:

Come, let us wor-ship the Lord, the King of a-pos-tles (al - le - lu - ia).

66. Several Martyrs or One Martyr:

Come, let us wor-ship Christ, the King of mar-tyrs (al-le-lu - ia).

67. Pastors:

Come, let us wor-ship Christ, chief shep-herd of the flock

(al - le - lu - ia).

68. Doctors:

Come, let us wor-ship the Lord, fount of all

wis-dom (al - le - lu - ia).

69. Virgins:

The ho-ly vir-gins praise their Lord and King; come, let us join in their wor-ship (al-le - lu - ia).

OR

Come, let us wor-ship the Lamb with the vir - gins who fol-lowed him (al - le-lu - ia).

70. Holy Men and/or Holy Women - Religious, those who worked for the underprivileged, teachers:

Come, let us wor-ship God, won-der-ful in the saints (al-le-lu - ia).

OR

Let us sing praise to God, as we ac-claim Saint ..... (al-le-lu - ia).

71. Office for the Dead:

Come, let us wor-ship the Lord; all things live for God.

Come, O Long-Awaited Jesus 1

1. Come, O long-a-wait-ed Je-sus, Free-dom to your
2. Is-rael's strength and con-so-la-tion, Hope to all the
3. Born your peo-ple to de-liv-er, Born a child, and
4. Born that we might all in-her-it Your great love and
5. Wor-ship, hon-or, glo-ry, bless-ing To the Fa-ther

peo-ple bring; From our sins and fears re-lease us
earth im-part; Dear de-sire of ev-'ry na-tion,
yet a king, Born to reign in us for ev-er,
life and light, By your all-suf-fi-cient mer-it
and the Son, With the ev-er-last-ing Spir-it,

That our hearts with joy may sing.
Joy of ev-'ry long-ing heart.
Now your gra-cious king-dom bring.
Raise us to your hon-ored right.
While un-end-ing a-ges run.

Text: Charles Wesley, 1707-1788, *Hymns for the Nativity of the Lord*, 1744, alt.
Tune: STUTTGART, 8 7 8 7; Charles Friedrich Witt, 1660-1716, in Witt's and A.C. Ludwig's *Psalmodia Sacra*, Gotha, 1715; adapt. by Henry John Gauntlett, 1805-1876

2 Come, Thou Long-Expected Jesus

1. Come, thou long-ex-pect-ed Je-sus, Born to set thy peo-ple free;
2. Born thy peo-ple to de-liv-er, Born a child and yet a king,

From our fears and sins re-lease us; Let us find our rest in thee.
Born to reign in us for-ev-er, Now thy gra-cious king-dom bring.

Is-rael's strength and con-so-la-tion, Hope of all the earth thou art,
By thine own e-ter-nal Spir-it Rule in all our hearts a-lone;

Dear de-sire of ev-'ry na-tion, Joy of ev-'ry long-ing heart.
By thine all-suf-fi-cient mer-it Raise us to thy glo-rious throne.

Text: Charles Wesley, 1707-1788, *Hymns for the Nativity of the Lord*, 1744
Tune: JEFFERSON, 8 7 8 7 D; William Walker's *Southern Harmony*, 1855; acc. by Sr. Theophane Hytrek, OSF, 1980, © 1981, ICEL

Comfort, Comfort Now My People   3

1. "Com - fort, com-fort now my peo - ple; Tell of peace," so says our God.
2. For the her-ald's voice is cry - ing In the des - ert far and near,
3. Straight shall be what long was crook - ed, And the rough - er plac - es plain!

Com-fort those who sit in dark - ness Mourn-ing un - der sor-row's load.
Call - ing us to true re - pen - tance, Since the King-dom now is here.
Let your hearts be true and hum - ble, As be - fits his ho - ly reign!

To God's peo - ple now pro-claim That God's par - don waits for them!
Oh, that warn - ing cry o - bey! Now pre - pare for Christ a way!
For the glo - ry of the Lord Now on earth is shed a - broad,

Tell them that their war is o - ver; God will reign in peace for-ev - er!
Let the val - leys rise to meet him, And the hills bow down to greet him!
And all flesh shall see the to - ken That God's word is nev - er bro - ken.

Text: Johann G. Olearius, 1611-1684; tr. by Catherine Winkworth, 1826-1878, alt.
Tune: FREU DICH SEHR, 8 7 8 7 7 7 8 8; Trente quatre psaumes de David, Geneva, 1551.

4 Creator of the Stars of Night

1. Cre - a - tor of the stars of night, Your peo - ple's ev - er - last - ing light, Je - sus, Re - deem - er, save us all, And hear your serv - ants when they call.
2. Now griev - ing that the an - cient curse Should doom to death a un - i - verse, You heal all those who need your grace And come to save our fall - en race.
3. You came when old world drew towards night, Ap - pear - ing not in prince - ly might, But born of Mar - y, moth - er mild, Be - came the vic - tim un - de - filed.
4. At your great name ma - jes - tic now, All knees must bend, all hearts must bow; All things in heav'n and earth a - dore, And own you, King for ev - er - more.
5. Great judge of all in that last day, Be pres - ent then with us we pray; Your scat - tered peo - ple, Lord, u - nite, In vic - t'ry o - ver Sa - tan's might.
6. To God the Fa - ther, God the Son, And God the Spir - it, Three in One, Praise, hon - or, might, and glo - ry be From age to age e - ter - nal - ly.

This hymn may also be sung to the Latin chant CREATOR ALME SIDERUM.

Text: *Creator alme siderum*, anon. 7th c.; tr. by John Mason Neale, 1818-1866, and others, *Hymnal Noted*, 1852, alt.
Tune: NIGHT LIGHT, 8 8 8 8; Henry Bryan Hays, OSB, *Swayed Pines Song Book*, © 1981, Order of St. Benedict, Inc.

O Gracious Maker of the Stars 5

1. O gra-cious mak-er of the stars That curb the dark-ness of the night, To you we raise our hum-ble prayers And trust in your re-deem-ing light.
2. For in your mer-cy grieved to see Our world so torn by sin and death You came on earth to touch our wounds And heal us with your liv-ing breath.
3. The world was drift-ing on its way To dark de-spair and deep-'ning gloom When calm-ly as the Bridge-groom comes, You came from Mar-y's vir-gin womb.
4. Be-fore your might, O gen-tle Lord, May ev-'ry crea-ture bend the knee And may the si-lent plan-ets praise The God who comes to set us free.
5. This eve-ning keep us, ho-ly Lord, With-in your pres-ence all the while That in your king-dom we may live For-ev-er safe from Sa-tan's guile.
6. May pow'r and praise and glo-ry be To God the Fa-ther and the Son Who came on earth that we might be With-in the Spir-it ev-er one. A-men.

This hymn may also be sung to NIGHT LIGHT.

Text: *Creator alme siderum*, anon. 7th C.; tr. by Ralph Wright, OSB, b.1938, © 1989, GIA Publications, Inc.
Tune: CREATOR ALME SIDERUM, 8 8 8 8; Plainsong, Mode IV; acc. by Theodore Mairer, 1980, © 1981, ICEL.

6 O Son of God, O Sovereign Word

1. O Son of God, O sov-'reign Word, What hu-man thought may span
2. Bring light in-to our hearts and touch With fire our lan-guid minds;
3. That when as judge you come to pay The wag-es of de-sire,
4. We may not then in pride join those Who spurn your gra-cious word,
5. We sing of glo-ry, might, and praise To Fa-ther and to Son,

The mys-ter-y of how in time You came as Son of Man.
The her-ald bids us loose with love What-ev-er sin still binds,
To give your King-dom to the just And to the wick-ed fire,
But with the blest e-ter-nal-ly May sing your prais-es, Lord.
Who with the Spir-it live and reign In joy for ev-er one.

Text: Ralph Wright, OSB, b.1938, © 1989, GIA Publications, Inc.
Tune: LONDON NEW, CM; *The Psalms of David in Prose and Meter*, 1635, alt.

Rejoice, Rejoice, Believers 7

1. Re-joice, re-joice, be-liev - ers, And let your lights ap-pear;
2. The watch-ers on the moun - tain Pro-claim the bride-groom near;
3. The saints, who here in pa - tience Their cross and suf-f'rings bore,
4. Our hope and ex-pec-ta - tion, O Je - sus, now ap-pear;

The eve-ning is ad-vanc - ing, And dark-er night is near.
Go forth as he ap-proach - es With al-le-lu - ias clear.
Shall live and reign for-ev - er When sor-row is no more.
A-rise, O Sun, and ban - ish The dark-ness of our fear!

The bride-groom is now ris - ing And soon he will draw nigh.
The mar-riage feast is wait - ing; The gates wide o-pen stand.
A-round the throne of glo - ry The Lamb they shall be-hold;
With hearts and hands up-lift - ed, We plead, O Lord, to see

Up, watch in ex-pec-ta - tion! At mid-night come the cry.
A-rise, O heirs of glo - ry; The bride-groom is at hand.
In tri-umph cast be-fore him Their di-a-dems of gold.
The day of earth's re-demp - tion That sets your peo-ple free!

Text: Laurentius Laurentii, 1660-1722; tr. by Sarah B. Findlater, 1823-1907,alt.
Tune: HAF TRONES LAMPA FÄRDIG, 7 6 7 6 D; Swedish Folk Tune; harm. *Lutheran Book of Worship*, © 1978

8 Awake, Awake: Fling Off the Night!

1. A - wake, a - wake: fling off the night! For God has
2. Let in the light; all sin ex - pose To Christ, whose
3. A - wake, and rise up from the dead, And Christ his
4. Then sing for joy, and use each day; Give thanks for

sent us glo - rious light; And we who live in
life no dark - ness knows. Be - fore his cross for
light on you will shed. Its power will wrong de -
ev - 'ry - thing al - ways. Lift up your hearts; with

Christ's new day Must works of dark - ness put a - way.
guid - ance kneel; His light will judge and, judg - ing, heal.
sires de - stroy, And your whole na - ture fill with joy.
one ac - cord Praise God through Je - sus Christ our Lord.

Text: Based on Ephesians 5:6-20, John Raphael Peacey, 1896-1971, © Mrs. M.E. Peacey
Tune: DEUS TUORUM MILITUM (GRENOBLE), LM; *Grenoble Antiphoner*, 1753; harm. *BBC Hymnbook*, © Oxford University Press

Come, Lord, and Tarry Not   9

1. Come, Lord, and tar - ry not!
2. Come, for your saints still wait;
3. Come, for cre - a - tion longs,
4. Come, and make all things new,
5. Come, and be - gin your reign,

Bring the long looked - for day!
Dai - ly as - cends their sigh;
Im - pa - tient of de - lay,
Come, save this long - ing earth;
Of ev - er - last - ing peace;

Oh, why these years of wait - ing here,
The Spir - it and the Bride say "Come!"
And yearns for end - less years of good,
Trans - form all crea - tures in your love,
Come, take the king - dom to your - self,

These ag - es of de - lay?
Do you not hear the cry?
Bright ag - es of your stay.
Cre - a - tion's sec - ond birth.
Great King of right - eous - ness!

Text: Attr. to Horatius Bonar, 1808-1889, *Kelso Tracts*, 1846, alt.
Tune: ST. BRIDE (ST. BRIDGET), SM; Samuel Howard, 1710-1782, William Riley's *Parochial Harmony*, 1762; harm. by Richard Proulx, b. 1937, © 1975, GIA
    Publications, Inc.

10 Hark! A Herald Voice Is Calling

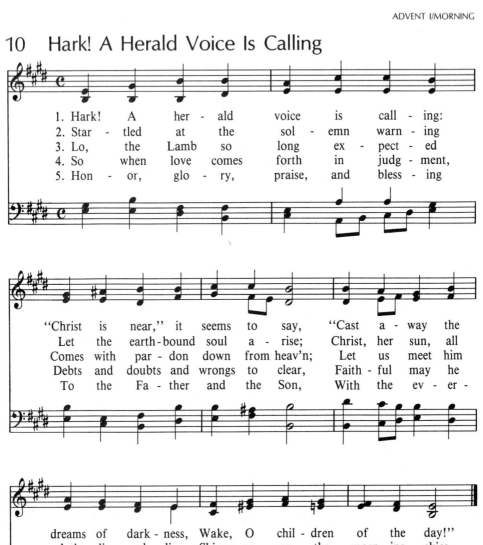

1. Hark! A her - ald voice is call - ing:
2. Star - tled at the sol - emn warn - ing
3. Lo, the Lamb so long ex - pect - ed
4. So when love comes forth in judg - ment,
5. Hon - or, glo - ry, praise, and bless - ing

"Christ is near," it seems to say, "Cast a - way the
Let the earth-bound soul a - rise; Christ, her sun, all
Comes with par - don down from heav'n; Let us meet him
Debts and doubts and wrongs to clear, Faith - ful may he
To the Fa - ther and the Son, With the ev - er -

dreams of dark - ness, Wake, O chil - dren of the day!"
sloth dis - pel - ling, Shines up - on the morn - ing skies.
with re - pen - tance, Pray that we may be for - giv'n.
find his ser - vants Watch - ing till the dawn ap - pear.
last - ing Spir - it, While e - ter - nal ag - es run.

Text: *Vox clara ecce intonat*, anon., Latin, 10th C.; tr. by Edward Caswall, 1814-1878, and others, *Lyra Catholica*, 1849, alt.
Tune: MERTON, 8 7 8 7; William Henry Monk, 1823-1889, *Parish Choir*, 1850.

Hills of the North, Rejoice 11

1. Hills of the north, re - joice, Ri - ver and moun- tain spring, Hear now the ad - vent voice, Val - ley and low - land sing: Though ab - sent long, your Lord is near, And soon in tri - umph will ap - pear.

2. Isles of the south - ern sea, Deep in your co - ral caves, Stilled be each war - ring breeze, Lulled by your rest - less waves: He comes to reign with bound- less sway, And waste-lands make his great high - way.

3. Lands of the east, a - wake, Soon you shall be set free; Sleep of the a - ges break, Ris - ing in li - ber - ty: On your far hills, long cold and grey, Has dawned the e - ver - last - ing day.

4. Shores of the far - most west, You that have wait - ed long, You that have been so blest, Break out in surg - ing song: Raise high the note that Je - sus died, Yet lives and reigns, the Cru - ci - fied.

5. Shout while you jour - ney home, Songs be in ev - ery mouth; See, from the north we come, From east and west and south: The Lord our God has set us free, We come to live e - ter - nal - ly.

Text: Charles E. Oakley, 1832-1865; adapt. by A.G. Petti, alt. © 1971, Faber Music Ltd.
Tune: DARWALL'S 148th, 6 6 6 6 8 8; John Darwall, 1731-1789, Aaron Williams' New *Universal Psalmodist*, 1770

12 O Day of God, Draw Nigh

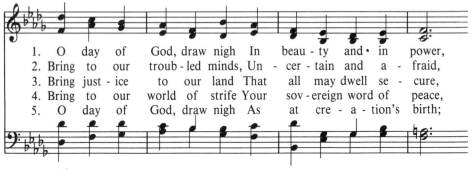

1. O day of God, draw nigh In beau-ty and in power,
2. Bring to our troub-led minds, Un - cer - tain and a - fraid,
3. Bring just - ice to our land That all may dwell se - cure,
4. Bring to our world of strife Your sov - ereign word of peace,
5. O day of God, draw nigh As at cre - a - tion's birth;

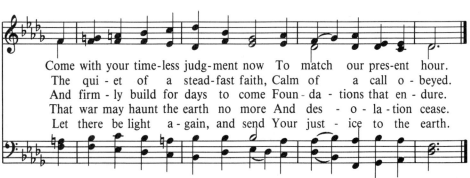

Come with your time-less judg-ment now To match our pres-ent hour.
The qui - et of a stead-fast faith, Calm of a call o - beyed.
And firm - ly build for days to come Foun - da - tions that en - dure.
That war may haunt the earth no more And des - o - la-tion cease.
Let there be light a - gain, and send Your just - ice to the earth.

Text: Robert Balgarnie Young Scott, b.1899, alt, © Emmanuel College, University of Toronto
Tune: BELLWOODS, SM; James Hopkirk, 1908-1972

O Savior, Rend the Heavens Wide   13

1. O Sav - ior, rend   the heav - ens   wide;   Come down, come
2. O Morn - ing Star, O   ra - diant Sun,   When will our
3. Sin's dread - ful doom up - on us   lies;   Grim death looms
4. There shall we all   our prais - es bring Ev - er to

down   with might - y   stride;   Un - lock the gates,   the doors break
hearts be - hold your   dawn?   O Sun, a - rise;   with - out   your
fierce be - fore our   eyes.   Oh, come, lead us   with might - y
you,   our Sav - ior   King;   There shall we laud   you and   a -

down;   Un - bar   the   way   to   heav - en's   crown.
light   We grope in   gloom   and   dark of   night.
hand   From ex - ile   to   our   prom - ised   land.
dore   For ev - er   and   for   ev - er   more.

Text: German Spiritual Song, Köln, 1623; tr. by Martin L. Seltz, 1909-1967, alt.
Tune: O HEILAND, REISS DIE HIMMEL AUF, LM; *Gesangbuch,* Augsburg, 1666
© 1969, Concordia Publishing House

14 On Jordan's Bank the Baptist's Cry

1. On Jor - dan's bank the Bap - tist's cry An -
2. Then cleansed be ev - 'ry heart from sin; Make
3. We hail you as our sav - ior, Lord, Our
4. To heal the sick stretch out your hand, And
5. To God the Son all glo - ry be Whose

nounc - es that the Lord is nigh; A - wake and heark - en
straight the way for God with - in, And let each heart pre -
ref - uge, and our great re - ward: With - out your grace we
bid the fall - en sin - ner stand; Shine forth, and let your
ad - vent set your peo - ple free; Whom with the Fa - ther

for he brings Glad tid - ings of the King of kings.
pare a home Where such a might - y guest may come.
waste a - way, Like flow'rs that with - er and de - cay.
light re - store Earth's own true love - li - ness once more.
we a - dore And Ho - ly Spir - it ev - er - more.

Text: *Jordanis oras, praevia*, Charles Coffin, 1675-1749, *Paris Breviary*, 1736, and *Hymni Sacri*, 1736; tr. by John Chandler, 1806-1875, *Hymns of the Primitive Church*, 1837, alt.
Tune: WINCHESTER NEW, LM; melody adapt. by William Henry Havergal, 1793-1870, from a chorale in *Musikalisches Hand-Buch*, Hamburg, 1690

The King Shall Come When Morning Dawns   15

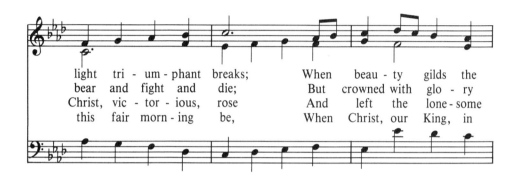

1. The King shall come when morn - ing dawns And
2. Not as of old a lit - tle child, To
3. O bright - er than the ris - ing morn, When
4. O bright - er than that glo - rious morn Shall

light tri - um - phant breaks; When beau - ty gilds the
bear and fight and die; But crowned with glo - ry
Christ, vic - tor - ious, rose And left the lone - some
this fair morn - ing be, When Christ, our King, in

east - ern hills And life to joy a - wakes.
like the sun That lights the morn - ing sky.
place of death, De - spite the rage of foes.
beau - ty comes And we his face shall see.

5. The King shall come when morning dawns
   And earth's dark night is past;
   O haste the rising of that morn,
   For ever it shall last.

6. The King shall come when morning dawns
   And light and beauty brings;
   Hail! Christ the Lord; your people pray
   Come quickly, King of kings.

Text: From a Greek text, tr. by John Brownlie, 1859-1925, *Hymns of the Russian Church,* alt.
Tune: MORNING SONG (CONSOLATION), CM; A. Davisson, *Kentucky Harmony,* 1816, harm. by Richard Proulx, © 1975, GIA Publications, Inc.

16 Throughout a World in Shadow

1. Through-out a world in shad - ow, John's ur - gent
2. He gives a new be - gin - ning To those who
3. His veiled but cer - tain splen - dor Be - gins to
4. With all who wait with long - ing, Give thanks that

voice we hear; Pre - pare for Christ your Sav - ior!
turn from sin, Who an - swer love with lov - ing
shine from far; He comes, his saints a - round him:
nev - er cease, For him whom God is send - ing

The Son of God is near.
By turn - ing back to him.
The bright and morn - ing star.
To vis - it us in peace.

Text: *The Stanbrook Abbey Hymnal*, rev. ed., 1974, © Stanbrook Abbey Music
Tune: SPLENDOR PATERNAE GLORIAE IV, 7 6 7 6; Mode IV alt., acc. by Frank Quinn, OP, b.1932, © 1989, GIA Publications, Inc.

SECOND TUNE - 16

1. Through-out a world in shad - ow, John's ur - gent
2. He gives a new be - gin - ning To those who
3. His veiled but cer - tain splen - dor Be - gins to
4. With all who wait with long - ing, Give thanks that

voice we hear; Pre - pare for Christ your Sav - ior!
turn from sin, Who an - swer love with lov - ing
shine from far; He comes, his saints a - round him:
nev - er cease, For him whom God is send - ing

The Son of God is near.
By turn - ing back to him.
The bright and morn - ing star.
To vis - it us in peace. A - men.

Text : *The Stanbrook Abbey Hymnal*, rev. ed., 1974, © Stanbrook Abbey Music
Tune : HEAVENLY LIGHT, 7 6 7 6; Mode IV; Columba Kelly, OSB, b.1930; acc. by Samuel Weber, OSB, b.1947; © 1987, Saint Meinrad Archabbey

17 Comfort My People and Quiet Her Fear

1. Com - fort my peo - ple and qui - et her fear;
2. Say to the cit - ies of Ju - dah: "Be - hold!
3. Moun - tains and hills shall be - come like a plain.

Tell her the time of sal - va - tion draws near.
Gen - tle, yet might - y, the arm of the Lord
Van - ished are mourn - ing and hun - ger and pain:

Tell her I come to re - move all her shame;
Res - cues the cap - tives of dark - ness and sin,
Nev - er a - gain shall these war a - gainst you;

"She that is pit - ied" shall be her new name.
Bring - ing them jus - tice and joy with - out end."
"See, he comes quick - ly to make all things new!"

Text: Based on Isaiah 40; St. Joseph's Abbey, 1967, alt., ©
Tune: CONSOLAMINI, 10 10 10 10; F.V. Stahan, 1972; harm. by Jerry R. Brubaker; © Catholic Liturgy Book

Hark, the Glad Sound! 18

1. Hark, the glad sound! The Sav - ior comes, The Sav - ior
2. He comes to set the pris - 'ners free In Sa - tan's
3. He comes the bro - ken heart to bind, The bleed - ing
4. Our glad ho - san - nas, Prince of peace, Your wel - come

prom - ised long; Let ev - 'ry heart pre -
bond - age held; The gates of brass be -
soul to cure; And with the trea - sures
shall pro - claim, And heav'n's ex - alt - ed

pare a throne And ev - 'ry voice a song.
fore him burst, The i - ron fet - ters yield.
of his grace En - rich - es all the poor.
arch - es ring With your be - lov - ed name.

Text : Philip Doddridge, 1705-1751, in his and Job Orton's *Hymns*, 1755, alt.
Tune : CHESTERFIELD, CM; Thomas Haweis, 1734-1820

19 Lift Up Your Heads, You Mighty Gates

1. Lift up your heads, you might - y gates; Be -
2. O blest the land, the cit - y blest, Where
3. Fling wide the por - tals of your heart; Make
4. So come, my Sov - 'reign, en - ter in! Let

hold the King of glo - ry waits! The
Christ the rul - er is con - fessed! O
it a tem - ple set a - part; Loud
new and no - bler life be - gin; Your

King of kings is draw - ing near; The
hap - py hearts and hap - py homes To
al - le - lu - ias now em - ploy, Sing
Ho - ly Spir - it guide us on Un -

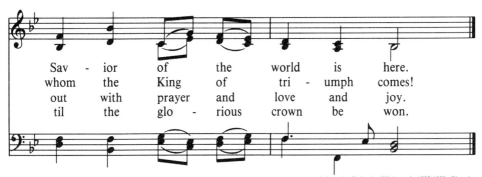

Sav - ior of the world is here.
whom the King of tri - umph comes!
out with prayer and love and joy.
til the glo - rious crown be won.

Text : Based on Ps. 24(23); 7-10; *Macht hoch die thur,* Georg Weissel, 1590-1635, *Preussiche Fest-Lieder,* 1642; tr. by Catherine Winkworth, 1827-1870, *Chorale-Book for England,* 1863, alt.
Tune : TRURO, LM; Thomas William's *Psalmodia Evangelica,* Part II, 1789

20 My Burden Is Light

1. Come to us, Fa - ther, with gifts of new vi - sion,
2. Come, Ho - ly Spir - it, with - in the day's te - dium,
3. Bring to your broth - ers and sis - ters, O Je - sus, Your

Come at the end of each night; Bring to your chil-dren who
Touch what is drab with de - light; Help us to toil till the
gen - tle - ness, wis-dom and might, Help us to shoul-der your

wait in the dark - ness The vi - sion, the bur-den of light. The
cool of the eve - ning And car - ry the bur-den of light, Of
yoke in the dark-ness, Come, for your bur-den is light.

bur - den of see - ing that all have been giv - en The
be - ing new hope for our broth - ers and sis - ters, Pro -
Be with us al - ways, O Lord, in your mer - cy And

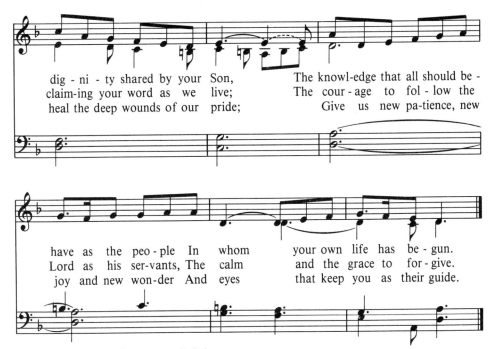

dig - ni - ty shared by your Son,
claim-ing your word as we live;
heal the deep wounds of our pride;

The knowl-edge that all should be -
The cour - age to fol - low the
Give us new pa-tience, new

have as the peo - ple In whom
Lord as his ser-vants, The calm
joy and new won-der And eyes

your own life has be - gun.
and the grace to for - give.
that keep you as their guide.

Text: Ralph Wright, OSB, b. 1938. © 1978, Daughters of St. Paul
Tune: LIGHT BURDEN, 11 7 11 8 12 8 12 8; Margaret Daly
© 1989, GIA Publications, Inc.

21 O Quickly, Come, Great Judge of All

1. O quick-ly, come, great Judge of all; For glo-rious will your
2. O quick-ly, come, true life of all; Death's might-y pow'rs do
3. O quick-ly, come, O come and save! Reign all a-round us

com - ing be All sha-dows from the truth will fall,
still a - bound; In ev-'ry place sin's shad - ows fall,
and with - in. Let sin no more our souls en - slave,

O come and heal that we may see! O quick-ly, come! for
On ev-'ry heart sin's mark is found: O quick-ly, come! for
Let pain and sor - row die with sin: O quick-ly, come! for

doubt and fear Dis-solve like cloud when you are near.
grief and pain Shall nev - er cloud your mar-vel-ous reign.
you a - lone Can make your scat - tered peo - ple one.

Text : Lawrence Tuttiette, 1825-1897, *Hymns for Churchmen*, 1854, alt.
Tune : DAS NEUGEBORNE KINDELEIN (JENA), 8 8 8 8 8 8; Melchior Vulpius, c.1560-1616, harmony from J.S. Bach, 1685-1750

Prepare the Way, O Zion 22

1. Pre - pare the way, O Zi - on, Your Christ is draw-ing near!
2. He brings God's rule, O Zi - on; He comes from heav'n a - bove.
3. Fling wide your gates, O Zi - on; Your Sav - ior's rule em - brace.

Let ev - 'ry hill and val - ley A lev - el way ap - pear.
His rule is peace and free - dom, And just - ice, truth, and love.
His tid - ings of sal - va - tion Pro-claim in ev - 'ry place.

Greet One who comes in glo - ry, Fore-told in sa - cred sto - ry.
Lift high your praise re - sound - ing, For grace and joy a - bound - ing
All lands will bow be - fore him, Their voic - es will a - dore him.

Oh, blest is Christ that came In God's most ho - ly name.
Oh, blest is Christ that came In God's most ho - ly name.
Oh, blest is Christ that came In God's most ho - ly name.

Text : Frans Mikael Franzen, 1772-1847; tr. composite; adapt. by Charles P. Price, b.1920, © 1982
Tune : BEREDEN VÄG FÖR HERRAN, 7 6 7 6 7 7 with refrain; melody from *Then Swenska Psalmboken*, 1697 ; harm. *Koralbok for Svenska Kyrkan*, 1939, alt.

23 The Bridegroom Will Be Coming

1. The Bride-groom will be com - ing in the mid - dle of the night
2. Be - ware, my soul, be watch - ful, lest slum-ber bring you down
3. That day, the day of fear, will come; my soul per - sist in toil,
4. Be - ware, my soul; be-ware, be-ware, lest deep in sleep you lie

And hap - py will those vir - gins be whose lamps are burn-ing bright.
And in the sleep of death you fall, to lose the gold - en crown.
So light your lamp, and feed it well, and make it bright with oil;
And like the Five, re - main out - side, and knock and vain - ly cry;

But woe to those dull serv-ants, whom the Mas - ter will sur - prise
But stay a - wake, be so - ber, with a watch-ful eye and thus
For no one knows how soon may sound the cry at ev - en - tide
But watch and keep your lamp un-dimmed and so with Christ put on

With lamps un-trimmed, un - burn-ing, and with slum-ber in their eyes.
Cry "Ho - ly, ho - ly, ho - ly God, have mer - cy up - on us."
"Be - hold the Bride-groom comes! A-rise! Go out to meet the bride."
The glo-rious wed - ding robe of light, the glo - ry of the Son.

Text: *Idou ho nymphios erchetai*, from the *Horologion* of the Eastern Church; tr. by Gerard Moultrie, "Behold the Bridegroom Cometh," *Lyra Messianica*, 1864,
and *Hymns and Lyrics*, 1867; extensively revised by Ralph Wright, OSB, b.1938, © 1989, GIA Publications, Inc.
Tune: SECOND MODE MELODY, CMD; Thomas Tallis, c.1515-1585

The Voice of God
Goes Out through All the World   24

1. The voice of God goes out through all the world: God's glo-ry speaks a-
2. The Lord has said: "Re-ceive my mes-sen-ger, My prom-ise to the
3. The bro-ken reed he will not tram-ple down, Nor set his heel up-
4. A-noint-ed with the Spir-it and with power, He comes to crown with
5. His touch will bless the eyes that dark-ness held, The lame shall run, the

cross the u-ni-verse. The great King's her-ald cries from star to
world, my pledge made flesh, A lamp to ev-'ry na-tion, light from
on the dy-ing flame, He binds the wounds, and health is in his
com-fort all the weak, To show the face of jus-tice to the
halt-ing tongue shall sing, And pris-'ners laugh in light and lib-er-

star: With pow'r, with jus-tice, he will walk his way.
light: With pow'r, with jus-tice, he will walk his way."
hand: With pow'r, with jus-tice, he will walk his way.
poor: With pow'r, with jus-tice, he will walk his way.
ty: With pow'r, with jus-tice, he will walk his way.

Text: Luke Connaughton, 1919-1979, © 1970, McCrimmon Publishing Co. Ltd.
Tune: TOULON, 10 10 10 10; *Genevan Psalter*, 1551; harm. by Louis Bourgeois, c.1510-1561

25 "Sleepers, Wake!" A Voice Astounds Us

1. "Sleep-ers, wake!" A voice a - stounds us, The
2. Zi - on hears the watch - man sing - ing; Her
3. Lamb of God, the heav'ns a - dore you; Let

shout of ram - part - guards sur - rounds us: "A -
heart with joy - ful hope is spring - ing, She
saints and an - gels sing be - fore you, As

wake, Je - ru - sa - lem, a - rise!" Mid - night's peace their
wakes and hur - ries through the night. Forth he comes, her
harps and cym - bals swell the sound. Twelve great pearls, the

cry has bro - ken, Their ur - gent sum-mons clear - ly spo -
Bride-groom glo - rious In strength of grace, in truth vic - to -
cit - y's por - tals: Through them we stream to join the im-mor -

ken: "The time has come, O maid - ens wise!
rious: Her star is ris'n, her light grows bright.
tals As we with joy your throne sur - round.

Rise up, and give us light; The Bride - groom is in
Now come, most wor - thy Lord, God's Son, In - car - nate
No eye has known the sight, No ear heard such de -

sight. Al - le - lu - ia! Your lamps pre - pare and
Word, Al - le - lu - ia! We fol - low all and
light: Al - le - lu - ia! There - fore we sing to

has - ten there, That you the wed - ding feast may share."
heed your call To come in - to the ban - quet hall.
greet our King; For ev - er let our prais - es ring.

Text: Matthew 25:1-13; *Wachet auf, ruft uns die Stimme*, Philipp Nicolai, 1556-1608; tr. by Carl P. Daw, Jr., b.1944, © 1982
Tune: WACHET AUF, 89 8 89 8 66 4 44 8; Hans Sachs, 1494-1576; adapt. by Philipp Nicolai, 1556-1608; arr. and harm. by Johann Sebastian Bach, 1685-1750

26 O Come, Divine Messiah

1. O come, Di - vine Mes - si - ah; The
world in si - lence waits the day When hope shall sing its
tri - umph And sad - ness flee a - way.

2. O Christ, whom na - tions sigh for, Whom
priest and proph - et long fore-told, Come break the cap - tives'
fet - ters, Re - deem the long lost fold.

3. You come in peace and meek - ness And
low - ly will your cra - dle be; All clothed in hu - man
weak - ness Shall we your God - head see.

Dear Sav-ior, haste! Come, come to earth. Dis-pel the night and show your face, And bid us hail the dawn of grace. O come, Di-vine, Mes-si - ah; The world in si - lence waits the day When hope shall sing its tri - umph And sad - ness flee a - way.

Text : *Venez, Divin Messie*, Abbe Pellegrin, 1663-1745, *Noels Nouveau*, 1708; tr. by Sister Mary of St. Phillip, *Sunday School Hymn Book*, 1887, alt.
Tune : VENEZ, DIVIN MESSIE, Irregular, with refrain; 16th Century Noel, c.1544; arr. by Arthur Hutchings, 1980, © 1981, ICEL

27 Praise We the Lord This Day

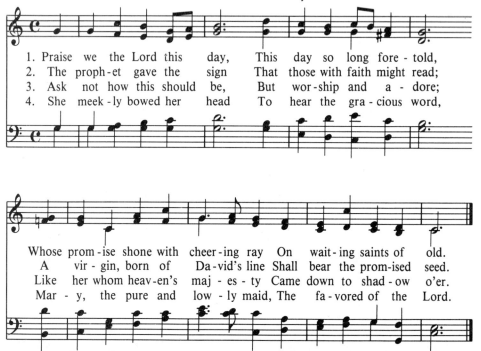

1. Praise we the Lord this day, This day so long fore-told,
Whose prom-ise shone with cheer-ing ray On wait-ing saints of old.

2. The proph-et gave the sign That those with faith might read;
A vir-gin, born of Da-vid's line Shall bear the prom-ised seed.

3. Ask not how this should be, But wor-ship and a-dore;
Like her whom heav-en's maj-es-ty Came down to shad-ow o'er.

4. She meek-ly bowed her head To hear the gra-cious word,
Mar-y, the pure and low-ly maid, The fa-vored of the Lord.

5. Blessed shall be her name
In all the Church on earth,
Through whom that wondrous mercy came,
The incarnate Savior's birth.

6. Jesus, the virgin's son,
We praise you and adore,
Who are with God the Father one
And Spirit evermore.

Text : Anonymous, *Hymns for the Festivals and Saints' Days of the Church of England*, 1846, alt.
Tune : SANDYS, SM; Trad. English Carol; William Sandys' *Christmas Carols, Ancient and Modern*, London, 1833; harm. by John Ainslie, ©

Watchman, Tell Us of the Night   28

1. Watch-man, tell us of the night, What its signs of prom-ise are.
2. Watch-man, tell us of the night; High-er yet that star as-cends.
3. Watch-man, tell us of the night, For the morn-ing seems to dawn.

Trav-'ler, o'er yon moun-tain's height, See that glo - ry - beam-ing star.
Trav-'ler, bless-ed - ness and light, Peace and truth its course por-tends.
Trav-'ler, dark-ness takes its flight, Doubt and ter - ror are with-drawn.

Watch-man, does its beau-teous ray Aught of joy or hope fore-tell?
Watch-man, will its beams a - lone Gild the spot that gave them birth?
Watch-man, let thy wan-d'rings cease; Hie thee to thy qui - et home.

Trav-'ler, yes; it brings the day, Prom-ised day of Is - ra - el.
Trav-'ler, a - ges are its own; See, it bursts o'er all the earth.
Trav-'ler, lo! the Prince of Peace, Lo! the Son of God is come!

Text : John Bowring, 1792-1827, *Hymns,* 1825
Tune : ABERYSTWYTH, 7 7 7 7 D; Joseph Parry, 1841-1903

29 Behold a Virgin Bearing Him

1. Be - hold a vir - gin bear - ing him Who comes to save us from our sin; The proph-ets cry; pre-pare his way! Make straight his path to Christ-mas Day.

2. Be - hold our hope and life and light, The prom-ise of the ho - ly night; We lift our prayer and bend our knee To his great love and maj - es - ty.

Text: Michael Gannon, b.1927, © 1955, World Library Publications, Inc.
Tune: O HEILAND, REISS DIE HIMMEL AUF, LM; *Gesangbuch*, Augsburg, 1666, harm. © 1969, Concordia Publishing House

O Child of Promise, Come! 30

1. O Child of prom-ise, come! O come, Em-man-u - el!
2. The Lord's true Ser - vant, come, In whom is his de - light,
3. O come, a - noint-ed One, To show blind eyes your face!
4. O Man of sor - rows, come, De-spised and cast a - side!

Come, prince of peace, to Da-vid's throne; Come, God, with us to dwell!
On Whom his ho - ly Spri-it rests, The Gen-tiles' prom-ised light!
Good ti - dings to the poor an-nounce; Pro-claim God's year of grace!
O bear our griefs, and by your wounds Re - deem us from our pride!

5. O come, God's holy Lamb;
   To death be meekly led!
   O save the many by your Blood,
   For sin so gladly shed!

6. O come, Messiah King,
   To reign in endless light,
   When heav'nly peace at last goes forth
   From Sion's holy height!

Text: James Quinn, SJ, b.1919, *New Hymns for All Seasons*, © 1969
Tune: CAMBRIDGE, 6 6 8 6; Ralph Harrison, 1748-1810

31 Redeemer of the Nations

1. Re - deem - er of the na - tions Make known your won-drous birth
2. The root of Jes - se blos - somed, Her spot - less womb con - ceived,
3. Pro - ceed-ing from your Fa - ther, Ac - cord-ing to his plan,
4. To you, Lord Je - sus, glo - ry And praise with one ac - cord;

Which so be - fits your gran - deur And sanc - ti - fies the earth.
And she brought forth Sal - va - tion To all who have be - lieved.
You blessed our hu - man na - ture, Be - com-ing Son of Man.
We ear - nest - ly im - plore you, To be our sav - ing Lord,

A vir - gin was your moth - er, O ho - ly mys-ter - y!
For, ris - ing out of Mar - y As from a cloud-less sky,
And hav - ing, by your pas - sion, Re-deemed the hu - man race,
That you to whom our weak - ness And sin - ful - ness are known,

Let all cre - a - tion mar - vel At that na - tiv - i - ty.
You came to bring to cap - tives Re - demp-tion from on high.
You reign now with the Fath - er, Our source of life and grace.
May sanc - ti - fy our na - ture Which you have made your own.

Text: *Veni, Redemptor gentium*, St. Ambrose 340-397; tr. by Frank C. Quinn, OP, b.1932, alt., © 1989, GIA Publications, Inc.
Tune: ROCKPORT, 7 6 7 6 D; T. Tertius Noble, 1938; from *The Hymnal,* © 1969, United Church Press

1. Re - deem - er of the na - tions Make known your
2. A vir - gin was your moth - er, O ho - ly
3. The root of Jes - se blos - somed, Her spot - less
4. For, ris - ing out of Mar - y As from a
5. Pro - ceed - ing from your Fa - ther, Ac - cord - ing

won - drous birth Which so be - fits your gran - deur
mys - ter - y! Let all cre - a - tion mar - vel
womb con - ceived, And she brought forth Sal - va - tion
cloud - less sky, You came to bring to cap - tives
to his plan, You blessed our hu - man na - ture,

And sanc - ti - fies the earth.
At that na - tiv - i - ty.
To all who have be - lieved.
Re - demp - tion from on high.
Be - com - ing Son of Man. A - men.

Stanzas 6, 7 and 8 overleaf.

6. And having, by your passion,
   Redeemed the human race,
   You reign now with the Father,
   Our source of life and grace.

7. To you, Lord Jesus, glory
   And praise with one accord;
   We earnestly implore you,
   To be our saving Lord,

8. That you to whom our weakness
   And sinfulness are known,
   May sanctify our nature
   Which you have made your own.

Text: *Veni, Redemptor gentium*, St. Ambrose 340-397; tr. by Frank C. Quinn, OP, b.1932, alt., © 1989, GIA Publications, Inc.
Tune: DAY OF SPLENDOR , 7 6 7 6; Mode VII; Columba Kelly, OSB, b.1930; acc. by Samuel Weber, OSB, b.1947; © 1987, Saint Meinrad Archabbey

32 Reveal Your Might, O God, and Come

1. Re - veal your might, O God, and come, De - scend to
   earth in maj - es - ty, In maj - es - ty of
   pov - er - ty, In pow - er of hu - mil - i - ty.

2. Be seen, O God, om - nip - o - tent, En - throned on
   wood of crib and tree; Be fore - most now in
   sac - ri - fice, Sur - ren - dered, slay in - iq - ui - ty.

3. O Son of Man, o - be - di - ent, The pris - on -
   ers of sin set free; The lame, the weak, the
   blind re - prieve, Pro - claim your day of lib - er - ty.

4. Come man - i - fest, most mer - ci - ful, In flesh cre -
   a - tion's des - ti - ny; That we may see your
   love re - vealed, Your per - fect love, O Trin - i - ty.

Text: Anonymous; adapt. by Ralph Wright, OSB, © 1989, GIA Publications, Inc.
Tune: EIN KIND GEBOR'N, LM; adapt. by Geoffrey Laycock from a 16th C. German Carol, © 1971, Faber Music Ltd.

Savior of the Nations, Come! 33

1. Sav - ior of the na - tions, come!
2. Won - drous birth! Oh, won - drous child
3. Thus on earth the Word ap - pears,
4. Come, O Fa - ther's sav - ing Son,

Vir - gin's Son, make here your home. Mar - vel now, both
of the Vir - gin un - de - filed! Might - y God and
grac - ing his cre - a - ted spheres; hence to death and
who o'er sin the vic - t'ry won. Bound-less shall your

heav'n and earth, that the Lord chose such a birth.
Mar - y's Son, ea - ger now his race to run!
hell de - scends, then the heav'n - ly throne as - cends.
king - dom be; grant that we its glo - ries see.

Text: Martin Luther, 1483-1546, after Ambrose of Milan, 340-397; tr. by William M. Reynolds, 1812-1876, and James Waring McCrady, b.1938, vs. 3-4.
© 1982, James Waring McCrady
Tune: NUN KOMM, DER HEIDEN HEILAND, 7 7 7 7; *Erfurt Enchiridia*, 1524

34 Send, Lord, Like Dew

1. Send, Lord, like dew to soothe the earth Your prom-ised
2. For-give our sins, for-get our sins; And though our
3. We lose your pres-ence through our sin, We choose our
4. Look on our sor-row and our need, Send Christ to
5. We trust you, Lord, for you are God, We know your

help, your Ho-ly One; And let him come, like
hearts have turned a-way From praise and love of
will and not your way; We fall like leaves, we
save us and for-give; With-out his love we
love, we need not fear; The Lamb of God who

spring's new life, Your Sav-ior Christ, your on-ly Son.
you, our God, Have pit-y on our hearts, we pray.
fall and die, Send, Lord, your Sav-ior Christ, we pray.
can-not love, With-out his life we can-not live.
takes our sins, Your prom-ised Sav-ior, Christ, is near.

Text: Brian Foley, b.1919, © 1971, Faber Music Ltd.
Tune: OAKLEY, 8 8 8 8; Ralph Vaughan Williams, 1872-1958, © Oxford University Press

The Coming of Our God 35

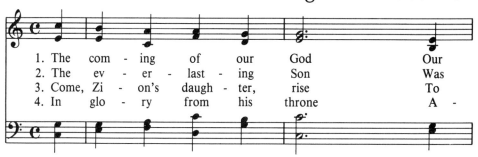

1. The com - ing of our God Our
2. The ev - er - last - ing Son Was
3. Come, Zi - on's daugh - ter, rise To
4. In glo - ry from his throne A -

thoughts must now em - ploy; Then let us meet him
born to make us free; And he a ser - vant's
greet your in - fant king; Nor let your stub - born
gain will Christ de - scend, And sum - mon all that

on the road With songs of ho - ly joy.
form put on To gain our lib - er - ty.
heart de - spise The par - don he will bring.
are his own To joys that nev - er end.

5. Let deeds of darkness fly
Before the approaching morn,
For unto sin we choose to die,
And serve the virgin-born.

6. Sing praise to Christ the Son,
Who comes to set us free,
With Father, Spirit, ever one
Through all eternity.

Text : *Instantis adventum Die,* Charles Coffin, 1676-1749, *Paris Breviary,* 1736; tr. by Robert Campbell, 1814-1868, and others, *St. Andrew's Hymnal,* 1850, alt.
Tune : OPTATUS VOTIS OMNIUM, SM; Anonymous, *Songs of Syon,* 1910; acc. by Arthur Hutchings, 1980, © 1981, ICEL

36 The People That in Darkness Walked

1. The people that in darkness walked Have
2. To hail you, Son of righteousness, The
3. To us a child of hope is born, To
4. His name shall be the Prince of peace, For
5. His pow'r increasing still shall spread, His

seen a glorious light; The light has shone on
gath'ring nations come; Rejoicing as when
us a son is giv'n; Him shall the tribes of
evermore adored, The Wonderful, the
reign no end shall know; Justice shall guard his

them who dwelt In death's surrounding night.
reapers bear Their harvest treasures home.
earth obey, Him all the hosts of heav'n.
Counselor, The great and mighty Lord.
throne above And peace abound below.

Text : Para. of Isaiah 9:2-8; John Morison, 1750-1798, *Scottish Translations Paraphrases*, 1781, alt.
Tune : CREDITON, CM; Thomas Clark, 1775-1859, *A Second Set of Psalm Tunes (for) Country Choirs*, c.1807

O Christ Redeemer, Lord of All 37

1. O Christ Re - deem - er, Lord of all, E - ter - nal -
2. You are the ech - o of his light, The un-known
3. Re - mem-ber, Lord, how long a - go You took with -
4. Each year this fes - tal day pro-claims To all with
5. The earth, the sky, the sea and all That lives and

ly the Fa-ther's Son, We mar-vel how, be - fore the
glo - ry of his face. To you in hope we raise our
in the Vir-gin's womb Our na - ture and as Son of
joy the sol-emn word: Now from his Fa-ther Christ has
teems be-neath the waves, Re - ech - o this great word of

dawn, You are with his own bright - ness one.
prayer, O hear us, Sav - ior of our race!
Man You touched and healed us of our wounds.
come, The Word of Peace to save the world.
hope To - day and give the Fa - ther praise.

Stanzas 6 and 7 overleaf.

6. And we, your servants, whom the blood
   of Jesus cleansed from ev'ry sin,
   proclaim this day that he is born
   who brings the joy of this new hymn.

7. We offer God our Father praise
   and praise the virgin-born, the Son,
   that in the Spirit we may be
   for ever in their glory one.

Text: Ralph Wright, OSB, © 1989, GIA Publications Inc.
Tune: CREATING GOD, LM; Hal Hopson, © 1989, Hope Publishing Co.

O Savior of Our Fallen Race   38

1. O   Sav - ior   of   our   fall - en   race,   O
2. O   Je - sus,   ve - ry   Light   of   light,   Our
3. Re - mem - ber,   Lord   of   life   and   grace,   How
4. To - day,   as   year   by   year   its   light   Bathes
5. For   from   the   Fa - ther's throne   you   came,   His

Bright - ness   of   the   Fa - ther's face,   O   Son   who shared the
con - stant   star   in   sin's   deep night: Now   hear   the prayers your
once,   to   save   our   fall - en   race, You   put   our   hu - man
all   the   world   in   ra - diance bright, One   pre - cious truth   out -
ban - ished chil - dren   to   re - claim; And   earth   and   sea   and

Fa - ther's might Be - fore   the   world   knew day   or   night,
peo - ple   pray Through-out   the   world   this   ho - ly   day.
ves - ture   on   And   came   to   us   as   Mar - y's son.
shines   the   sun: Sal - va - tion   comes   from you   a - lone.
sky   re - vere   The   God   of   love   who sent   you here.

6. And we are jubilant today,
   For you have washed our guilt away.
   Oh, hear the glad new song we sing
   On this, the birthday of our king!

7. O Christ, redeemer, virgin-born,
   Let songs of praise your name adorn.
   Whom with the Father we adore
   And Holy Spirit evermore.

Text : Latin office hymn, c.6th C.; tr. by Gilbert E. Doan, b.1930, alt.; © 1978, *Lutheran Book of Worship*
Tune : REX GLORIOSAE, LM; Rouen Antiphoner, 1728

38 – SECOND TUNE

1. O Sav-ior of our fall-en race, O Bright-ness of the Fa-ther's face,
2. O Je-sus, ve-ry Light of light, Our con-stant star in sin's deep night:
3. Re-mem-ber, Lord of life and grace, How once, to save our fall-en race,
4. To-day, as year by year its light Bathes all the world in ra-diance bright,
5. For from the Fa-ther's throne you came, His ban-ished chil-dren to re-claim;

O Son who shared the Fa-ther's might Be-fore the world knew day or night,
Now hear the prayers your peo-ple pray Through-out the world this ho-ly day.
You put our hu-man ves-ture on And came to us as Mar-y's son.
One pre-cious truth out-shines the sun: Sal-va-tion comes from you a-lone.
And earth and sea and sky re-vere The God of love who sent you here.

A - men.

6. And we are jubilant today,
   For you have washed our guilt away.
   Oh, hear the glad new song we sing
   On this, the birthday of our king!

7. O Christ, redeemer, virgin-born,
   Let songs of praise your name adorn.
   Whom with the Father we adore
   And Holy Spirit evermore.

Text: Latin office hymn, c.6th C.; tr. by Gilbert E. Doan, b.1930, alt, © 1978, *Lutheran Book of Worship*
Tune: JESU DULCIS MEMORIA, LM: Mode I: acc. by Samuel Weber, OSB, b.1947, © 1987, Saint Meinrad Archabbey

39　From East to West, from Shore to Shore

1. From east to west, from shore to shore Let ev-
2. Be - hold! the world's Cre - a - tor wears The form
3. For this how won - drous - ly God wrought! A maid,
4. When Mar - y heard the an - gel's word, Ac - cept-
5. He shrank not from the ox - en's stall Nor scorned

'ry heart a - wake and The ho - ly child whom
and fash - ion of a slave; Our hu - man flesh the
in low - ly hu - man place Be - came, in ways be-
ing all the Fath - er willed, Then sud - den - ly the
the low - ly man - ger bed; For he who feeds and

Mar - y bore, The Christ, the ev - er - last - ing King!
God - head shares, A hu - man race God comes to save.
yond all thought, The chos - en ves - sel of God's grace.
prom - ised One That pure and hal - lowed tem - ple filled.
cares for all At Mar - y's breast him - self was fed.

6. To shepherds poor the Lord most high,
   The one great Shepherd, was revealed
   While angel choirs in the sky
   Sang praise above the silent field:

7. "All glory be to God above
   And on the earth let there be peace
   To all who long to taste God's love,
   Till time itself shall come to cease."

Alternate doxology, when verses 6 and 7 are not used:
All glory for this blessed morn
To God, the Father, ever be;
All praise to you, O virgin-born,
And to the Spirit, one and three.

All the stanzas may be sung or:
a. On Christmas day and the Octave of Christmas, vss. 1,2,5,6,7, may be used.
b. On January 1, the feast of Mary, Mother of God, vss. 1,2,3,4, with alternate doxology may be used.

Text : *A solis ortu cardine*, Coelius Sedulius, c.450; tr. by John Ellerton, 1826-1898, rev. and adapt.
Tune: JESU, DECUS ANGELICUM, LM: Mode II; *Antiphonarium Sacri Ordinis Praedicatorum pro Diurnis Horis*, Rome, 1933

39 – SECOND TUNE

1. From east to west, from shore to shore   Let ev - 'ry
2. Be - hold! the world's Cre - a - tor wears   The form and
3. For this how won-drous - ly   God wrought! A maid, in
4. When Mar - y heard the an - gel's word,   Ac - cept - ing
5. He shrank not from the ox - en's stall   Nor scorned the

heart a - wake and sing   The ho - ly child whom Mar - y
fash - ion of a slave;   Our hu - man flesh the God-head
low - ly hu - man place   Be - came, in ways be - yond all
all the Fath - er willed,   Then sud - den - ly the prom-ised
low - ly man - ger bed;   For he who feeds and cares for

bore,   The Christ, the ev - er - last - ing King!
shares,   A hu - man race God comes to save.
thought,   The chos - en ves - sel of God's grace.
One   That pure and hal lowed tem - ple filled.
all   At Mar - y's breast him - self was fed.   A - men.

6. To shepherds poor the Lord most high,
   The one great Shepherd, was revealed
   While angel choirs in the sky
   Sang praise above the silent field:

7. "All glory be to God above
   And on the earth let there be peace
   To all who long to taste God's love,
   Till time itself shall come to cease."

Alternate doxology, when verses 6 and 7 are not used:

All glory for this blessed more
To God, the Father, ever be
All praise to you, O virgin-born,
And to the Spirit, one and three.

All the stanzas may be sung or:
a. On Christmas day and the Octave of Christmas, vss. 1,2,5,6,7 may be used.
b. On January 1, the feast of Mary, Mother of God, vss. 1,2,3,4 with alternate doxology may be used.

Text : *A solis ortu cardine,* Coelius Sedulius, c.450; tr. by John Ellerton, 1826-1898, rev. and adapt.
Tune : LASST UNS IM FESTE HEUT BEGEHN, LM: Mode VIII; *Antiphonale zum Stundengebet,* Muensterschwarzach, 1979; acc. by Samuel Weber, OSB,
   © 1987, St. Meinrad Archabbey

40 Sing, O Sing, This Blessed Morn

1. Sing, O sing, this bless - ed morn! Un - to us a child is born,
2. God of God, and Light of Light, Comes with mer-cies in - fi-nite,
3. God with us, Em - man - u - el, Deigns for ev - er now to dwell;
4. Je - sus comes that we may rise, Raised by him be - yond the skies,
5. O re - new us, Lord, we pray, In your Spir-it day by day,

Un - to us a Son is giv'n, God, as Sav-ior, comes from heav'n:
Join-ing in a won - drous plan, Comes to earth as Son of Man:
Now on Ad-am's fall - en race Sheds the full-ness of God's grace:
Christ is Son of Man that we With our God may al-ways be:
That in us the world may see Your own love and so be-lieve:

Sing, O sing, this bless - ed morn, Je - sus Christ to - day is born.
Sing, O sing, this bless - ed morn, Je - sus Christ to - day is born.
Sing, O sing, this bless - ed morn, Je - sus Christ to - day is born.
Sing, O sing, this bless - ed morn, Je - sus Christ to - day is born.
Sing, O sing, this bless - ed morn, Je - sus Christ to - day is born.

Text : Christopher Wordsworth, 1807-1885; revised by Ralph Wright, OSB, b.1938
Tune : JUBILATE DEO, 77 77 77; George Thalben-Ball, *The BBC Hymn Book*, © Oxford University Press

Angels, from the Realms of Glory 41

1. An-gels, from the realms of glo-ry, Wing your flight o'er all the earth;
2. Shep-herds in the field a-bid-ing, Watch-ing o'er your flocks by night,
3. Sag-es, leave your con-tem-pla-tion; Bright-er vi-sions beam a-far:
4. Though an in-fant now we view him, He shall fill his Fa-ther's throne,

You, who sang cre-a-tion's sto-ry, Now pro-claim Mes-si-ah's birth:
God with you is now re-sid-ing; Yon-der shines the in-fant Light:
Seek the great De-sire of na-tions; You have seen his na-tal star:
Gath-er all the na-tions to him; Ev-'ry knee shall then bow down:

Come and wor-ship, come and wor-ship, Wor-ship Christ, the new-born King.

5. Saints before the alter bending,
   Watching long in hope and fear.
   Suddenly the Lord, descending,
   In his temple shall appear:
   Come and worship, come and worship,
   Worship Christ, the newborn King.

6. All creation join in praising
   God, the Father, Spirit, Son,
   Evermore your voices raising,
   To the eternal Three in One:
   Come and worship, come and worship,
   Worship Christ, the newborn King.

Text : James Montgomery, 1771-1854, in *Iris*, Sheffield newspaper, 1816, alt.
Tune : REGENT SQUARE, 8 7 8 7 8 7; Henry Thomas Smart, 1813-1879, *Psalms and Hymns for Divine Worship*, 1867

42 A Child Is Born in Bethlehem

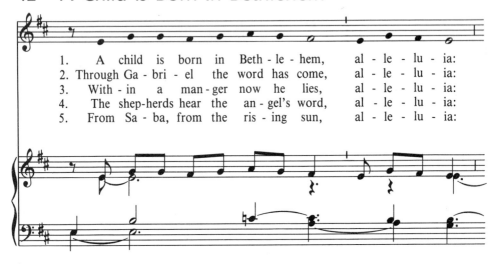

1. A child is born in Beth - le - hem, al - le - lu - ia:
2. Through Ga - bri - el the word has come, al - le - lu - ia:
3. With - in a man - ger now he lies, al - le - lu - ia:
4. The shep-herds hear the an - gel's word, al - le - lu - ia:
5. From Sa - ba, from the ris - ing sun, al - le - lu - ia:

So leap with joy, Je - ru - sa - lem, al - le - lu - ia, al - le - lu - ia.
The Vir - gin will con-ceive a son, al - le - lu - ia, al - le - lu - ia.
Who reigns on high be-yond the skies, al - le - lu - ia, al - le - lu - ia.
This child is tru - ly Christ the Lord, al - le - lu - ia, al - le - lu - ia.
With in-cense, gold, and myrrh they come, al - le - lu - ia, al - le - lu - ia.

A new song let us sing For Christ is born

let us a - dore and let our glad - ness ring.

6. Till with their gifts they enter in,
   alleluia:
   And kings adore the newborn King,
   alleluia, alleluia.

7. From virgin's womb this child is born,
   alleluia:
   The Light from Light who brings the dawn,
   alleluia, alleluia.

8. He comes to free us from our strife,
   alleluia:
   And share with us the Father's life,
   alleluia, alleluia.

9. At this the coming of the Word,
   alleluia:
   O come let us adore the Lord,
   alleluia, alleluia.

10. To Father, Son, and Spirit praise,
    alleluia:
    From all his creatures all their days,
    alleluia, alleluia.

By a selection of verses this hymn could be used more specifically on certain feasts of the Christmas Season, e.g.:

verses 1,3,4,9,10 = Christmas Day
verses 1,2,7,8,10 = Jan. 1, Mother of God
verses 1,5,6,9,10 = Jan. 6, Epiphany
verses 1,7,8,9,10 = Throughout the Christmas Season

Text: *Puer Natus in Bethlehem*, Latin 14th C., from a Benedictine Processional; tr. by Ralph Wright, OSB
Tune: Plainchant, Mode I; acc. by Theodore Marier
© 1981, ICEL

43 From Heaven Above to Earth I Come

1. From heav'n a - bove to earth I come To
2. To you this night is born a child Of
3. This is the Christ, God's Son most high, Who
4. The bless - ing which the Fa - ther planned The

bring good news to ev - 'ry - one! Glad ti - dings of great
Mar - y, chos - en vir - gin mild; This new - born child of
hears your sad and bit - ter cry; He will him - self your
Son holds in his in - fant hand, That in his king - dom,

joy I bring To all the world, and glad - ly sing:
low - ly birth Shall be the joy of all the earth.
Sav - ior be And from all sin will set you free.
bright and fair, You may with us his glo - ry share.

5. These are the signs which you will see
To let you know that it is he:
In manger-bed, in swad'ling clothes
The child who all the earth upholds.

6. How glad we'll be to find it so!
Then let us with the shepherds go.
The Father has great marvels done
In sending us the only Son.

7. My heart for very joy now leaps;
My voice no longer silence keeps;
I too must join the angel-throng
To sing with joy his cradle-song:

8. "Glory to God in highest heav'n,
Who unto us the Son has giv'n."
With angels sing in pious mirth:
A glad new year to all the earth!

Not all verses have to be sung; verses 1-4, for example, could be sung without the rest of the stanzas.

Text: Martin Luther, 1483-1546; tr. © 1978, *Lutheran Book of Worship*, alt.
Tune: VOM HIMMEL HOCH, LM; Martin Luther, *Geistliche lieder auffs neu gebessert und gemehrt*, 1539

Alternate version

Tune: VOM HIMMEL HOCH, LM: Martin Luther; harm. by Johann Sebastian Bach, 1685-1750, *Christmas Oratorio*

44   Of the Father's Love Begotten

1. Of the Fa - ther's love be - got - ten
2. Oh, that birth for ev - er bless - ed,
3. Let the heights of heav'n a - dore him;
4. Christ, to thee, with God the Fa - ther,

Ere the worlds be - gan to be,
When the vir - gin, full of grace,
An - gel hosts, his prais - es sing;
And, O Spir - it blest, to thee,

He is Al - pha and O - me - ga,
By the Ho - ly Ghost con - ceiv - ing,
Pow'rs, do - min - ions, bow be - fore him
Hymn and chant and high thanks - giv - ing

He the source, the end - ing he,
Bore the Sav - ior of our race,
And ex - tol our God and King;
And un - wea - ried prais - es be:

Of the things that are, that have been,
And the babe, the world's re - deem - er,
Let no tongue on earth be si - lent,
Hon - or, glo - ry, and do - min - ion,

And that fu - ture years shall see, Ev-er-more and ev - er - more.
First re-vealed his sa - cred face, Ev-er-more and ev - er - more.
Ev - 'ry voice in con-cert ring Ev-er-more and ev - er - more.
And e - ter - nal vic - to - ry Ev-er-more and ev - er - more!

Text: *Corde natus ex Parentis;* Marcus Aurelius Clemens Prudentius, 348-413; tr. by John M. Neale, 1818-1866, and Henry W. Baker, 1821-1877
Tune: DIVINUM MYSTERIUM, 87 87 877; 12th C.; Mode V; acc. by Richard Proulx, b.1937, © 1985, GIA Publications, Inc.

Metrical version

1. Of the Fa - ther's love be - got - ten Ere the worlds be -
2. Oh, that birth for ev - er bless - ed, When the vir - gin,
3. Let the heights of heav'n a - dore him; An - gel hosts, his
4. Christ, to thee, with God the Fa - ther, And, O Spir - it

gan to be, He is Al - pha and O - me - ga,
full of grace, By the Ho - ly Ghost con - ceiv - ing,
prais - es sing; Pow'rs, do - min - ions, bow be - fore him
blest, to thee, Hymn and chant and high thanks-giv - ing

He the source, the end - ing he, Of the things that
Bore the Sav - ior of our race, And the babe, the
And ex - tol our God and King; Let no tongue on
And un - wea - ried prais - es be: Hon - or, glo - ry,

are,   that   have   been,   And   that   fu - ture
world's re - deem   -   er,   First re - vealed his
earth   be   si   -   lent,   Ev - 'ry voice   in
and   do - min   -   ion,   And   e - ter - nal

years shall see,   Ev - er - more and ev - er - more.
sa - cred face,   Ev - er - more and ev - er - more.
con - cert ring   Ev - er - more and ev - er - more.
vic - to - ry   Ev - er - more and ev - er - more!

Text : *Corde natus ex Parentis;* Marcus Aurelius Clemens Prudentius, 348-413; tr. by John Mason Neal, 1818-1866, and Henry Williams Baker, 1821-1877, alt.
Tune : DIVINUM MYSTERIUM, 8 7 8 7 8 7; with refrain; Sanctus trope, 11th C.; adapt. *Piae Cantiones,* 1582; acc. by Bruce Neswick, b.1956, © 1984

45 Good Christian Friends, Rejoice

1. Good Chris-tian friends, re - joice With heart and soul and voice;
2. Good Chris-tian friends, re - joice With heart and soul and voice;
3. Good Chris-tian friends, re - joice With heart and soul and voice;

Give ye heed to what we say: Je - sus Christ is born to-day;
Now ye hear of end - less bliss: Je - sus Christ was born for this!
Now ye need not fear the grave; Je - sus Christ was born to save!

Ox and ass be - fore him bow, And he is in the man-ger now.
He has o - pened heav-en's door, And we are blest for ev - er-more.
Calls you one and calls you all To gain his ev - er - last-ing hall.

Christ is born to - day! Christ is born to - day!
Christ was born for this! Christ was born for this!
Christ was born to save! Christ was born to save!

Text : Medieval Latin Carol; tr. by John Mason Neale, 1818-1866, alt.
Tune : IN DULCI JUBILO, 66 77 78 55; Klug's *Geistliche Lieder*, Wittenberg, 1535

To Us a Child of Hope Is Born 46

1. To us a child of hope is born, To
2. His name shall be the Prince of peace, For
3. His pow'r in - creas - ing still shall spread, His

us a son is giv'n; Him shall the tribes of
ev - er - more a - dored, The Won - der - ful, the
reign no end shall know: Jus - tice shall guard his

earth o - bey, Him all the hosts of heav'n.
Coun - se - lor, The great and might - y Lord.
throne a - bove And peace a - bound be - low.

Text : Para. of Isaiah 9:2-8; from "The People That in Darkness Walked," John Morison, 1750-1798, *Scottish Translations and Paraphrases*, 1781, alt.
Tune : PISGAH, CM: American Folk Hymn, attr. to J.C. Lowry, 1818; adapt. and harm. in *Songs of Praise*, 1925

47 When Christ Was Born at Bethlehem

1. When Christ was born at Beth - le - hem The heed - less world slept on And on - ly sim - ple shep - herds heard That God's own Word had come.
2. But when the Sav - ior comes a - gain With thun - der or with fire, The cos - mos will it - self be - hold His splen - dor and his pow'r.
3. Then shall the pure of heart be blest; As mild he comes to them As when up - on the Vir - gin's breast He lay at Beth - le - hem.
4. He gen - tly came to those with faith But strong - er now to save For hav - ing felt the sting of death And hav - ing burst the grave.

5. Come, dwell in us, O Lord, that we
May know you as our friend.
Come share with us beyond our pain
That joy that cannot end.

6. O Father, hear this song of hope
Brought by your saving Son,
That in your Spirit we may live
And praise you ever one.

Text: J. Anstice, 1808-1836, *English Hymnal*, 1906; freely adapt by Ralph Wright, OSB, b.1938
Tune: THIS ENDRIS NYGHT, CM; English Carol Melody, c.15th C.; harm. by Ralph Vaughan Williams, 1872-1958, *English Hymnal*, © Oxford University Press

Behold a Mystical Rose 48

1. Be-hold a Mys-ti-cal Rose From thorn-y stem has sprung;
2. Be-hold the Moth-er of God, Yet low-li-est daugh-ter of Eve;
3. Be-hold the Cause of our Joy, Who brought to the world God's child,

Of Da-vid's lin-e-age God chose To give to the world his Son.
At her as-sent-ing nod God's Son in her womb was con-ceived.
The Child who was to de-stroy the e-vil that kept us be-guiled.

All hail, O House of Gold, Of whom an-cient proph-ets fore-told;
All hail, O Morn-ing Star, Who brought bless-ed Light from a-far,
All hail, O Gate of Heav'n, Through you all grac-es are giv'n:

Your roy-al prais-es we sing; Your womb was the Court of our King.
Dis-pel the dark-ness of night, Il-lu-mine our path with your Light.
Through you Sal-va-tion came; All praised and blest be your name.

Text: Richard Cross, alt.; adapt. by Ralph Wright, OSB, b.1938
Tune: OLD BRETON AIR, Irregular; acc. by Richard Cross
© 1964, World Library Publications, Inc.

49 Virgin-born, We Bow before Thee

1. Vir - gin - born, we bow be - fore Thee: Bless - ed was the womb that bore Thee: Mar - y, Moth-er meek and mild; Bless - ed was she in her Child.

2. Bless - ed she by all cre - a - tion, Who brought forth the world's Sal - va - tion; Bless - ed they, for ev - er blest, Most who love, and serve Thee best.

Blessed was the breast that fed Thee, Blessed
Virgin-Born we bow before Thee; Blessed

was the hand that led Thee, Blessed was the parent's
was the womb that bore Thee: Mary, Mother meek and

eye Watched Thy slumb'ring infancy.
mild; Blessed was she in her Child.

Text: Reginald Heber, 1783-1820
Tune: PSALM 86 [MON DIEU, PRETE-MOI L'OUREILLE], 87 87 D; *Genevan Psalter*, 1543, Louis Bourgeois, c.1510-1561; harm. by Claude Goudimel, c.1510-1572;
    soprano and tenor inverted.

50 Brightest and Best of the Stars of the Morning

1. Bright - est and best of the stars of the morn - ing,
2. Cold on his cra - dle the dew - drops are shin - ing,
3. Shall we than yield him, in cost - ly de - vo - tion,
4. Vain - ly we of - fer each am - ple ob - la - tion,
5. Bright - est and best of the stars of the morn - ing,

Dawn on our dark - ness and lend us thine aid;
Low lies his head with the beasts of the stall;
O - dors of E - dom, and of - f'rings di - vine,
Vain - ly with gifts would his fa - vor se - cure,
Dawn on our dark - ness and lend us thine aid;

Star of the east, the hor - i - zon a - dorn - ing,
An - gels a - dore him in slum - ber re - clin - ing,
Gems of the moun - tain, and pearls of the o - cean,
Rich - er by far is the heart's a - dor - a - tion,
Star of the east, the hor - i - zon a - dorn - ing,

Guide where our in - fant Re - deem - er is laid.
Mak - er and Mon - arch and Sav - ior of all.
Myrrh from the for - est, and gold from the mine?
Dear - er to God are the prayers of the poor.
Guide where our in - fant Re - deem - er is laid.

Brightest and best of the stars of the morning,
Dawn on our darkness, and lend us thine aid;
Star of the east, the horizon adorning,
Guide where our infant Redeemer is laid.

Text: Reginald Heber, 1783-1826, alt.
Tune: STAR IN THE EAST, 11 10 11 10 with refrain; *The Southern Harmony*, 1835; harm. by Thomas Foster, © 1984

51 The Only Son from Heaven

1. The on - ly Son from heav - en, Fore - told by an - cient seers,
2. Oh, time of God ap - point - ed, Oh, bright and ho - ly morn!
3. O Fa - ther, here be - fore you With God the Ho - ly Ghost,

By God the Fa - ther giv - en, In hu - man form ap - pears.
He comes, the king a - noin - ted, The Christ, the vir - gin - born,
And Je - sus, we a - dore you, O pride of an - gel - host:

No sphere his light con - fin - ing, No star so bright - ly
Grim death to van - quish for us, To o - pen heav'n be -
Be - fore you mor - tals low - ly Cry "Ho - ly, ho - ly,

shin - ing As he, our Morn - ing Star.
fore us And bring us life a - gain.
ho - ly, O bless - ed Trin - i - ty!"

Text: Elizabeth Cruciger, c.1500-1535; tr. by Arthur T. Russel, 1806-1874, alt.
Tune: HERR CHRIST DER EINIG GOTTS SOHN, 76 76 776; *Enchiridion*, Erfurt, 1524; harm. from *Lutheran Book of Worship*, © 1978

As with Gladness Men of Old 52

1. As with glad-ness men of old Did the guid-ing star be-hold, As with joy they hailed its light, Lead-ing on-ward, beam-ing bright, So, most gra-cious God, may we Ev-er-more be led to thee.

2. As with joy-ful steps they sped To that low-ly man-ger bed, There to bend the knee be-fore Him whom heav'n and earth a-dore; So may we with will-ing feet Ev-er seek thy mer-cy seat.

3. As they of-fered gifts most rare At that man-ger rude and bare; So may we with ho-ly joy, Pure and free from sin's al-loy, All our cost-liest treas-ures bring, Christ, to thee, our heav'n-ly King.

4. Ho-ly Je-sus, ev-'ry day Keep us in the nar-row way; And, when earth-ly things are past, Bring our ran-somed souls at last Where they need no star to guide, Where no clouds thy glo-ry hide.

5. In the heav'n-ly coun-try bright Need they no cre-at-ed light; Thou its light, its joy, its crown, Thou its sun which goes not down; There for ev-er may we sing Al-le-lu-ias to our King.

Text : William Chatterton Dix, 1837-1898, *Hymns of Love and Joy,* 1861
Tune : DIX, 77 77 77; arr. by William Henry Monk, 1823-1889, from the chorale *Treuer Heiland* by Conrad Kocher, 1786-1872, *Stimmen aus dem Reiche Gottes,* Stuttgart, 1838

53 Earth Has Many a Noble City

1. Earth has man-y a no-ble cit-y;
2. Fair-er than the sun at morn-ing
3. East-ern sag-es at his cra-dle
4. Sa-cred gifts of sol-emn mean-ing:
5. Je-sus whom the Gen-tiles wor-shiped

Beth-le-hem does all ex-cel; From it came the
Was the star that told his birth, To the world its
Make their of-f'rings rich and rare; See them give, in
In-cense does their God dis-close; Gold the King of
At your glad e-piph-a-ny, Un-to you with

Lord from heav-en Came to rule his Is-ra-el.
God an-nounc-ing Seen in hu-man form on earth.
deep de-vo-tion Gold and frank-in-cense and myrrh.
kings pro-claim-ing; Myrrh his sep-ul-cher fore-shows.
God the Fa-ther And the Spir-it, glo-ry be.

Text: Matthew 2:1-11; *O sola magnarum urbium*, Marcus Aurelius Clemens Prudentius, 348-c.413; tr. by Edward Caswall, 1814-1878, *Lyra Catholica*, 1849; rev. in *Hymns Ancient and Modern*, 1861, alt.
Tune: STUTTGART, 87 87; Christian Friedrich Witt, 1660-1716, Witt's and A.C. Ludwig's *Psalmodia Sacra*, Gotha, 1715; adapt. by Henry John Gauntlett, 1805-1876

Hail to the Lord's Anointed 54

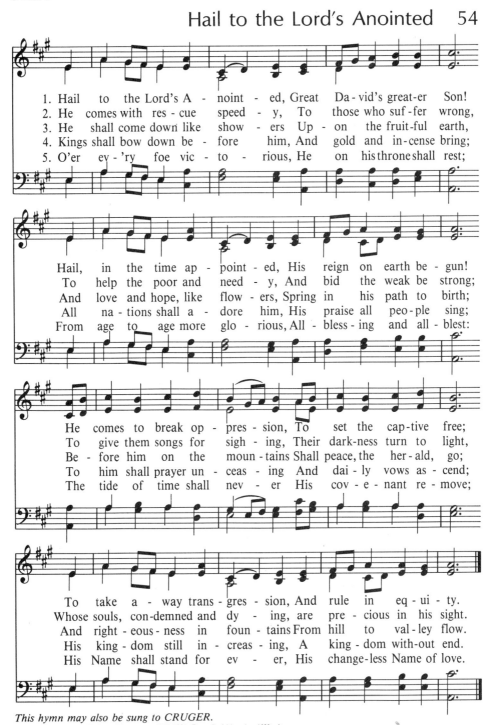

1. Hail   to   the Lord's A - noint - ed, Great   Da - vid's great-er   Son!
2. He   comes with res - cue   speed - y,   To   those who suf-fer   wrong,
3. He   shall come down like   show - ers   Up - on   the fruit-ful   earth,
4. Kings shall bow down be - fore   him, And   gold   and in-cense bring;
5. O'er   ev - 'ry   foe vic - to - rious, He   on   his throne shall rest;

Hail,   in   the time ap - point - ed, His   reign   on   earth be - gun!
To   help   the poor and   need - y, And   bid   the weak be   strong;
And   love   and hope, like   flow - ers, Spring in   his   path to   birth;
All   na - tions shall a - dore   him, His   praise all   peo-ple   sing;
From   age   to   age more   glo - rious, All - bless-ing   and all - blest:

He   comes to break op - pres - sion, To   set   the   cap-tive   free;
To   give them songs for   sigh - ing, Their   dark-ness turn to   light,
Be - fore him   on   the   moun - tains Shall peace, the   her - ald,   go;
To   him shall prayer un - ceas - ing And   dai - ly   vows as - cend;
The   tide   of   time shall   nev - er   His   cov - e - nant re - move;

To   take   a - way trans - gres - sion, And   rule   in   eq - ui - ty.
Whose souls, con-demned and   dy - ing, are   pre - cious in his sight.
And   right - eous - ness   in   foun - tains From hill   to   val - ley flow.
His   king - dom still   in - creas - ing, A   king - dom with-out end.
His   Name shall stand for   ev - er, His   change-less Name of love.

This hymn may also be sung to CRUGER.

Text : Based on Psalm 72; James Montgomery, 1771-1854, *Evangelical Magazine*, 1822, alt.
Tune : ELLACOMBE, 7 6 7 6 D; From *Gesangbuch ... der Herzogl. Wirtembergischen katholischen Hofkapelle*, 1784, alt; adapt. *Katholischen Gesangbuch*, 1863;
   harm. William Henry Monk, 1823-1889

55 How Brightly Shines

1. How bright-ly shines the morn-ing star, With sud-den ra-diance from a-far, To cheer us with its shin-ing! God's bright-ness dawns up-on our night, And fills our dark-ened souls with light, Which long for truth were pin-ing. Your word,

2. Through you a-lone can we be blest, Then deep be on our hearts im-pressed The love which you have borne us; So make us read-y to ful-fill With fer-vent zeal your ho-ly will, Though some may mock and scorn us. Sa-vior,

3. All praise to him who came to save, Who con-quered death and scorned the grave; For ev-er sing his prais-es. A-dore the Lamb who once was slain, The friend whom none shall trust in vain, Who fills us with his grac-es. High-est

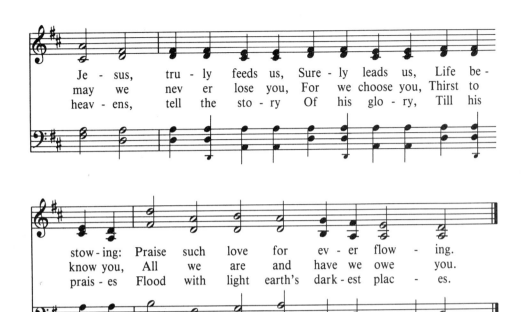

Je - sus, tru - ly feeds us, Sure - ly leads us, Life be -
stow - ing: Praise such love for ev - er flow - ing.

may we nev er lose you, For we choose you, Thirst to
know you, All we are and have we owe you.

heav - ens, tell the sto - ry Of his glo - ry, Till his
prais - es Flood with light earth's dark - est plac - es.

Text: *Wie schön leuchtet der Morgenstern;* Philipp Nicolai, 1556-1608, and Johann Adolf Schlegel, 1721-1793; tr. by Catherine Winkworth, 1827-1878; adapt. by A.G. Petti, alt., © 1971, Faber Music Ltd.
Tune: WIE SCHÖN LEUCHTET, 88 7 88 7 22 44 48; Philipp Nicolai, 1556-1608; harm. by Johann H. Schein, 1586-1630

55 – SECOND TUNE

1. How bright-ly shines the morn-ing star, With sud-den ra-diance
2. Through you a - lone can we be blest, Then deep be on our
3. All praise to him who came to save, Who con-quered death and

from a - far, To cheer us with its shin - ing! God's
hearts im-pressed The love which you have borne us; So
scorned the grave; For ev - er sing his prais - es. A -

bright-ness dawns up - on our night, And fills our dark-ened
make us read - y to ful - fill With fer - vent zeal your
dore the Lamb who once was slain, The friend whom none shall

souls with light, Which long for truth were pin - ing. Your word,
ho - ly will, Though some may mock and scorn us. Sa - vior,
trust in vain, Who fills us with his grac - es. High - est

Je - sus, tru - ly feeds us, Sure - ly leads us, Life be -
may we nev - er lose you, For we choose you, Thirst to
heav - ens, tell the sto - ry Of his glo - ry, Till his

stow - ing: Praise such love for ev - er flow - ing.
know you, All we are and have we owe you.
prais - es Flood with light earth's dark - est plac - es.

Text: *Wie schön leuchtet der Morgenstern;* Philipp Nicolai, 1556-1608, and Johann Adolf Schlegel, 1721-1793; tr. by Catherine Winkworth, 1827-1878; adapt.
by A.G. Petti, alt., © 1971, Faber Music Ltd.
Tune: WIE SCHÖN LEUCHTET, 88 7 88 7 22 44 48; Philipp Nicolai, 1556-1608; harm. by J.S. Bach, 1685-1750

56 O Tyrant Herod, Why This Fear

1. O ty-rant Her-od, why this fear That tears your tor-tured soul a-part?
2. The Ma-gi see the sud-den star And fol-low as it shows the way.
3. The sin-less Lamb by John is led To Jor-dan's wa-ter and bap-tized.
4. At Ca-na there is joy and calm, With wed-ding laugh-ter as they dine.
5. O ech-o songs! Be loud with praise! The Fa-ther's Son is now re-vealed.

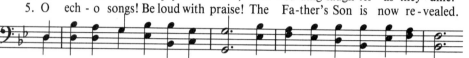

He has not come to strip your pow'r Who brings a king-dom of the heart.
They come with gifts and jour-ney far To reach the fi-nal Light of day.
He bears the bur-den of the dead, En-a-bling all who fall to rise.
His moth-er speaks with-out a-larm, He hears and wa-ter flows as wine.
His Spir-it gen-tle, un-a-fraid, He wel-comes all who would be healed.

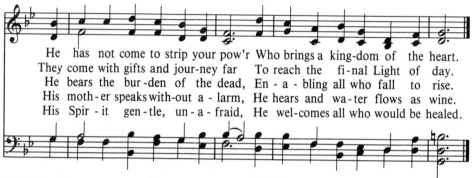

Text: *Hostis Herodis impie*, Coelius Sedulius, c.5th C.; tr. by Ralph Wright, OSB, b.1938
Tune: TYRANT HEROD, LM; David N. Johnson
© 1989, GIA Publications, Inc.

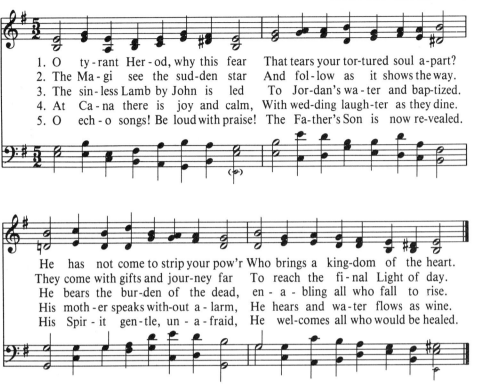

1. O ty-rant Her-od, why this fear That tears your tor-tured soul a-part?
2. The Ma-gi see the sud-den star And fol-low as it shows the way.
3. The sin-less Lamb by John is led To Jor-dan's wa-ter and bap-tized.
4. At Ca-na there is joy and calm, With wed-ding laugh-ter as they dine.
5. O ech-o songs! Be loud with praise! The Fa-ther's Son is now re-vealed.

He has not come to strip your pow'r Who brings a king-dom of the heart.
They come with gifts and jour-ney far To reach the fi-nal Light of day.
He bears the bur-den of the dead, en-a-bling all who fall to rise.
His moth-er speaks with-out a-larm, He hears and wa-ter flows as wine.
His Spir-it gen-tle, un-a-fraid, He wel-comes all who would be healed.

Text: *Hostis Herodis impie*, Coelius Sedulius, c.5th C.; tr. by Ralph Wright, OSB, b.1938, © 1989, GIA Publications, Inc.
Tune: ERHALT UNS, HERR, LM; *Geistliche Lieder*, Wittenberg, 1543

57 Songs of Thankfulness and Praise

1. Songs of thank-ful - ness and praise, Je - sus, Lord, to you we raise;
2. Man - i - fest in Jor - dan's stream, Proph-et, Priest, and King su-preme;
3. Grant us grace to see you, Lord, Pres - ent in your ho - ly World;

Man - i - fest - ed by the star To the Ma - gi from a - far,
And at Ca - na wed - ding guest In your God-head man - i - fest;
Grace to im - i - tate you here, Liv - ing lives that know no fear,

Branch of roy - al Da - vid's stem In your birth at Beth - le - hem:
Man - i - fest in pow'r di - vine, Chang-ing wa - ter in - to wine;
That your face we then may see At your great e - piph - a - ny.

An-thems be to you ad-dressed, God in flesh made man - i - fest.
An-thems be to you ad-dressed, God in flesh made man - i - fest.
Now we praise you, ev - er blest, God in flesh made man - i - fest.

Text: Christopher Wordsworth, 1807-1885, The Holy Year, 1862; adapt. by David F. Wright, OP, 1984, © 1989, GIA Publications, Inc.
Tune: SALZBURG, 77 77 D; Jacob Hintze, 1622-1702, Praxis Pietatis Melica, Berlin, 1678; harm. by Johann Sebastian Bach, 1685-1750

What Star Is This, with Beams So Bright   58

1. What star is this, with beams so bright,
2. 'Tis now ful - filled what God de - creed,
3. O Je - sus, while the star of grace
4. To God the Fa - ther, heav'n - ly Light,

More love - ly than the noon - day light,
"From Ja - cob shall a star pro - ceed";
Im - pels us on to seek your face,
To Christ, re - vealed in earth - ly night,

'Tis sent to an - nounce a new - born King,
And lo! the East - ern sag - es stand,
Let not our sloth - ful hearts re - fuse
To God the Spir - it now we raise

Glad ti - dings of our God to bring.
To read in heav'n the Lord's com - mand.
The guid - ance of your light to use.
An end - less song of thank - ful praise!

Text: Charles Coffin, 1736; rev. by John Chandler, 1837,alt.
Tune: PUER NOBIS NASCITUR, LM; Trier MS, 15th C.; adapt. by Michael Praetorius, 1609; harm. by George R. Woodward, 1902

59 Worship the Lord in the Beauty of Holiness

1. Wor-ship the Lord in the beau-ty of ho-li-ness!
2. Low at his feet lay thy bur-den of care-ful-ness,
3. Fear not to en-ter his courts in the slen-der-ness
4. These, though we bring them in trem-bling and fear-ful-ness,
5. Wor-ship the Lord in the beau-ty of ho-li-ness!

Bow down be-fore him, his glo-ry pro-claim; With
High on his heart he will bear it for thee,
Of the poor wealth thou wouldst reck-on as thine:
He will ac-cept for the name that is dear;
Bow down be-fore him, his glo-ry pro-claim; With

gold of o-be-dience, and in-cense of low-li-ness,
Com-fort thy sor-rows, and an-swer thy prayer-ful-ness,
Truth in its beau-ty, and love in its ten-der-ness,
Morn-ings of joy give for eve-nings of tear-ful-ness,
gold of o-be-dience, and in-cense of low-li-ness,

Kneel and a-dore him, the Lord is his name!.
Guid-ing thy steps as may best for thee be.
These are the of-f'rings to lay on his shrine.
Trust for our trem-bling and hope for our fear.
Kneel and a-dore him, the Lord is his name!

Text: J.S.B. Monsell, 1811-1875, *Hymns of Love and Praise*, 1853; rev. *Parish Hymnal*, 1873
Tune: WAS LEBET, WAS SCHWEBET, 12 10 12 10; from the *Rheinhardt M.S.*, Uttingen, 1754

When Jesus to the Jordan Came 60

1. When Je - sus to the Jor - dan came— The
2. A voice like thun - der then was heard, The
3. The voice said, "This is my dear Son. O
4. O praise the Fa - ther of the Word! O

sin - less one— to know our shame, The wa - ters of the
Fa - ther wit - nessed to the Word. The Spir - it like a
hear his words for he has come To save the world, to
praise our sav - ior, Christ the Lord! The Spir - it, liv - ing

earth were giv'n The pow'r to cleanse our hearts for heav'n.
dove came down And glo - ry set - tled on the Son.
do my will; In him all things will be ful - filled."
in our hearts, Will make our praise a joy - ful task.

Text: Ralph Wright, OSB, b.1938, © 1989, GIA Publications, Inc.
Tune: WINDHAM, LM; Daniel Read, *The American Singing Book*, 1785

60 – SECOND TUNE

1. When Je - sus to the Jor - dan came— The sin - less one— to
2. A voice like thun - der then was heard, The Fa - ther wit - nessed
3. The voice said, "This is my dear Son. O hear his words for
4. O praise the Fa - ther of the Word! O praise our sav - ior,

know our shame, The wa - ters of the earth were giv'n
to the Word. The Spir - it like a dove came down
he has come To save the world, to do my will;
Christ the Lord! The Spir - it, liv - ing in our hearts,

The pow'r to cleanse our hearts for heav'n.
And glo - ry set - tled on the Son.
In him all things will be ful - filled."
Will make our praise a joy - ful task. A - men.

Text: Ralph Wright, OSB, b.1938, © 1989, GIA Publications, Inc.
Tune: TE LUCIS ANTE TERMINUM VIII, LM; Mode VIII; *Antiphonale Monasticum pro Diurnis Horis*, Rome, 1934; adapt. Columba Kelly, OSB, b.1930; acc. by
Samuel Weber, OSB, b.1947, © 1987, Saint Meinrad Archabbey

When John Baptized by Jordan's River 61

1. When John bap-tized by Jor-dan's riv - er In faith and
2. There as the Lord, bap-tized and pray - ing, Rose from the
3. O Son of Man, our na-ture shar - ing, In whose o -

hope the peo - ple came, That John and Jor-dan might de - liv - er
stream, the sin - less one, A voice was heard from heav-en say - ing,
be - dience all are blest, Sav - ior, our sins and sor - rows bear-ing,

Their trou-bled souls from sin and shame. They came to seek a new be-
"This is my own be - lov-ed Son." There as the Fa - ther's word was
Hear us and grant us this re-quest: Dai - ly to grow, by grace de-

gin - ning, The hu-man spir - it's age - less quest, Re - pent-ance,
spo - ken, Not in the pow'r of wind and flame, But of his
fend - ed, Filled with the Spir - it from a - bove; In Christ bap-

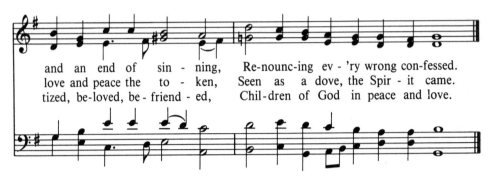

and an end of sin - ning, Re-nounc-ing ev - 'ry wrong con-fessed.
love and peace the to - ken, Seen as a dove, the Spir - it came.
tized, be-loved, be - friend - ed, Chil-dren of God in peace and love.

Text : Timothy Dudley-Smith, b. 1926, © 1984, Hope Publishing Co.
Tune : RENDEZ À DIEU, 9 8 9 8 D; Louis Bourgeois, c.1510-1561

Jesus Calls Us Out of Darkness 62

1. Je-sus calls us out of dark-ness To the won - der of his light.
2. Turn a - way from all cor-rup-tion, Be a sign be-fore the world
3. Fa-ther, hear your chil-dren call you In the name of Christ your Son;

See your dig - ni - ty, O Chris-tian, Res-cued from e - ter-nal night.
Of the love the Fa-ther shows us In his gen - tle might-y Word.
Send the Spir - it whom he prom-ised That in him we may be one.

See the glo - ry of your call - ing, Broth-ers, sis - ters of the Lord,
Be the light up - on the lamp-stand, Be the cit - y on the hill.
Then the world will come to know you In the Son who came and died,

Call-ing God a - lone your Fa - ther Through the love he has out - poured.
Be the men and wo-men toil - ing, Seek-ing but the Fa - ther's will.
For your love will be re - flect - ed In the mir-ror of our lives.

Text: Ralph Wright, OSB, b.1938, © 1989, GIA Publications, Inc.
Tune: OUT OF DARKNESS, 8 7 8 7 D; Austin Rennick, OSB, ©

63　Lord Jesus, As We Turn from Sin

1. Lord Jesus, as we turn from sin With
2. We call on you whose liv - ing word Has
3. Your glance at Pe - ter helped him know The
4. Reach out and touch with heal - ing pow'r The
5. Then stay with us when eve - ning comes And

strength and hope re - stored, Re - ceive the hom - age
made the Fa - ther known, O Shep - herd, we have
love he had de - nied, Now gaze on us and
wounds we have re - ceived, That in for - give - ness
dark - ness makes us blind, O stay un - til the

that we bring To you our ris - en Lord.
wan - dered far, Find us and lead us home.
heal us, Lord, Of self - ish - ness and pride.
we may love And may no long - er grieve.
light of dawn May fill both heart and mind.

Text: Ralph Wright, OSB, b.1938
Tune: FORGIVENESS, CM; Austin Rennick, OSB
© 1981, ICEL

Lord Jesus, Think on Me 64

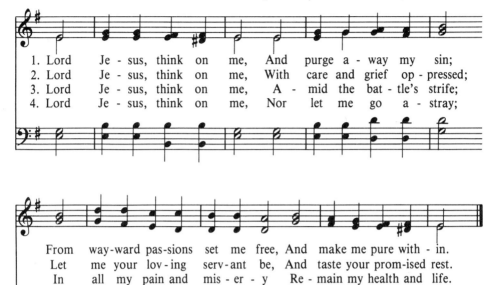

1. Lord Je - sus, think on me, And purge a - way my sin;
2. Lord Je - sus, think on me, With care and grief op - pressed;
3. Lord Je - sus, think on me, A - mid the bat - tle's strife;
4. Lord Je - sus, think on me, Nor let me go a - stray;

From way-ward pas-sions set me free, And make me pure with - in.
Let me your lov - ing serv-ant be, And taste your prom-ised rest.
In all my pain and mis - er - y Re - main my health and life.
Through dark-ness and per - plex - i - ty Re - veal the heav'n - ly way.

5. Lord Jesus, think on me,
   When flows the tempest high,
   When onwards rush the enemy,
   O Saviour dear, be nigh.

6. Lord Jesus, think on me,
   That when the flood is past,
   Eternal brightness I may see,
   And share your joy at last.

Text : Bishop Synesius, 375-430; tr. by A.W. Chatfield, 1808-1896; adapt. by Anthony G. Petti, © 1971, Faber Music Ltd.
Tune : SOUTHWELL, SM; Damon's *Psalmes*, 1579, later form of third phrase

65 Lord, Who throughout These Forty Days

1. Lord, who through - out these for - ty days, For
2. As you with Sa - tan did con - tend And
3. As you did hun - ger and did thirst, So
4. And through these days of pen - i - tence, And
5. A - bide with us, that through this life of

us did fast and pray, Teach us to o - ver -
did the vic - t'ry win, O give us strength in
teach us, gra - cious Lord, To die to self and
through your pas - sion - tide, For ev - er - more, in
doubts and hopes and pain, An East - er of un -

come our sins And close by you to stay.
you to fight, In you to con - quer sin.
so to live By your most ho - ly word.
life and death, O Lord, with us a - bide.
end - ing joy We may at last at - tain.

Text : Claudia Frances Hernaman, 1838-1898, *A Child's Book of Praise*, 1873, alt.
Tune : ST. FLAVIAN, CM; *John Day's Psalter*, 1562

Make Speed, O God of Mercy, Lord   66

1. Make speed, O God of mercy, Lord,
2. You know our thoughts, you un - der - stand,
3. Give us the strength to win con - trol
4. Re - ceive, most ho - ly Trin - i - ty,

To hear the hum - ble prayers
Our weak - ness proves your power;
Of ev - 'ry swift de - sire,
The of - fer - ings we raise;

We of - fer in these Lent - en days
As we re - turn, for - give with love
That fast - ing from all taste of sin
O Lord of all sim - plic - i - ty,

Of pen - i - tence and tears.
The fail - ures of the hour.
Our love may nev - er tire.
In - crease our lov - ing praise.

Text: *Audi, benigne conditor;* adapt. by Ralph Wright, OSB, b.1938
Tune: GOD OF MERCY, CM; Margaret Daly
© 1989, GIA Publications, Inc.

67 O God, Creator of Us All

1. O God, cre - a - tor of us all, From
2. For - give us all the wrong we do, And
3. The fast by law and proph - ets taught, By
4. O God of mer - cy, hear our prayer, With

whom we come, to whom we go, You look with pit - y
pu - ri - fy each sin - ful soul. What we have dark - ened,
you, O Christ, was sanc - ti - fied. Bless all our pen - ance,
Christ your Son, and Spir - it blest, Tran - scend - ent Trin - i -

on our hearts, The weak - ness of our wills you know.
heal with light, And what we have de - stroyed, make whole.
give us strength To share the cross on which you died.
ty in whom Cre - at - ed things all come to rest.

Text: *The Stanbrook Abbey Hymnal*, rev. ed., © Stanbrook Abbey Music
Tune: CHRISTE QUI LUX ES ET DIES, LM; Mode II; *Antiphonarium SOP*, Rome 1933; acc. by Frank Quinn, OP, b.1932, © 1989, GIA Publications, Inc.

Take Up Your Cross, the Savior Said 68

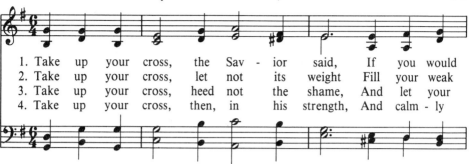

1. Take up your cross, the Sav - ior said, If you would
2. Take up your cross, let not its weight Fill your weak
3. Take up your cross, heed not the shame, And let your
4. Take up your cross, then, in his strength, And calm - ly

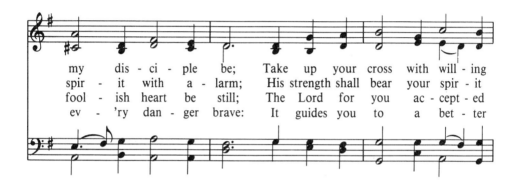

my dis - ci - ple be; Take up your cross with will - ing
spir - it with a - larm; His strength shall bear your spir - it
fool - ish heart be still; The Lord for you ac - cept - ed
ev - 'ry dan - ger brave: It guides you to a bet - ter

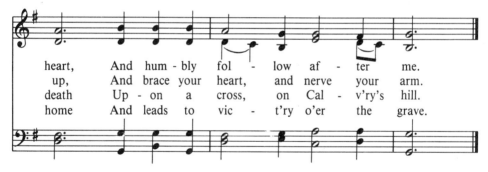

heart, And hum - bly fol - low af - ter me.
up, And brace your heart, and nerve your arm.
death Up - on a cross, on Cal - v'ry's hill.
home And leads to vic - t'ry o'er the grave.

5. Take up your cross, and follow Christ,
   Nor think till death to lay it down;
   For only those who bear the cross
   May hope to wear the glorious crown.

6. To you, great Lord, the One in Three,
   All praise for evermore ascend;
   O grant us here below to see
   The heav'nly life that knows no end.

Text : Charles William Everest, 1814-1877, *Vision of Death,* 1833, alt.
Tune : BRESLAU, LM; *As Hymnodus Sacer,* Leipzig, 1625, as melody of "Herr Jesu Christ, mein Lebens Licht," adapt. by Felix Mendelssohn-Bartholdy, 1809-1847

68 SECOND TUNE

1. Take up your cross, the Sav - ior said, If you would my dis -
2. Take up your cross, let not its weight Fill your weak spir - it
3. Take up your cross, heed not the shame, And let your fool - ish
4. Take up your cross, then, in his strength, And calm - ly ev - 'ry

ci - ple be; Take up your cross with will - ing heart,
with a - larm; His strength shall bear your spir - it up,
heart be still; The Lord for you ac - cept - ed death
dan - ger brave: It guides you to a bet - ter home

And hum - bly fol - low af - ter me.
And brace your heart, and nerve your arm.
Up - on a cross, on Cal - v'ry's hill.
And leads to vic - t'ry o'er the grave. A - men.

5. Take up your cross, and follow Christ,
Nor think till death to lay it down;
For only those who bear the cross
May hope to wear the glorious crown.

6. To you, great Lord, the One in Three,
All praise for evermore ascend;
O grant us here below to see
The heav'nly life that knows no end.

Text: Charles William Everest, 1814-1877, *Vision of Death*, 1833, alt.
Tune: MERCIFUL REDEEMER, LM; Mode IV; acc. by Samuel Weber, OSB, b.1947, © 1987, Saint Meinrad Archabbey

May We Observe These Forty Days 69

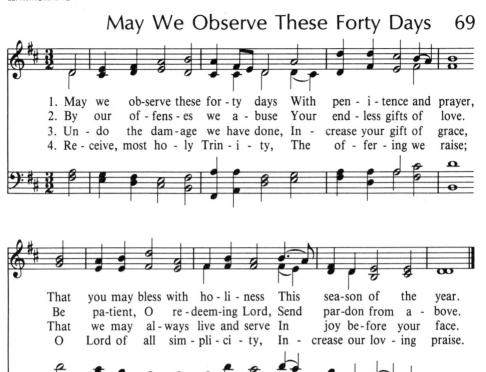

1. May we ob-serve these for-ty days With pen-i-tence and prayer,
2. By our of-fens-es we a-buse Your end-less gifts of love.
3. Un-do the dam-age we have done, In-crease your gift of grace,
4. Re-ceive, most ho-ly Trin-i-ty, The of-fer-ing we raise;

That you may bless with ho-li-ness This sea-son of the year.
Be pa-tient, O re-deem-ing Lord, Send par-don from a-bove.
That we may al-ways live and serve In joy be-fore your face.
O Lord of all sim-pli-ci-ty, In-crease our lov-ing praise.

Text: Ralph Wright, OSB, b.1938, © 1989, GIA Publications, Inc.
Tune: LIVERPOOL, CM; American Folk Hymn, attr. to M.C.H. Davis, *Mercer's Cluster*, 1823

70 O God of Pity

1. O God of pity, turn to us, your chil - dren;
2. Look down in mer - cy from your throne in glo - ry;
3. O Christ, true light and good - ness, life of all things,
4. All praise to God the Fa - ther ev - er - last - ing,

In - cline your ear in your great lov - ing
Pour on our world the ra - diance of your
Joy of the whole world, in - fi - nite in
All praise for ev - er to the sole be -

kind - ness. And, as your peo - ple's song is now as -
pres - ence; Drive from our wea - ry hearts the shades of
kind - ness, Who by the crim - son flow - ing of your
got - ten, With whom the Ho - ly Spir - it, with them

cend - ing, We beg you, hear us.
dark - ness; Light - en our foot - steps.
life - blood To life re - store us.
e - qual, Reigns through the ag - es.

Text : *Aures ad nostras*, Ante-Tridentine Breviary; tr. by Alan G. McDougal, b.1895, alt.
Tune : HERZLIEBSTER JESU, 11 11 11 5; John Cruger, 1640; adapt by J.S. Bach, 1685-1750

O Sun of Justice, Fill Our Hearts   71

1. O Sun of Jus - tice, fill our hearts, Where sin - ful-
2. Make this a fit - ting time for us, A time to
3. So sanc - ti - fy our pen - ance, Lord, That strength-ened
4. As spring a - wakes the fro - zen earth, So East - er
5. O ev - er - last - ing Trin - i - ty, We soon shall

ness has brought de - cay; Dis - pel the dark - ness of our
change and turn to you; Please hear our prayer, most pa - tient
by the grac - es won, We may a - mend our sin - ful
blooms from Lent's re - straints. Re - joice! for Christ will con - quer
see that day of days When all cre - a - tion, born a-

souls   As now the night gives place to day.
Lord,   Re - pen - tance in our hearts re - new.
lives   And toward our goal more sure - ly run.
death   And bring his grace to make us saints.
gain,   Will sing an East - er song of praise.

Text: *Jam Christe, Sol Justitiae*, c. 6th C.: tr. by Frank C. Quinn, OP, b.1932
Tune: JAM CHRISTE SOL JUSTITIAE. LM; MODE VIII, alt.; *Antiphonarium SOP*, Rome, 1933; acc. by Frank Quinn, OP, b.1932

71 – SECOND TUNE

1. O   Sun   of   Jus - tice,   fill   our   hearts,   Where
2. Make   this   a   fit - ting   time   for   us,   A
3. So   sanc - ti - fy   our   pen - ance,   Lord,   That
4. As   spring a - wakes   the   fro - zen   earth,   So
5. O   ev - er - last - ing   Trin - i - ty,   We

sin - ful - ness has   brought de - cay; Dis - pel   the   dark-ness
time to change and   turn to   you; Please hear   our   prayer, most
strength-ened by the   grac - es   won,   We   may   a - mend our
East - er blooms from   Lent's re - straints. Re - joice! for   Christ will
soon shall see that   day   of   days When all   cre - a - tion,

of   our souls As   now   the   night gives place to   day.
pa - tient Lord, Re - pen - tance in   our   hearts re - new.
sin - ful lives And   toward our   goal more sure - ly   run.
con - quer death And   bring his   grace to   make us   saints.
born a - gain, Will   sing   an   East - er   song of   praise.

Text: *Jam Christe, Sol Justitiae*, c. 6th C.: tr. by Frank C. Quinn, OP, b.1932, © 1989, GIA Publications, Inc.
Tune: ERHALT UNS, HERR (SPIRES), LM; J. Klug's *Geistliche Lieder*, 1543

The Glory of These Forty Days 72

1. The glo - ry of these for - ty days we
2. A - lone and fast - ing Mo - ses saw the
3. So Dan - iel trained his mys - tic sight, de -
4. Then grant us, Lord, like them to do such
5. O Fa - ther, Son, and Spir - it blest, to

cel - e - brate with songs of praise; for Christ by whom all
lov - ing God who gave the law; and to E - li - jah,
liv - ered from the li - ons' might; and John, the Bride-groom's
things as bring great praise to you; our spir - its strength-en
you be ev - 'ry prayer ad - dressed, who are by all your

things were made, him - self has fast - ed and has prayed.
fast - ing, came the steeds and char - i - ots of flame.
friend, be - came the her - ald of Mes - si - ah's name.
with your grace, and give us joy to see your face.
works a - dored, from age to age, the on - ly Lord.

Text : *Clarum decus jejunii*, 6th C.; tr. by Maurice F. Bell, 1862-1947, © Oxford University Press
Tune : ERHALT UNS, HERR (SPIRES), LM; J. Klug's *Geistliche Lieder*, 1543

73 Forty Days and Forty Nights

1. For-ty days and for-ty nights You were fast-ing
2. Shall we not your vig-il share, And from world-ly
3. And if e-vil on us press Our en-deav-ors
4. So shall peace di-vine be ours, Last-ing glad-ness
5. Guard and keep us, Sav-ior dear, ev-er con-stant

in the wild; For-ty days and for-ty nights
joys ab-stain, With you watch-ing, fast in prayer,
to as-sail, Vic-tor in the wil-der-ness,
ours shall be; Come to us an-gel-ic pow'rs
by your side, that with you we may ap-pear

Tempt-ed, and still un-be-guiled.
With you strong to suf-fer pain?
Help us not to swerve or fail.
Who ac-claimed your vic-to-ry.
at the e-ter-nal East-er-tide.

Text : George Hunt Smyttan, 1822-1870, *Penny Post*, 1856; alt. by Francis Pott, 1832-1909, *Hymns Ancient and Modern*, 1861, and others; alt.
Tune : HEINLEIN, 7 7 7 7; *Nurnbergisches Gesang-Buch*, 1676, attr. to Martin Herbst, 1654-1681

How Good, Lord, to Be Here! 74

1. How good, Lord to be here! Your glo-ry fills the night; Your
2. How good, Lord, to be here! Your beau-ty to be-hold Where
3. Be-fore we taste of death, We see your king-dom come; We
4. How good, Lord, to be here! Yet we may not re-main; But

face and gar-ments, like the sun, Shine with un-bor-rowed light.
Mo-ses and E-li-jah stand, Your mes-sen-gers of old.
long to hold the vi-sion bright And make this hill our home.
since you bid us leave the mount, Come with us to the plain.

Text : Joseph A. Robinson, 1858-1933, alt., © Miss Esmé D.E. Bird
Tune : POTSDAM, SM; Mercer, *Church Psalter*, 1854

75 More Ancient Than the Primal World

1. More an - cient than the pri - mal world And old - er
2. Your im - age is the Lord of Life, Your Son from
3. Trans - fig - ured Christ, be - lieved and loved, In you our
4. O Fa - ther, Son and Spir - it blest, With hearts trans -

than the morn - ing star, Be - fore the first things
all e - ter - ni - ty; All that must per - ish,
on - ly hope has been; Grant us, in your un -
fig - ured by your grace, May we your match - less

took their shape, Cre - a - tor of them all, you are.
he re - stores, In him all re - con-ciled will be.
fath - omed love, Those things no eye has ev - er seen.
splen - dor praise And see the glo - ry of your Face.

Text : *The Stanbrook Abbey Hymnal*, rev. ed., 1974, © Stanbrook Abbey Music
Tune : ANGEL'S SONG, LM; melody and bass by Orlando Gibbons, 1623

SECOND TUNE – 75

1. More an-cient than the pri-mal world And old-er than the
2. Your im-age is the Lord of Life, Your Son from all e-
3. Trans-fig-ured Christ, be-lieved and loved, In you our on-ly
4. O Fa-ther, Son and Spir-it blest, With hearts trans-fig-ured

morn-ing star, Be-fore the first things took their
ter-ni-ty; All that must per-ish, he re-
hope has been; Grant us, in your un-fath-omed
by your grace, May we your match-less splen-dor

shape, Cre-a-tor of them all, you are.
stores, In him all re-con-ciled will be.
love, Those things no eye has ev-er seen.
praise And see the glo-ry of your Face. A-men.

Text : *The Stanbrook Abbey Hymnal*, rev. ed., 1974, © Stanbrook Abbey Music
Tune : IAM CHRISTE SOL IUSTITIAE, LM; Mode II; *Antiphonale Monasticum pro Diurnis Horis*, Rome, 1934; acc. by Samuel Weber, OSB, b.1947,
© 1987, Saint Meinrad Archabbey

76 O Raise Your Eyes on High and See

1. O raise your eyes on high and see There
2. We glimpse the splen-dor and the pow'r Of
3. Of ev-'ry creed and na - tion King, In
4. The proph-ets stand and with great joy Give
5. This glo-ry that to - day our eyes Have

stands our sov-'reign Lord. His glo - ry is this
him who con-quered death, The Christ in whom the
him all strife is stilled; The prom-ise made to
wit - ness as they gaze; The Fa - ther with a
glimpsed of God's own Son Will help us ev - er

day re - vealed, His word a two-edged sword.
u - ni - verse Knows God's cre - at - ing breath.
A - bra - ham In him has been ful - filled.
sign has sealed Our trust, our hope, our praise.
sing with love Of three who are but One.

Text: Ralph Wright, OSB, b.1938, © 1989, GIA Publications, Inc.
Tune: PEAKED ACRES OLD, CM; Prinknash Tone; Charles Watson, OSB; acc. by Br. Ashenden; © 1976, The Panel of Monastic Musicians—Liturgy in Community

1. O raise your eyes on high and see There
2. We glimpse the splen - dor and the pow'r Of
3. Of ev - 'ry creed and na - tion King, In
4. The proph - ets stand and with great joy Give
5. This glo - ry that to - day our eyes Have

stands our sov - 'reign Lord. His glo - ry is this
him who con - quered death, The Christ in whom the
him all strife is stilled; The prom - ise made to
wit - ness as they gaze; The Fa - ther with a
glimpsed of God's own Son Will help us ev - er

day re - vealed, His word a two - edged sword.
u - ni - verse Knows God's cre - at - ing breath.
A - bra - ham In him has been ful - filled.
sign has sealed Our trust, our hope, our praise.
sing with love Of three who are but One.

Text: Ralph Wright, OSB, b.1938, © 1989, GIA Publications, Inc.
Tune: MORNING SONG, 8 6 8 6; *Kentucky Harmony;* harm. by C. Winfred Douglas, 1867-1944, © 1943,1971, 1981, Church Pension Fund

77 O Wondrous Type! O Vision Fair!

1. O won - drous type! O vi - sion fair Of glo - ry
2. With Mo - ses and E - li - jah nigh The in - car - nate
3. With shin - ing face and bright ar - ray, Christ deigns to
4. And faith - ful hearts are raised on high By this great
5. O Fa - ther, with the e - ter - nal Son, And Ho - ly

that the church may share, Which Christ up - on the
Lord holds con - verse high; And from the cloud the
man - i - fest to - day What glo - ry shall be
vi - sion's mys - ter - y; For which in joy - ful
Spir - it, ev - er one, Vouch-safe to bring us

moun-tain shows, Where bright - er than the sun he glows!
Ho - ly One Bears wit - ness to the on - ly Son.
theirs a - bove Who joy in God with per - fect love.
strains we raise The voice of prayer, the hymn of praise.
bu thy grace To see thy glo - ry face to face.

Text : 15th C. Office Hymn (Sarum); tr. by John Mason Neale, 1818-1866, alt.
Tune : AGINCOURT, LM; "The Agincourt Song," 15th C. English Melody; adapt. by Lawrence Francis Bartlett, b.1933, © 1977, The Australian Hymn Book Pty.
Limited

Again We Keep This Solemn Fast 78

1. A - gain we keep this sol - emn fast, A gift of
   faith from ag - es past, This Lent which binds us
   lov - ing - ly To faith and hope and char - i - ty.

2. The law and proph - ets from of old In fig - ured
   ways this Lent fore - told, Which Christ, all a - ges'
   King and Guide, In these last days has sanc - ti - fied.

3. More spar - ing, there - fore, let us make The words we
   speak, the food we take, Our sleep, our laugh - ter,
   ev - 'ry sense; Learn peace through ho - ly pen - i - tence.

4. Let us a - void each harm - ful way That lures the
   care - less mind a - stray; By watch - ful prayer our
   spir - its free From schem - ing of the En - e - my.

5. We pray, O bless - ed Three - in - One, Our God while
   end - less ag - es run, That this, our Lent of
   for - ty days, May bring us growth and give you praise.

Text : *Ex more docti mystico*, ascr. to Gregory the Great, d.604; tr. by Peter Scagnelli, b.1949, ©
Tune : A LA VENUE DE NOËL, LM; *Fleurs des noëls*, 1535

79 Eternal Lord of Love

1. E - ter - nal Lord of love, be - hold your Church
2. So dai - ly dy - ing to the way of self,
3. If dead in you, so in you we a - rise,

Walk - ing once more the pil - grim way of Lent,
So dai - ly liv - ing to your way of love,
You the first - born of all the faith - ful dead;

Led by your cloud by day, by night your fire,
We walk the road, Lord Je - sus, that you trod,
And as through ston - y ground the green shoots break,

Moved by your love and toward your pres - ence bent,
Know - ing our - selves bap - tized in - to your death:
Glo - rious in spring - time dress of leaf and flow'r,

Far off yet here— the goal of all de - sire.
So we are dead and live with you in God.
So in the Fa - ther's glo - ry shall we wake.

Text : Thomas H. Cain, 1931, © 1982
Tune : OLD 124th, 10 10 10 10 10; *Pseaumes octante trois de David,* 1551; harm. by Charles Winfred Douglas, 1867-1944

80 Father of Heaven, Whose Love Profound

1. Fa - ther of heav'n, whose love pro - found
2. Al - might - y Son, in - car - nate Word,
3. E - ter - nal Spir - it, by whose breath
4. Thrice Ho - ly! Fa - ther, Spir - it, Son;

A ran - som for our souls has found,
Our Proph - et, Priest, Re - deem - er, Lord,
The soul is raised from sin and death,
Mys - te - rious God - head, Three in One,

Be - fore your throne we sin - ners bend,
Be - fore your throne we sin - ners bend,
Be - fore your throne we sin - ners bend,
Be - fore your throne we sin - ners bend,

To us your par - d'ning love ex - tend.
To us your sav - ing grace ex - tend.
To us your quick - 'ning pow'r ex - tend.
Grace, par - don, life to us ex - tend.

Text : Edward Cooper, 1770-1833, *Selections of Psalms and Hymns*, 1805, alt.
Tune : SONG 5, LM; adapt. from melody and bass by Orlando Gibbons, 1583-1625, Wither's *Hymnes and Songs of the Church*, 1623, rhythm slightly alt.

SECOND TUNE – 80

1. Fa - ther of heav'n, whose love pro-found   A ran - som for our
2. Al-might - y Son, in - car -nate Word,   Our Proph - et, Priest, Re -
3. E - ter - nal Spir - it,   by whose breath   The soul is raised from
4. Thrice Ho - ly!   Fa - ther, Spir - it, Son;   Mys - te - rious God-head,

souls has found,   Be - fore your throne we   sin - ners bend,
deem - er, Lord,   Be - fore your throne we   sin - ners bend,
sin   and death,   Be - fore your throne we   sin - ners bend,
Three   in   One,   Be - fore your throne we   sin - ners bend,

To   us   your par - d'ning love ex - tend.
To   us   your sav - ing grace ex - tend.
To   us   your quick -'ning pow'r ex - tend.
Grace, par - don, life   to   us   ex - tend.   A - men.

Text : Edward Cooper, 1770-1833, *Selections of Psalms and Hymns*, 1805, alt.
Tune : TE LUCIS ANTE TERMINUM II, alt., LM; Mode II; *Antiphonale Monasticum pro Diurnis Horis*, Rome, 1934; acc. by Samuel Weber, OSB, b.1947,
   © 1987, Saint Meinrad Archabbey

81 God, You Are Clothed with Light

1. God you are clothed with light, As with a gar-ment fair, And
2. Give me a robe of light That I may walk with you: Bright
3. But can a sin-ner dare, In rags, and sore a-shamed, Lift
4. O Christ, I lift my eyes; Your love for me I own; In

in your ho-ly sight The saints your beau-ty wear; The
as the stars are bright, Pure as their light is pure; Whose
up to God the prayer Which now my lips have framed, While
your great sac-ri-fice Re - mains my hope a - lone; The

heav'ns and all there-in ex-press The glo-ry of your ho-li-ness.
tex-ture sin shall nev-er stain, But ev-er un-de-filed re-main.
glow-ing ser-aphs fold their wings, And pour their sin-less of-fer-ings?
robe is mine, my soul to dress, Of ev-er-last-ing right-eous-ness.

Text : Hymn from the Russian Church; tr. John Brownlie, 1857-1925, alt.
Tune : HAREWOOD, 66 66 88; Samuel Sebastian Wesley, 1810-1876

Have Mercy, Lord, on Us 82

1. Have mer - cy, Lord, on us, For
2. Lord, wash a - way our guilt, And
3. The joy your grace can give, Let
4. To God the Fa - ther, Son, And

you are ev - er kind; Though we have sinned be -
cleanse us from our sin; For we con - fess our
us a - gain ob - tain, And may your Spir - it's
Spir - it glo - ry be, Who was, and is, and

fore you, Lord, Your mer - cy let us find.
wrongs, and see How great our guilt has been.
firm sup - port Our spir - its then sus - tain.
shall be so For all e - ter - ni - ty.

Text: Psalm 52; Nahum Tate, 1652-1715, and Nicholas Brady, 1659-c.1726, *New Version of the Psalms*, 1696, alt.
Tune: SOUTHWELL, SM; William Damon's *Psalmes*, later form of 3rd phrase

83 Have Pity, God of Grace

1. Have pit - y, God of grace, on me, a sin - ner;
2. True hearts a - lone, O God of truth, de - light you;
3. Let me, I pray, live al - ways in your pres - ence;
4. All glo - ry be to God, the gra - cious Fa - ther,

My sin - ful heart in your great love con - sole.
My heart of hearts to truth make ev - er true.
Give me your Spir - it, Lord, to guide me still.
All glo - ry be to God, the on - ly Son,

Cleanse me O fount of grace, from sin's de - file - ment;
Give me a wis - er heart to learn true wis - dom;
Give me a - new the joy of your sal - va - tion;
All glo - ry be to God, the Ho - ly Spir - it,

Bathe me, O heal - ing spring, and make me whole.
By stead - fast love my way - ward - ness un - do.
Re - new my spir - it and up - hold my will.
Who dwell in us by grace and make us one.

Text : Based on Psalm 51; James Quinn, SJ, b.1919, *New Hymns for All Seasons*, © 1969
Tune : INTERCESSOR, 11 10 11 10; Charles Hubert Hastings Perry, 1848-1918

Lord, We Are Blind 84

1. Lord, we are blind; the world of sight Is as a shad-ow in the
2. Lord, we are blind; the world a - round Con fus - es us, al-though we
3. Lord, we are blind; our sight, our life By our own ef - forts can-not

All:

dark. Yet we have eyes; Lord, give us light That we may see.
see. In Christ the pat - tern is re - found; He sets us free.
be. Breathe on our clay and touch our eyes; We would serve thee.

Text: "Men Born Blind," David Edge, b.1932, ©
Tune: GODMANSTONE, 8 8 8 4; Cyril Taylor, b.1907, © 1989, Hope Publishing Co.

85 Now Let Us All with One Accord

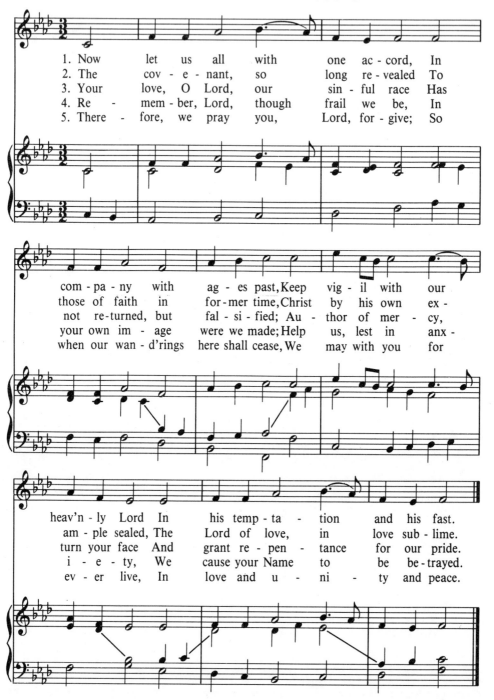

1. Now let us all with one ac-cord, In com-pa-ny with ag-es past, Keep vig-il with our heav'n-ly Lord In his temp-ta - tion and his fast.
2. The cov-e-nant, so long re-vealed To those of faith in for-mer time, Christ by his own ex - am-ple sealed, The Lord of love, in love sub-lime.
3. Your love, O Lord, our sin-ful race Has not re-turned, but fal-si-fied; Au-thor of mer - cy, turn your face And grant re-pen - tance for our pride.
4. Re - mem-ber, Lord, though frail we be, In your own im - age were we made; Help us, lest in anx-i - e - ty, We cause your Name to be be-trayed.
5. There - fore, we pray you, Lord, for-give; So when our wan-d'rings here shall cease, We may with you for ev - er live, In love and u - ni - ty and peace.

Text : Attr. to Gregory the Great, 540-604; tr. James Quinn, SJ, b.1919, *Praise the Lord*, 1972, alt., © Geoffrey Chapman
Tune : BOURBON, LM; attr. to Freeman Lewis, 1780-1859; harm. by Thomas Foster, b.1938, © 1984

1. New let us all with one ac-cord, In com-pa-ny with
2. The cov-e-nant, so long re-vealed To those of faith in
3. Your love, O Lord, our sin-ful race Has not re-turned, but
4. Re-mem-ber, Lord, though frail we be, In your own im-age
5. There-fore, we pray you, Lord, for-give; So when our wan-d'rings

ag - es past, Keep vig - il with our heav'n - ly Lord
for - mer time, Christ by his own ex - am - ple sealed,
fal - si - fied; Au - thor of mer - cy, turn your face
were we made; Help us, lest in anx - i - e - ty,
here shall cease, We may with you for ev - er live,

In his temp - ta - tion and his fast.
The Lord of love, in love sub - lime.
And grant re - pen - tance for our pride.
We cause your Name to be be - trayed.
In love and u - ni - ty and peace. A - men.

Text : Attr. to Gregory the Great, 540-604; tr. by James Quinn, SJ, b.1919, *Praise the Lord*, 1972, alt., © Geoffrey Chapman
Tune : TE LUCIS ANTE TERMINUM II, alt., LM; Mode II; *Antiphonale Monasticum pro Diurnis Horis*, Rome, 1934; acc. by Samuel Weber, OSB, b.1947,
© 1987, Saint Meinrad Archabbey

86 Creator of the Earth and Skies

1. Cre - a - tor of the earth and skies, To whom the words of life be - long, Grant us your truth to make us wise: Grant us your pow'r to make us strong.
2. We have not known you; to the skies Our mon - u - ments of fol - ly soar, And all our self - wrought mis - er - ies Have made us trust our - selves the more.
3. We have not loved you: far and wide The wreck - age of our hat - red spreads, And e - vils wrought by hu - man pride Re - coil on un - re - pent - ant heads.
4. For this, our fool - ish con - fi - dence, Our pride of knowl - edge and our sin, We come to you in pen - i - tence; In us the work of grace be - gin.
5. Teach us to know and love you, Lord, And hum - bly fol - low in your way. Speak to our souls the quick - 'ning word, And turn our dark - ness in - to day.

Text : David W. Hughes, 1911-1967, alt.; © J. Donald P. Hughes
Tune : UFFINGHAM, LM; Jeremiah Clarke, 1670-1707, alt.

1. Cre - a - tor of the earth and skies, To whom the words of
2. We have not known you; to the skies Our mon - u - ments of
3. We have not loved you: far and wide The wreck-age of our
4. For this, our fool - ish con - fi - dence, Our pride of knowl-edge
5. Teach us to know and love you, Lord, And hum - bly fol - low

life be - long, Grant us your truth to make us wise:
fol - ly soar, And all our self-wrought mis - er - ies
hat - red spreads, And e - vils wrought by hu - man pride
and our sin, We come to you in pen - i - tence;
in your way. Speak to our souls the quick-'ning word,

Grant us your pow'r to make us strong.
Have made us trust our - selves the more.
Re - coil on un - re - pent - ant heads.
In us the work of grace be - gin.
And turn our dark - ness in - to day. A - men.

Text : David W. Hughes, 1911-1967, alt.; © J. Donald P. Hughes
Tune : TE LUCIS ANTE TERMINUM IIa, alt., LM; Mode II; *Antiphonale Monasticum pro Diurnis Horis*, Rome, 1934; acc. by Samuel Weber, OSB, b.1947,
© 1987, Saint Meinrad Archabbey

87 O Christ, You Are the Light and Day

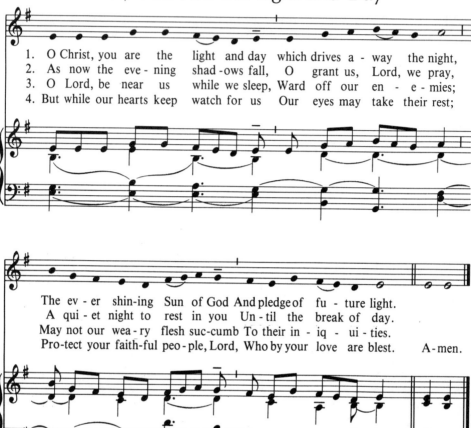

1. O Christ, you are the light and day which drives a - way the night,
2. As now the eve - ning shad -ows fall, O grant us, Lord, we pray,
3. O Lord, be near us while we sleep, Ward off our en - e - mies;
4. But while our hearts keep watch for us Our eyes may take their rest;

The ev - er shin-ing Sun of God And pledge of fu - ture light.
A qui - et night to rest in you Un - til the break of day.
May not our wea - ry flesh suc-cumb To their in - iq - ui - ties.
Pro-tect your faith-ful peo - ple, Lord, Who by your love are blest. A-men.

5. Regard, O Lord, our helplessness,
   And come to our defense;
   May we be governed by your love,
   In true obedience.

6. Remember us, poor mortals all,
   We humbly ask, O Lord,
   And may your presence in our souls
   Be now our great reward.

Text: *Christe, qui Lux es et Dies*, c.800; tr. by Frank C. Quinn, OP, b.1932, © 1989, GIA Publications, Inc.
Tune: PRINKNASH PARK, CM; Prinknash Tone, © Trustees of Prinknash Abbey; acc. by Br. Ashenden, ©

Behold the Royal Cross on High 88

1. Be - hold the roy - al cross on high, Re - splend - ent in its mys - ter - y, The cross on which the Lord of all Once suf - fered hu - man ag - o - ny.

2. From nails which bound his feet and hands Christ's tor - tured bod - y hung in pain. Thus was the vic - tim sac - ri - ficed Who for the sins of all was slain.

3. But when his sa - cred side was pierced, A sym - bol of his love was seen: Christ's blood with wa - ter is - sued forth To purge our souls and wash us clean.

4. O ho - ly and re - splend - ent Tree Once wa - tered by that pre - cious flood Which blessed your trunk and col - ored it The pur - ple hue of roy - al blood.

5. O holy Cross in whom alone
The world's salvation is assured,
May Christ impart to us the grace
Which by his passion he procured.

6. Now may the blessed Trinity
By ev'ry creature be adored,
Who through the myst'ry of the Cross
From death to life has been restored.

Text: *Vexilla Regis prodeunt*, Venantius Fortunatus, 569; tr. by Frank C. Quinn, OP, b.1932, © 1989, GIA Publications, Inc.
Tune: ILLSLEY, LM; M. Bishop, c.1665-1773

88 – SECOND TUNE

1. Be - hold the roy - al cross on high, Re-splend-ent in its
2. From nails which bound his feet and hands Christ's tor-tured bod - y
3. But when his sa - cred side was pierced, A sym - bol of his
4. O ho - ly and re-splend-ent Tree Once wa - tered by that

mys - ter - y, The cross on which the Lord of all
hung in pain. Thus was the vic - tim sac - ri - ficed
love was seen: Christ's blood with wa - ter is - sued forth
pre - cious flood Which blessed your trunk and col - ored it

Once suf - fered hu - man ag - o - ny.
Who for the sins of all was slain.
To purge our souls and wash us clean.
The pur - ple hue of roy - al blood. A - men.

5. O holy Cross in whom alone
   The world's salvation is assured,
   May Christ impart to us the grace
   Which by his passion he procured.

6. Now may the blessed Trinity
   By ev'ry creature be adored,
   Who through the myst'ry of the Cross
   From death to life has been restored.

Text: *Vexilla Regis prodeunt*, Venantius Fortunatus, 569; tr. by Frank C. Quinn, OP, b.1932, © 1989, GIA Publications, Inc.
Tune: MERCIFUL REDEEMER, LM; Mode II; acc. by Samuel Weber, OSB, b.1947, © 1987, Saint Meinrad Archabbey

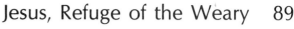

Jesus, Refuge of the Weary   89

1. Je - sus, ref - uge of the wea - ry, Blest re - deem - er, whom we love,
2. Do we pass that cross un - heed-ing, Breath-ing no re - pen-tant vow,
3. Je - sus, may our hearts be burn-ing With more fer - vent love for you;

Foun - tain of life's des - ert drea - ry, Sav - ior from the world a - bove:
Though we see you wound-ed, bleed-ing, See your thorn-en - cir - cled brow?
May our eyes be ev - er turn - ing To be - hold your cross a - new;

Of - ten have your eyes, of - fend - ed, Gazed up - on the sin - ner's fall;
Yet your sin - less death has brought us Life e - ter - nal, peace, and rest;
Till in glo - ry, part - ed nev - er From the bless - ed Sav - ior's side,

Yet up - on the cross ex - tend - ed, You have borne the pain of all.
On - ly what your grace has taught us Calms the sin - ner's deep dis - tress.
Grav - en in our hearts for ev - er, Dwell the cross, the Cru - ci - fied.

Text : Girolomo Savonarola, 1452-1498; tr. by Jane F. Wilde, 1826-1896, alt.
Tune : O DU LIEBE MEINER LIEBE, 87 87 D; Herrnhut, c.1735

90 My Song Is Love Unknown

1. My song is love un-known, My sav-ior's love to me, Love
*2. He came from his blest throne Sal-va-tion to be-stow: But
3. Some-times they strew his way And his sweet prais-es sing, Re-
4. Why, what has my Lord done? What makes this rage and spite? He
5. They rise and needs will have My dear Lord made a-way; A

to the love-less shown, That they might love-ly be. O
men made strange, and none The longed-for Christ would know. But
sound-ing all the day Ho-san-nas to their King. Then
made the lame to run, He gave the blind their sight. Sweet
mur-der-er they save: The prince of life they slay. Yet

who am I That for my sake My Lord should take Frail flesh, and die?
O my friend! My friend in-deed, Who at my need His life did spend.
"Cru-ci-fy!" Is all they breathe, And for his death They thirst and cry.
in-jur-ies! Yet they at these Them-selves dis-please, And 'gainst him rise.
cheer-ful he To suf-f'ring goes, That he his foes, From thence might free.

6. In life, no house, no home
My Lord on earth might have;
In death, no friendly tomb
But what a stranger gave.
What may I say?
Heav'n was his home;
But mine the tomb
Wherein he lay.

7. Here might I stay and sing—
No story so divine;
Never was love, dear King,
Never was grief like thine.
This is my friend,
In whose sweet praise
I all my days
Could gladly spend.

Note: Vs. 2 contains a generic "men" which given the antiquity and beauty of this poem has not been changed. Thus, those who do not wish to sing it can avoid the verse.

Text: Samuel Crossman, c.1624-1684
Tune: LOVE UNKNOWN, 66 66 4444; John Nicholson Ireland, 1879-1962, © John Ireland Trust

O Cross of Christ, Immortal Tree   91

1. O Cross of Christ, im - mor - tal tree   On which   our Sav - ior died,
2. From bit - ter death and bar - ren wood   The tree   of life is made;
3. O   faith-ful Cross, you stand un-moved While ag - es run their course:
4. Give glo - ry   to   the   ris - en Christ And   to   his Cross give praise,

The world is shel-tered by your arms   That bore the Cru - ci - fied.
Its branch-es bear un - fail- ing fruit   And leaves that nev - er   fade.
Foun - da - tion of the   u - ni - verse,   Cre - a - tion's bind-ing force.
The sign of God's un-fath-omed love,   The hope of   all   our   days.

Text : *The Stanbrook Abbey Hymnal*, rev. ed., 1974; © Stanbrook Abbey Music
Tune : CHESHIRE, CM; Este's *Psalter*, 1592, rhythm slightly altered

91 – SECOND TUNE

1. O Cross of Christ, im - mor - tal tree On
2. From bit - ter death and bar - ren wood The
3. O faith - ful Cross, you stand un - moved While
4. Give glo - ry to the ris - en Christ And

which our Sav - ior died, The world is shel - tered by your arms
tree of life is made; Its branch - es bear un - fail - ing fruit
ag - es run their course: Foun - da - tion of the u - ni - verse,
to his Cross give praise, The sign of God's un - fath-omed love,

That bore the Cru - ci - fied.
And leaves that nev - er fade.
Cre - a - tion's bind - ing force.
The hope of all our days. A - men.

Text : *The Stanbrook Abbey Hymnal*, rev. ed., 1974; © Stanbrook Abbey Music
Tune : LOVING HEARTS, CM; Mode IV; Columba Kelly, OSB, b.1930, alt.; acc. by Samuel Weber, OSB, b.1947, © 1987, Saint Meinrad Archabbey

The Regal Dark Mysterious Cross 92

1. The re - gal dark mys - te - rious cross In song is lift - ed high, The wood on which the Son of Man Was stretched a - gainst the sky.
2. Up - on this wood his bod - y bore The nails, the taunts, the spear, Till wa - ter flowed with blood to wash The whole world free of fear.
3. At last the song that Da - vid sang Is heard and un - der - stood: "Be - fore the na - tions God as king Reigns from his throne of wood."
4. This wood now spread with pur - ple wears The pag - eant - ry of kings; Of cho - sen stock it dares to hold On high his tor - tured limbs.
5. O bless - ed Tree, up - on whose arms The world's own ran - som hung; His bod - y pays our debt, and life From Sa - tan's grasp is wrung.

6. O sacred Cross, our steadfast hope,
   In this our Passiontide,
   Through you the Son obtained for all
   Forgiveness as he died.

7. May ev'ry living creature praise
   Our God both one and three,
   Who rules in everlasting peace
   All whom his cross makes free.

Text: *Vexilla Regis,* Venantius Honorius Fortunatus, 530-609; tr. by Ralph Wright, OSB, b.1938, © 1989, GIA Publications, Inc.
Tune: REGAL CROSS,CM; Austin Rennick, OSB, ©

93 O Sacred Head, Surrounded

1. O sacred head, surrounded By crown of pierc-ing thorn! O bleed-ing head, so wound-ed, Re-viled and put to scorn! Our
2. The Lord of ev-'ry na-tion Was hung up-on a tree; His death was our sal-va-tion, Our sins, his ag-o-ny. O
3. In this, your bit-ter Pas-sion, Good Shep-herd, think of me With your most kind com-pas-sion, Un-wor-thy though I be; Be-

sins have marred the glo - ry Of
Je - sus, by your Pas - sion, Your
neath your cross a - bid - ing For

your most ho - ly face, Yet an - gel hosts a -
life in us in - crease; Your death for us did
ev - er would I rest, In your dear love con -

dore you, And trem - ble as they gaze.
fash - ion Our par - don and our peace.
fid - ing, And with your pres - ence blest.

Text : St. 1, Henry W. Baker, 1821-1877, alt.; st. 2, Melvin L. Farrell, SS, b.1930, © 1961, World Library Publications, Inc.; st. 3, Arthur T. Russell, 1806-1874, alt.
Tune : PASSION CHORALE, 76 76 D; Hans L. Hassler, 1564-1612; harm. by Johann Sebastian Bach, 1685-1750

94A Sing in Triumph of Our Savior: PART I

1. Sing in tri - umph of our Sav - ior, Raise your voic - es, sing with pride, Of the gen - tle one who loves us And for us was cru - ci - fied, Stretched up - on the cross in tor - ment, Heal - ing ha - tred as he died.

2. Grieved by Sa - tan's swift de - cep - tion, Our cre - at - ing, sav - ing Lord, Pledged that death would not be fi - nal As the fruit of hu - man fraud, But that life one day would tri - umph, On an - oth - er tree re - stored.

3. Har - mo - ny with per - fect rhy - thm Per - me - ates the bal - anced plan, For the Prince of false - hood tum - bles— Meet - ing truth he can - not stand— And the wea - pon that once wound - ed Heals with - in the sur - geon's hand.

4. As the cho - sen hour of judge - ment Struck with light - ning's in - stant flash, From be - yond all time the god - head, At the Fa - ther's time - less wish, Came in - to the womb of Mar - y And put on our mor - tal flesh.

5. Stirring now he lies restricted
   in the cattle manger's hold.
   Now his mother binds his body
   in the bands against the cold.
   So the hands of her creator
   with her linen she enfolds.

6. May our praises and our wonder
   echo through the heart of light
   to the Father who creates us
   and the Son whose gentle might
   in the Spirit won us freedom
   from the grasp of endless night.

Text: *Pange lingua gloriosi proelium certaminis*, Venantius Honorius Fortunatus, 530-609; tr. by Ralph Wright, OSB, b. 1938, © 1989, GIA Publications, Inc.
Tune: FORTUNATUS NEW, 87 87 87; Carl F. Schalk, b.1929, © 1967, Concordia Publishing House

The Pange lingua, *parts I and II, is a single composition detailing the entire saving history of Jesus Christ. Part I is traditionally sung at morning prayer and part II at evening prayer.*

94B Sing in Triumph of Our Savior: PART II

1. Sing in tri - umph of our Sav - ior, Raise your voic - es,
2. Sing of gall, of nails, of spit - tle, Sing of sponge and
3. See the no - ble cross re - splend - ent Stand - ing tall and
4. Bend your boughs, O Tree, be gen - tle, Bring re - lief to

sing with pride, Of the gen - tle one who loves us
spear and rod, How the blows of sol - diers o - pened
with - out peer. Where, O Tree, have you a ri - val
God's own limbs, Bow in hom - age to bring com - fort

And for us was cru - ci - fied, Stretched up - on the
Wounds with - in the heart of God. And the world of
In the leaf or fruit you bear? Sweet the bur - den,
To the gen - tle King of kings. Ease the throne where

cross in tor - ment, Heal - ing ha - tred as he died.
pain found heal - ing, Bathed with - in the Sav - ior's blood.
sweet the ran - som, That through iron your branch - es bear.
your cre - a - tor Harsh - ly treat - ed, calm - ly reigns.

5. For of all the woods and forests
   You were chosen out to hold
   That fair prize that would win harbor
   For a drifting, storm-tossed world,
   You whose wood has now been purpled,
   By the Lamb's own blood enfurled.

6. May our praises and our wonder
   Echo through the heart of light
   To the Father who creates us
   And the Son whose gentle might
   In the Spirit won us freedom
   From the grasp of endless night.

Text: *Pange lingua gloriosi proelium certaminis*, Venantius Honorius Fortunatus, 530-609; tr. by Ralph Wright, OSB, b. 1938, © 1989, GIA Publications, Inc.
Tune: FORTUNATUS NEW, 87 87 87; Carl F. Schalk, b.1929, © 1967, Concordia Publishing House

95 What Wondrous Love Is This

1. What won-drous love is this, O my soul, O my soul?
2. To God and to the Lamb I will sing, I will sing;
3. And when from death I'm free, I'll sing on, I'll sing on;

What won-drous love is this, O my soul?
To God and to the Lamb, I will sing;
And when from death I'm free, I'll sing on;

What won-drous love is this That caused the Lord of Bliss
To God and to the Lamb Who is the great I am,
And when from death I'm free, I'll sing and joy - ful be,

To bear the dread-ful curse for my soul, for my soul;
While mil - lions join the theme, I will sing, I will sing;
And through e - ter - ni - ty I'll sing on, I'll sing on!

To   bear   the   dread - ful   curse   for   my   soul?
While   mil - lions join   the   theme,   I   will   sing.
And   through e - ter - ni - ty,   I'll   sing   on.

Text : Rev. Alexander Means, *Southern Harmony*, 1835
Tune : WONDROUS LOVE, 66 63 66 66 63; *Southern Harmony*, 1835; harm. *Cantate Domino, 1980*, © 1980, World Council of Churches

96 A Cheering, Chanting, Dizzy Crowd

1. A cheer-ing, chant-ing, diz-zy crowd Had
2. They laid their gar-ments in the road And
3. When day dimmed down to deep-'ning dark The
4. Lest we be fooled be-cause our hearts Have
5. In-stead of palms a wind-ing sheet Will

stripped the green trees bare, And hail-ing Christ as king a-
spread his path with palms And vows of last-ing love be-
crowd be-gan to fade 'Til on-ly tram-pled leaves and
surged with pass-ing praise, Re-mind us, God, as this week
have to be un-rolled, A car-pet much more fit to

loud, Waved branch-es in the air.
stowed With roy-al hymns and psalms.
bark Were left from the pa-rade.
starts Where Christ has fixed his gaze.
greet The king a cross will hold.

Text: Thomas H. Troeger, b.1945
Tune: KING'S WELCOME, CM; Carol Doran
© 1985, Oxford University Press

Ride On, Ride On in Majesty   97

1. Ride on, ride on in maj - es - ty, And hear them all ho-san - na cry; Your hum - ble beast pur - sues its way, Where crowds their palms and gar - ments lay.

2. Ride on, ride on in maj - es - ty, In sim - ple state ride on to die; Dear Christ, your tri - umphs now be - gin: To cap - ture death and con - quer sin.

3. Ride on, ride on in maj - es - ty, While hosts of an - gels fill the sky; They watch with sad and won - d'ring eyes, And see im - pend - ing sac - ri - fice.

4. Ride on, ride on in maj - es - ty, Your last and fierc - est fight is near; The Fa - ther, on his state - ly throne, A - waits his own a - noint - ed Son.

5. Ride on, ride on in maj - es - ty, In sim - ple state ride on to die; Sub - mit to suf - fer mor - tal pain, Re - sume then, God, your pow'r and reign.

Text : Henry Hart Milman, 1791-1868; adapt. by Anthony G. Petti, © 1971, Faber Music Ltd.
Tune : THE KING'S MAJESTY, LM; Graham George, b.1912, © Belwin Mills Publishing Corp.

97 – SECOND TUNE

1. Ride on, ride on in maj - es - ty, And hear them all ho -
2. Ride on, ride on in maj - es - ty, In sim - ple state ride
3. Ride on, ride on in maj - es - ty, While hosts of an - gels
4. Ride on, ride on in maj - es - ty, Your last and fierc - est
5. Ride on, ride on in maj - es - ty, In sim - ple state ride

san - na cry; Your hum - ble beast pur - sues its way,
on to die; Dear Christ, your tri - umphs now be - gin:
fill the sky; They watch with sad and won - d'ring eyes,
fight is near; The Fa - ther, on his state - ly throne,
on to die; Sub - mit to suf - fer mor - tal pain,

Where crowds their palms and gar - ments lay.
To cap - ture death and con - quer sin.
And see im - pend - ing sac - ri - fice.
A - waits his own a - noint - ed Son.
Re - sume then, God, your pow'r and reign.

Text: Henry Hart Milman, 1791-1868; adapt. by Anthony G. Petti, © 1971, Faber Music Ltd.
Tune: WINCHESTER NEW, LM; *Musikalisches Handbuch*, Hamburg, 1690, adapt.

Sunset to Sunrise Changes Now 98

1. Sun - set to sun - rise chang-es now, For God cre-ates the world a-new; On the Re-deem-er's thorn-crowned brow The won-ders of that dawn we view.

2. Al - though the sun with-holds its light Yet a more heav-'nly lamp shines here; And from the cross on Cal-v'ry's height Gleams of e-ter-ni-ty ap-pear.

3. Here in o'er-whelm-ing fi-nal strife The Lord of life has vic-to-ry; And sin is slain, and death brings life, And earth in-her-its heav-en's key.

Text: St. Clement of Alexandria, c.170-220; para. by Howard Chandler Robbins, 1876-1952, alt.
Tune: KEDRON, LM; attr. to Elkanah Kelsay Dare, 1782-1826; harm. by Alec Wyton, b.1921, © 1985, Church Pension Fund

99 Lord Christ, When First You Came to Earth

1. Lord Christ, when first you came to earth, Up-
2. O awe-some Love, which finds no room In
3. New ad-vent of the love of Christ, Will
4. O wound-ed hands of Je - sus, build In

on a cross they bound you. And mocked your sav - ing
life where sin de - nies you. And, doomed to death, shall
we a - gain re - fuse you. Till in the night of
us your new cre - a - tion: Our pride is dust, our

king-ship's worth By thorns with which they crowned you. And
bring to doom The pow'r which cru - ci - fies you, Till
hate and war We per - ish as we lose you? From
boast-ing stilled: We wait your rev - e - la - tion. O

still our wrongs may fash - ion now New thorns to pierce that
not a stone be left on stone, And then the na - tions'
an - cient doubts our minds re - lease To seek the king-dom
Love that tri - umphs o - ver loss, We bring our hearts be-

stead - y brow, And robe of sor - row round you.
pride, o'er-thrown, Will nev - er - more de - fy you!
of your peace, By which a - lone we choose you.
fore your cross To fin - ish your sal - va - tion.

Text : W. Russell Bowie, 1882-1969, alt.
Tune : MIT FREUDEN ZART, 8 7 8 7 88 7; Bohemian Brethren's *Kirchengesange*, 1566

100   O Darkness Great! Behold the Night!

slightly slower

1. O dark - ness great! Be - hold the night! O bur - den sharp and heav - y! See - ing God the Fa - ther's Son Car - ried out and bur - ied.
2. He cried a - loud With - in their streets, He whis - pered in the dark - ness. Gent - ly heal - ing all who came, Lis - t'ning to their sad - ness.
3. But some would rage When he would heal For he called God his Fa - ther. Rage dis - pels the Shep - herd's flock, All the sheep are scat - tered.
4. O see the night! O blind - ness deep! A dark when Light had per - ished. God the Fa - ther's on - ly Son, Mocked and nailed and bur - ied.

Text: Ralph Wright, OSB, b.1938, © 1989, GIA Publications, Inc.
Tune: O TRAURIGKEIT, O HERZELEID, 447 76; *Himlischer Lieder*, 1641, alt.; harm. *Hymnal 1982*, © 1985, Church Pension Fund

Daylight Fades 101

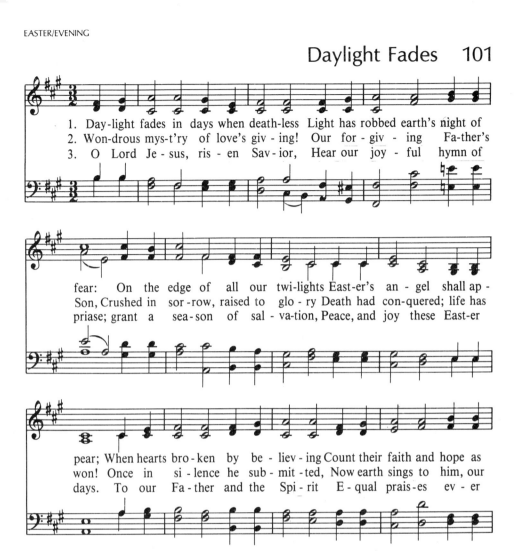

1. Day-light fades in days when death-less Light has robbed earth's night of
2. Won-drous mys-t'ry of love's giv-ing! Our for-giv-ing Fa-ther's
3. O Lord Je-sus, ris-en Sav-ior, Hear our joy-ful hymn of

fear: On the edge of all our twi-lights East-er's an-gel shall ap-
Son, Crushed in sor-row, raised to glo-ry Death had con-quered; life has
priase; grant a sea-son of sal-va-tion, Peace, and joy these East-er

pear; When hearts bro-ken by be-liev-ing Count their faith and hope as
won! Once in si-lence he sub-mit-ted, Now earth sings to him, our
days. To our Fa-ther and the Spi-rit E-qual prais-es ev-er

dead, Christ will greet them in each oth-er And in break-ing of the bread.
King; Fear will ev-er flee de-feat-ed When a heart in love can sing.
be; Born a-gain, we sing God's good-ness, Now and through e-ter-ni-ty.

Text: Based on Luke 24:28-35; Peter Scagnelli, b.1949, © 1973
Tune: DOMHNACH TRIONOIDE, 87 87 D; Gaelic Melody; harm. by Janet Stuart, 1914

102 At the Lamb's High Feast We Sing

1. At the Lamb's high feast we sing Praise to our vic-
2. Where the pas-chal blood is poured, Death's dark an-gel
3. Might-y vic-tim from the sky, Pow'rs of hell be-
4. East-er tri-umph, East-er joy, This a-lone can

to-rious King. He has washed us in the tide
sheathes his sword; Is-rael's hosts tri-um-phant go
neath you lie; Death is con-quered in the fight,
sin de-stroy; From the death of sin set free,

Flow-ing from his wound-ed side. Praise the Lord whose
Through the wave that drowns the foe. Christ the Lamb, whose
You have brought us life and light. Your vic-to-rious
Souls re-born, O Lord, we'll be. Hymns of glo-ry,

love di-vine Gives his sa-cred blood for wine,
blood was shed, Pas-chal vic-tim, pas-chal bread!
ban-ners wave; You have ris-en from the grave;
songs of praise, Fa-ther, un-to you we raise;

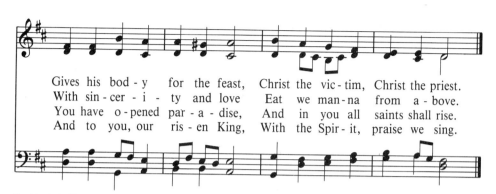

Gives his bod - y for the feast, Christ the vic - tim, Christ the priest.
With sin - cer - i - ty and love Eat we man - na from a - bove.
You have o - pened par - a - dise, And in you all saints shall rise.
And to you, our ris - en King, With the Spir - it, praise we sing.

Text: *Ad regias Agni dapes,* 1632; tr. by Robert Campbell, 1814-1868, *St. Andrew's Hymnal,* 1850, alt.
Tune: SALZBURG, 77 77 D; Jacob Hinze, 1622-1702, *Praxis Pietatis Melica,* Berlin, 1678; harm. by Johann Sebastian Bach, 1685-1750

102–SECOND TUNE

1. At the Lamb's high feast we sing Praise to our vic-
2. Praise the Lord, whose love di-vine Gives his sa-cred
3. Where the pas-chal blood is poured, Death's dark an-gel
4. Christ the Lamb, whose blood was shed, Pas-chal vic-tim,

to-rious King. He has washed us in the tide
blood for wine, Gives his bod-y for the feast,
sheathes his sword; Is-rael's hosts tri-um-phant go
pas-chal bread! With sin-cer-i-ty and love

Flow-ing from his wound-ed side. Al-le-lu-ia!
Christ the vic-tim, Christ the priest. Al-le-lu-ia!
Through the wave that drowns the foe. Al-le-lu-ia!
Eat we man-na from a-bove. Al-le-lu-ia!

5. Mighty victim from the sky,
   Pow'rs of hell beneath you lie;
   Death is conquered in the fight,
   You have brought us life and light.

6. Your victorious banners wave;
   You have risen from the grave;
   You have opened paradise,
   And in you all saints shall rise.

7. Easter triumph, Easter joy,
   This alone can sin destroy;
   From the death of sin set free,
   Souls reborn, O Lord, we'll be.

8. Hymns of glory, songs of praise,
   Father, unto you we raise;
   And to you, our risen King,
   With the Spirit, praise we sing.

Text: *Ad regias Agni dapes*, 1632; tr. by Robert Campbell, 1814-1868, *St. Andrew's Hymnal*, 1850, alt.
Tune: SONNE DER GERECHTIGKEIT, 77 77 with alleluia; *Kirchengesang*, 1566; acc. by Theophane Hytrek, OSF, © 1981, ICEL

103 Christ Jesus Lay in Death's Strong Bands

1. Christ Je - sus lay in death's strong bands, For our of - fens - es
2. It was a strange and dread - ful strife When life and death con -
3. So let us keep the fes - ti - val To which the Lord in -
4. Then let us feast this East - er day On the true bread of

giv - en, But now at God's right hand he stands, And
tend - ed; The vic - to - ry re - mained with life, The
vites us; Christ is him - self the joy of all, The
heav - en. The word of grace has purged a - way The

brings us life from heav - en: There-fore let us
reign of death was end - ed: Stripped of pow'r no
sun that warms and lights us; By his grace he
old and wick - ed leav - en; Christ a - lone our

joy - ful be, And sing God's prais - es
more it reigns, And emp - ty form a -
shall im - part e - ter - nal sun - shine
soul will feed, He is our meat and

thank - ful - ly With songs of Al - le -
lone re - mains; Death's sting is lost for
to the heart; The night of sin is
drink in - deed, Faith lives up - on no

lu - ia! Al - le - lu - ia!
ev - er. Al - le - lu - ia!
end - ed. Al - le - lu - ia!
oth - er. Al - le - lu - ia!

Text: Based on *Victimae Paschali Laudes*, attr. to Wipo of Burgundy, 10th C. German: *Christ lag in Todesbanden*, Martin Luther, 1483-1546; tr. by Richard Massie,
    Spiritual Songs, 1854, alt.
Tune: CHRIST LAG IN TODESBANDEN, 87 87 78 7 with alleluia; based on 12th C. Latin sequence; adapt. by Martin Luther, 1483-1546, Johann Walther's
    Geystliche gesangk Buchleyn, Wittenberg, 1524; later adapt. and arr. by Johann Sebastian Bach, 1685-1750

104   Rejoice, Angelic Choirs, Rejoice!

1. Re - joice, an - gel - ic choirs, re - joice! Re - joice now, all cre - a - tion! Let trum-pets loud-ly raise their voice To hail the Lord's sal - va - tion; Let all Christ's ho - ly priest-hood sing The tri - umph of their might-y king In fes - tive cel - e - bra - tion!

2. O earth, ex - ult in ra - diance bright, Il - lu - mined by Christ's splen - dor! Your dark-ness now is put to flight; To him due prais - es ren - der! Be glad, O Church! sing out your songs! Your tem - ples fill with shout-ing throngs To hail the glo - rious vic - tor!

3. Let all who gath - er round this flame, The sign of Christ's a - ris - ing, The death-less light of Christ ac - claim, His sav - ing mer - cy priz - ing; That all may live by faith in him Who con-quered death, des - pair, and sin To make us his for ev - er.

Text : Latin Hymn, 11th C.; tr. by Joel W. Lundeen, b.1918, © 1978, *Lutheran Book of Worship*
Tune : WÄCHTERLIED, 87 87 887; C. Engenolf, *Reutterliedlein*, 1535; harm. *Songs of Praise*, © Oxford University Press

Sing of One Who Walks beside Us   105

1. Sing of one who walks be - side us   And this day is   liv - ing still,
2. Strang-ers we have walked be - side him   The long jour-ney   of the day,
3. Stay with us, dear Lord, and raise us,   Once a - gain the   night is near.

One who now is   clos - er   to   us   Than the thoughts our hearts dis - till,
And have told him   of the dark-ness   That has swept our   hope a - way.
Dine with us   and   share your wis-dom,   Free our hearts from   ev - 'ry fear.

One who once up - on   a   hill-top, Raised a - gainst the   pow'r of sin,
He has of-fered words of com-fort, Words of   en - er - gy   and light,
In   the calm of   each new eve-ning, In   the fresh-ness   of each dawn,

Died in love as   his   own crea-tures Cru - ci - fied their   God and King!
And our hearts have blazed with-in   us   As   he saved us   from the night.
If   you hold us   fast   in friend-ship   We will nev - er   be   a - lone.

Text: Ralph Wright, OSB, b.1938, © 1989, GIA Publications, Inc.
Tune: HOLY MANNA, 8 7 8 7 D; American Folk Hymn Melody

106 The Sad Apostles

1. The sad a - pos - tles mourn him slain, Nor
2. With gen - tle voice the an - gel gave The
3. And while with fear and joy they pressed To
4. So when his sad A - pos - tles heard The

hope to see their Lord a - gain, Their Lord whom sin - ners
wom - en ti - dings at the grave; "Forth with you mas - ter
tell these ti - dings to the rest, Their Lord, their liv - ing
ti - dings of the faith-ful word, They hur - ried forth to

had de - filed, Ar - raigned, ac - cused, and doomed to die.
shall you see; He goes be - fore, to Gal - i - lee!"
Lord, they meet And see his form and kiss his feet.
Gal - i - lee, Their loved and lost once more to see.

5. Creation's author, now we pray,
Fulfill in us thy joy today;
When death assails, grant, Lord, that we
May share the paschal victory.

6. All praise be yours, O risen Lord,
From death to endless life restored;
All praise to God now be professed,
All praise, O Spirit, ever blessed.

Alternate doxology, after Ascension:
O risen Christ, ascended Lord,
All praise to you let earth accord,
Who are, while endless ages run,
With Father and with Spirit one.

Text: Tristes ereant apostoli, 4th, 5th C.; tr. by Lacey, © Oxford University Press
Tune: DISTRESS, LM; *Southern Harmony*, 1835

Through the Red Sea Brought At Last   107

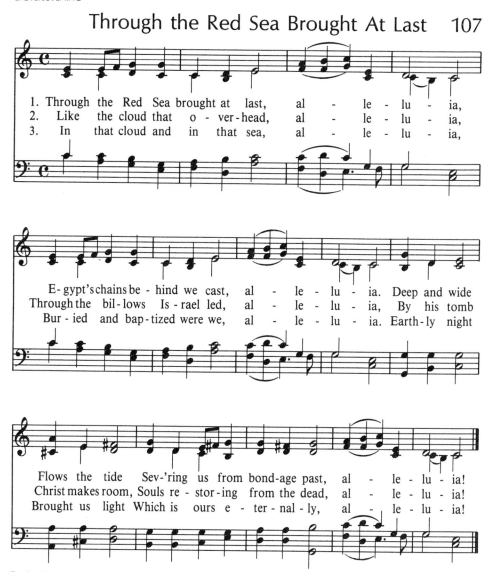

1. Through the Red Sea brought at last, al - le - lu - ia,
2. Like the cloud that o - ver - head, al - le - lu - ia,
3. In that cloud and in that sea, al - le - lu - ia,

E - gypt's chains be - hind we cast, al - le - lu - ia. Deep and wide
Through the bil - lows Is - rael led, al - le - lu - ia, By his tomb
Bur - ied and bap - tized were we, al - le - lu - ia. Earth - ly night

Flows the tide Sev - 'ring us from bond - age past, al - le - lu - ia!
Christ makes room, Souls re - stor - ing from the dead, al - le - lu - ia!
Brought us light Which is ours e - ter - nal - ly, al - le - lu - ia!

Text: Ronald A. Knox, © 1939, Burns and Oates
Tune: STRAF MICH NICHT, 77 33 7 with alleluias; *Hundert Arien*, Dresden, 1694; harm. by Alastair Cassels-Brown, 1977, © 1978, Church Pension Fund

108 We Celebrate the Lamb's High Feast

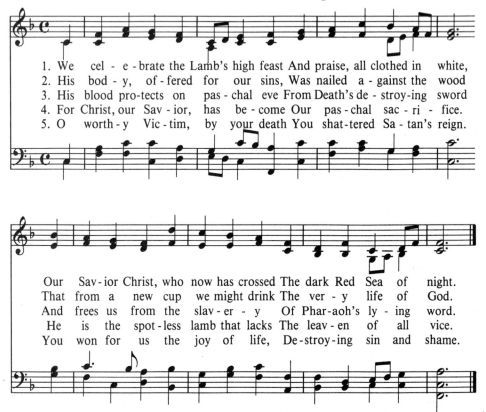

1. We cel - e - brate the Lamb's high feast And praise, all clothed in white,
2. His bod - y, of - fered for our sins, Was nailed a - gainst the wood
3. His blood pro-tects on pas - chal eve From Death's de - stroy-ing sword
4. For Christ, our Sav - ior, has be - come Our pas - chal sac - ri - fice.
5. O worth - y Vic - tim, by your death You shat-tered Sa - tan's reign.

Our Sav-ior Christ, who now has crossed The dark Red Sea of night.
That from a new cup we might drink The ver - y life of God.
And frees us from the slav - er - y Of Phar-aoh's ly - ing word.
He is the spot - less lamb that lacks The leav - en of all vice.
You won for us the joy of life, De-stroy-ing sin and shame.

6. Yes, Christ has risen from the tomb,
The conqueror of night.
The Prince of Darkness is in chains,
Unbarred the gates of light.

7. Protect your people, mighty Lord,
This joy-filled paschaltide,
From ev'ry sin that leads to death,
From lust, from hate, from pride.

8. We praise you, Father, for this day
From death you raised your Son
That in your Spirit we might live
And praise you ever one.

Text: *Ad cenam agni providi;* tr. by Ralph Wright, OSB, b.1938
Tune: HIGH FEAST, CM; David N. Johnson
© 1989, GIA Publications, Inc.

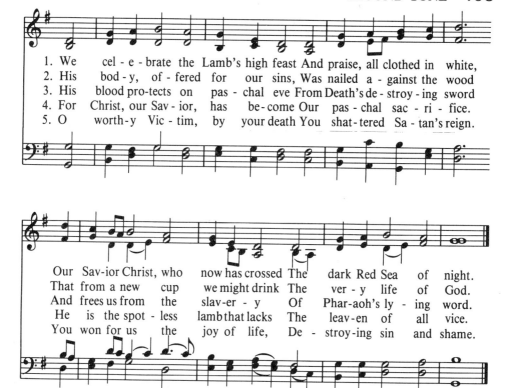

1. We cel - e - brate the Lamb's high feast And praise, all clothed in white,
2. His bod - y, of - fered for our sins, Was nailed a - gainst the wood
3. His blood pro-tects on pas - chal eve From Death's de - stroy - ing sword
4. For Christ, our Sav - ior, has be-come Our pas - chal sac - ri - fice.
5. O worth-y Vic - tim, by your death You shat-tered Sa - tan's reign.

Our Sav-ior Christ, who now has crossed The dark Red Sea of night.
That from a new cup we might drink The ver - y life of God.
And frees us from the slav-er - y Of Phar-aoh's ly - ing word.
He is the spot - less lamb that lacks The leav-en of all vice.
You won for us the joy of life, De - stroy-ing sin and shame.

6. Yes, Christ has risen from the tomb,
   The conqueror of night.
   The Prince of Darkness is in chains,
   Unbarred the gates of light.

7. Protect your people, mighty Lord,
   This joy-filled paschaltide,
   From ev'ry sin that leads to death,
   From lust, from hate, from pride.

8. We praise you, Father, for this day
   From death you raised your Son
   That in your Spirit we might live
   And praise you ever one.

Text: *Ad cenam agni providi*; tr. by Ralph Wright, OSB, b.1938, © 1989, GIA Publications, Inc.
Tune: TWENTY-FOURTH,CM; American Folk Hymn; attr. to Lucius Chapin, 1813

109 Alleluia! Alleluia!
Hearts and Voices Heavenward Raise

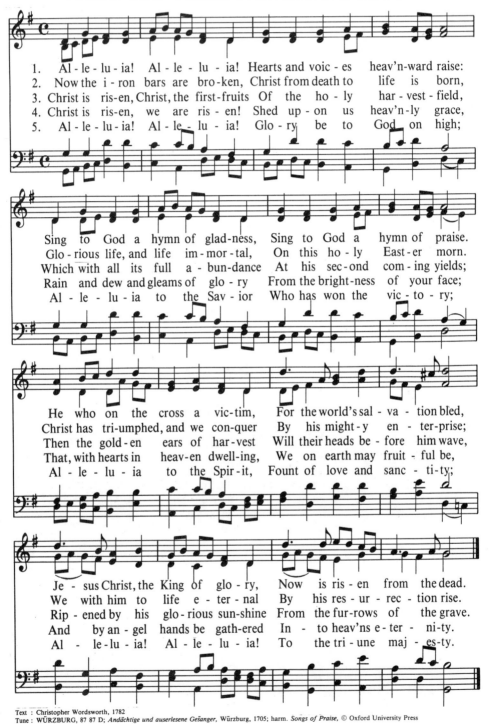

1. Al - le - lu - ia! Al - le - lu - ia! Hearts and voic - es heav'n-ward raise:
2. Now the i - ron bars are bro-ken, Christ from death to life is born,
3. Christ is ris-en, Christ, the first-fruits Of the ho - ly har - vest - field,
4. Christ is ris-en, we are ris - en! Shed up - on us heav'n-ly grace,
5. Al - le - lu - ia! Al - le - lu - ia! Glo - ry be to God on high;

Sing to God a hymn of glad-ness, Sing to God a hymn of praise.
Glo - rious life, and life im - mor - tal, On this ho - ly East-er morn.
Which with all its full a - bun-dance At his sec-ond com - ing yields;
Rain and dew and gleams of glo - ry From the bright-ness of your face;
Al - le - lu - ia to the Sav - ior Who has won the vic - to - ry;

He who on the cross a vic-tim, For the world's sal - va - tion bled,
Christ has tri-umphed, and we con-quer By his might-y en - ter-prise;
Then the gold-en ears of har-vest Will their heads be - fore him wave,
That, with hearts in heav-en dwell-ing, We on earth may fruit - ful be,
Al - le - lu - ia to the Spir-it, Fount of love and sanc - ti-ty;

Je - sus Christ, the King of glo - ry, Now is ris - en from the dead.
We with him to life e - ter - nal By his res - ur - rec - tion rise.
Rip - ened by his glo - rious sun-shine From the fur-rows of the grave.
And by an - gel hands be gath-ered In - to heav'ns e - ter - ni-ty.
Al - le - lu - ia! Al - le - lu - ia! To the tri - une maj - es-ty.

Text : Christopher Wordsworth, 1782
Tune: WÜRZBURG, 87 87 D; *Andächtige und auserlesene Gesänger*, Würzburg, 1705; harm. *Songs of Praise*, © Oxford University Press

Come, O Christian People, Sing   110

1. Come, O Chris-tian peo - ple, sing In tri - um-phant glad - ness;
2. Spring is in our hearts to - day; Christ has burst his pris - on
3. Now the queen of sea - sons, bright With the day of splen - dor,
4. Neith - er could the gates of death, Nor the tomb's dark por - tal,

God has res - cued Is - ra - el, Giv - en joy for sad - ness;
And from three days' sleep in death As a sun has ris - en.
With the roy - al feast of feasts, Far from bleak De - cem - ber,
Nor the watch-ers, nor the seal, Hold you as a mor - tal.

Freed from Phar-aoh's bit - ter yoke Ja - cob's sons and daugh - ters;
All the win - ter of our sins, Long and dark, is fly - ing
Comes to glad Je - ru - sa - lem, Who with true af - fec - tion,
But to - day a - mid your own You have stood be - stow - ing

Lead-ing them be - yond all death Through the Red Sea wa - ters.
From his light, to whom we give Song and praise un - dy - ing.
Wel-comes with un - tir - ing praise Je - sus' res - ur - rec - tion.
Your own peace which ev - er - more Pass - es hu - man know - ing.

Text: *Aisomen pantes laoi*, John of Damascus, c.740; tr. by John Mason Neale, 1859, alt.
Tune: AVE VIRGO VIRGINUM (GAUDEAMUS PARITER), 76 76 D; John Horn, 1544

111 Easter Glory Fills the Sky

1. East-er glo-ry fills the sky! Al - le - lu - ia!
2. See, the stone is rolled a - way Al - le - lu - ia!
3. Mar - y, Moth-er, greet your Son, Al - le - lu - ia!
4. Mag-d'len, wipe a - way your tears! Al - le - lu - ia!
5. Shep-herd, seek the sheep that strayed! Al - le - lu - ia!

Christ now lives, no more to die! Al - le - lu - ia!
From the tomb where once he lay! Al - le - lu - ia!
Ra-diant from his tri-umph won! Al - le - lu - ia!
He has come who calms all fears! Al - le - lu - ia!
Come to con-trite Pe-ter's aid! Al - le - lu - ia!

Dark-ness has been put to flight! Al - le - lu - ia!
He has ris-en as he said, Al - le - lu - ia!
By his cross you shared his pain, Al - le - lu - ia!
Hear the mas-ter speak your name; Al - le - lu - ia!
Strength-en him to be the rock; Al - le - lu - ia!

By the liv-ing Lord of light! Al - le - lu - ia!
Glo-rious first born from the dead! Al - le - lu - ia!
So for ev - er share his reign! Al - le - lu - ia!
Turn to him with heart a-flame! Al - le - lu - ia!
Make him shep-herd of your flock! Al - le - lu - ia!

6. Seek not life within the tomb;
   Christ stands in the upper room!
   Risen glory he conceals,
   Risen body he reveals!

7. Though we see his face no more,
   He is with us as before!
   Glory veiled, he is our priest,
   His true flesh and blood our feast!

8. Christ, the victor over death,
   Breathes on us the Spirit's breath!
   Paradise is our reward,
   Endless Easter with our Lord!

Text : James Quinn, SJ, b.1919, ©
Tune : FRANCOIS, 77 77 with alleluias; David Kingsley, © Geoffrey Chapman

112 Free As Is the Morning Sun

1. Free as is the morn-ing sun   Christ's new peo-ple
2. One man for the peo-ple dies,   Christ, the pas-chal
3. We, like those who crossed dry-shod   E-gypt's marsh-es
4. Christ him-self his peo-ple saves,   Har-vest of the

he will lead   To that home-land he has won;
lamb de-creed,   One man in whom all may rise;
and the reed,   Praise in lib-er-ty our God;
dy-ing seed   Spring-ing live-ly from the grave;

Christ is ris-en, Lord in-deed! Christ is ris-en, Lord in -

Text: Hamish Swanston
Tune: RESURREXIT, 77 77 with refrain; Robert Sherlaw Johnson
© 1971, Faber Music Ltd.

Simplified version

Tune: RESURREXIT, 77 77 with refrain; Robert Sherlaw Johnson, © 1971, Faber Music Ltd.

113 Let Us Rise in Early Morning

1. Let us rise in ear-ly morn-ing, And in-stead of oint-ment bring
2. Come, let us go out to meet him! Come with lamps in ev-'ry hand!

Hymns and prais-es to our mas-ter, And his res-ur-rec-tion sing;
From the sep-ul-cher he ris-es; Read-y for the Bride-groom stand;

We shall see the Sun of Jus-tice Ris'n with heal-ing in his wing.
And the Pasch of our sal-va-tion Hail with his tri-um-phant band.

Let us rise in ear-ly morn-ing, And his res-ur-rec-tion sing.
Come let us go out to meet him! Read-y for the Bride-groom stand!

Text: *Orthrisomen orthrou batheos*, John of Damascus, c.754; tr. by John Mason Neale, 1862; vs. 2, rev. by Ralph Wright, OSB, b.1938, © 1989, GIA Publications, Inc.
Tune: HYFRYDOL, 87 87 D; R.H. Prichard, 1831

Now the Green Blade Rises 114

1. Now the green blade ris - es from the bur - ied grain, Wheat that in
2. In the grave they laid him, love by ha - tred slain, Think - ing that
3. Forth he came at East - er, like the ris - en grain, He that for
4. When our hearts are win - try, griev-ing, or in pain, Your touch can

dark earth man - y days has lain; Love lives a - gain, that
he would nev - er wake a - gain, Laid in the earth like
three days in the grave had lain; Raised from the dead, my
call us back to life a - gain, Fields of our hearts that

with the dead has been:
grain that sleeps un - seen:
liv - ing Lord is seen: Love is come a - gain like wheat a - ris-ing green.
dead and bare have been:

Alternate harmonization overleaf.

Text : John M.C. Crum, 1872-1958, *The Oxford Book of Carols*, alt.
Tune : NOËL NOUVELET, 11 10 11 10; Medieval French Carol; harm. *The Oxford Book of Carols*
© Oxford University Press

Alternate harmonization

Tune : NOËL NOUVELET, 11 10 11 10; Medieval French Carol; harm. by Alastair Cassels-Brown, © 1978, Church Pension Fund

On Earth Has Dawned This Day   115

1. On earth has dawned this day of days, Where-on the faith-ful
2. The ser-pent's craft, sin, death, and hell, This day be-fore the
3. At ear-ly morn, with spic - es rare, The wom - en three as -
4. "Whom do you seek?" the an - gel said; Christ now is ris - en
5. So let our songs to heav - en wing, The vault with al - le -

give God praise! For Christ is ris - en from the tomb, And
con - q'ror fell: All suf - f'ring, sor - row, ill, the name Of
sem - bled there, All to a - noint fair Mar - y's Son, Who
from the dead; See where he lay; let joy be - gin, The
lu - ias ring, In praise of him; our ris - en Lord, To

light and joy have con-quered doom: Al - le - lu - ia!
Je - sus ris'n this day o'er - came: Al - le - lu - ia!
o - ver death had vic - t'ry won: Al - le - lu - ia!
tomb is emp - ty; en - ter in!" Al - le - lu - ia!
all sal - va - tion now af - fords. Al - le - lu - ia!

Text: *Erschienen is der herrlich Tag*, Nikolaus Hermann, 1560; st. 1,3, and 5, tr. by Charles S. Terry, 1928, alt., from *Bach's Four-Part Chorals*.
© Oxford University Press; st. 2, tr. by Arthur T. Russell, 1851
Tune: ERSCHIENEN IST DER HERRLICH TAG, 88 88 4; Nikolaus Herman, 1560; harm. by Gotthart Erträus, 1608

116 That Easter Day with Joy Was Bright

1. That East - er day with joy was bright, The sun shone
2. His ris - en flesh with ra - diance glowed; His wound - ed
3. O Je - sus, King of gen - tle - ness, Come now your -
4. O Lord of all, with us a - bide In this our
5. To God the Fa - ther let us sing; To God the

out with fair - er light, When, to their long - ing
hands and feet he showed Those scars their sol - emn
self our hearts pos - sess, That we may give you
joy - ful East - er - tide; Your own re - deemed for
Son, our ris - en King, And e - qual - ly let

eyes re - stored, The glad a - pos - tles saw their Lord.
wit - ness gave That Christ was ris - en from the grave.
all our days The trib - ute of our grate - ful praise.
ev - er shield From ev - 'ry weap - on death can wield.
us a - dore The Ho - ly Spir - it ev - er - more.

Text : *Claro paschali gaudio* (*Aurora lucis rutilat*). Latin, 5th C.; tr. by John Mason Neale, *Hymns Noted*, 1852, alt.
Tune : PUER NOBIS, LM; adapt. by Michael Praetorius, 1571-1621, *Musae Sionae*, VI, 1609; harm. by George R. Woodward, 1904

SECOND TUNE - 116

1. That East - er day with joy was bright, The sun shone
2. His ris - en flesh with ra-diance glowed; His wound-ed
3. O Je - sus, King of gen - tle - ness, Come now your -
4. O Lord of all, with us a - bide In this our
5. To God the Fa - ther let us sing, To God the

out with fair - er light, When, to their long - ing eyes re-stored,
hands and feet he showed; Those scars their sol - emn wit-ness gave
self our hearts pos-sess, That we may give you all our days
joy - ful East - er - tide; Your own re - deemed for ev - er shield
Son, our ris - en King, And e - qual - ly let us a - dore

The glad a - pos - tles saw their Lord.
That Christ was ris - en from the grave.
The tri - bute of our grate-ful praise.
From ev - 'ry weap - on death can wield.
The Ho - ly Spir - it ev - er more. A - men.

Text : *Claro paschali gaudio* (*Aurora lucis rutilat*), Latin, 5th C.; tr. by John Mason Neale, *Hymns Noted*, 1852, alt.
Tune : ETERNAL KING, LM; Mode VII; © Saint Meinrad Archabbey; harm. by Samuel Weber, OSB, b.1947, © 1987, Saint Meinrad Archabbey

117 This Day of God Destroys the Night

1. This day of God de-stroys the night, Al - le - lu - ia!
2. What could sur-pass this vic - to - ry? Al - le - lu - ia!
3. Lord Je - sus, ris - en ev - er - more, Al - le - lu - ia!

Se - rene and blest God's ho - ly light, Al - le - lu - ia!
Grace con-quers sin e - ter - nal - ly, Al - le - lu - ia!
Where sor - row rules, your joy re - store, Al - le - lu - ia!

Death and hate had sealed life's grave, Con-quered by the love he gave:
Love now reigns where fear brought strife; Death yields gift of last - ing life:
In the peace of East - er days, Born a - gain we sing your praise,

This is the day the Lord has made, Al - le - lu - ia!
Christ in our midst a - live a - gain, Al - le - lu - ia!
To Fa - ther, Son, and Spir - it blest, Al - le - lu - ia!

Text : *Hic est dies,* Ambrose of Milan, d.397; tr. by Peter Scagnelli, 1973, ©
Tune : DE HEER IS WAARLIJK OPGESTAAN, 84 84 77 84; Wim ter Burg, b.1914

All You on Earth 118

1. All you on earth, re-joice and sing; Give glo-ry to our ris-en King
2. Your death, O Lord, was but the seed From which a new life would pro-ceed!
3. The Lord has made this East-er day; To joy let sor-row now give way!

Raise your voic-es! Al-le - lu - ia! Our Lord, who died, now tru - ly lives;
Al-le - lu - ia, al-le-lu-ia! Our Lord, who rose by his own pow'r,
Cel-e-brate it! Al-le - lu - ia! All Chris-tians, who one faith de-clare,

To us this prom-ise he now gives. Al-le-lu - ia, al-le-lu - ia,
Will raise us all in that last hour. Al-le-lu - ia, al-le-lu - ia,
Sing praise to him whose life we share. Al-le-lu - ia, al-le-lu - ia,

Al-le-lu - ia, al-le-lu - ia, al-le-lu - ia!
Al-le-lu - ia, al-le-lu - ia, al-le-lu - ia!
Al-le-lu - ia, al-le-lu - ia, al-le-lu - ia!

Text : Omer Westendorf, b.1916, © 1970, World Library Publications, Inc.
Tune : LASST UNS ERFREUEN, 88 8 88 with alleluias, *Auser lesene Katolische Geistliche Kirchengesänge*, Cologne, 1623; harm. by Ralph Vaughan Williams, 1872-1958, *English Hymnal*, © Oxford University Press

119   Christ the Lord Is Risen Again

1. Christ the Lord is ris'n a - gain;   Christ has bro-ken ev 'ry chain;
2. He who gave for us his life,   Who for us en - dured the strife,
3. He who bore all pain and loss   Com-fort-less up - on the cross,
4. He who slum-bered in the grave   Is ex - alt - ed now to save;

Hark! the an - gels shout for joy,   Sing-ing ev - er - more on high:
Is our pas - chal Lamb to - day;   We too sing for joy, and say:
Lives in glo - ry now on high,   Pleads for us, and hears our cry:
Now through Chris-ten - dom it rings   That the Lamb is King of kings:

Al - le - lu - ia!   Al - le - lu - ia!   Al - le - lu - ia!   Al - le - lu - ia!

5. Now he bids us tell abroad
How the lost may be restored,
How the penitent forgiv'n,
How we too may enter heav'n:
Alleluia!

6. Christ our paschal Lamb indeed,
Christ, your ransomed people feed:
At the end of earthly strife
Raise us, Lord to endless life:
Alleluia!

Text: *Christus ist erstanden*, Michael Weisse, c. 1480-1534, Ein Neu Gesangbuch-lein, 1531; tr. by Catherine Winkworth, 1827-1878, *Lyra Germanica II*, 1858, alt.
Tune: CHRIST IST ERSTANDEN, 77 77 4 with refrain; 12th C.; harm. by Godfrey Ridout, 1971, © 1972 C.C.C.

Christ the Lord Is Risen Today, Alleluia! 120

1. Christ the Lord is ris'n to - day,
2. Love's re - deem - ing work is done,
3. Lives a - gain our glo - rious King,
4. Soar we now where Christ has led,

al - le - lu - ia!

All God's peo - ple, stand and say:
Fought the fight, the bat - tle won.
Where, O death, is now your sting?
Fol - l'wing our ex - alt - ed Head.

al - le - lu - ia!

Raise your joys and tri - umphs high,
Death in vain for - bids him rise;
Once he died our souls to save,
Made like him, like him we rise,

al - le - lu - ia!

Sing, you heav'ns, and earth re - ply:
Christ has o - pened par - a - dise.
Where your vic - to - ry, O grave?
Ours the cross, the grave, the skies.

al - le - lu - ia!

Text : Charles Wesley, 1707-1788, *Sacred Poems*, 1739, alt.
Tune : GWALCHMAI, 77 77 with alleluias; Joseph David Jones, 1832-1870, *Llyfr Tonau ac Emyau*, 1868

121 Christ the Lord Is Risen Today

1. Christ the Lord is ris'n to-day; Chris-tians, haste your vows to pay;
2. Christ, the vic-tim un-de-filed, God and sin-ners rec-on-ciled;
3. Tell us, Mar-y, let us know What you saw up-on the road.
4. Christ, who once for sin-ners bled, Now the first-born from the dead,

Of-fer now your prais-es meet At the Pas-chal Vic-tim's feet;
When in strange and dread-ful strife Met to-geth-er death and life;
"I have seen, where once he lay, An-gels and an emp-ty grave.
Throned in end-less might and pow'r, Lives and reigns for ev-er-more.

For the sheep the Lamb has bled, Sin-less in the sin-ner's stead.
Chris-tians, on this hap-py day Haste with joy your vows to pay.
I have seen the glo-ry bright Of the ris-en Lord of light;
Hail, e-ter-nal hope on high! Hail, our King of vic-to-ry!

Christ the Lord is ris'n on high; Now he lives, no more to die.
Christ the Lord is ris'n on high; Now he lives, no more to die.
Christ my hope is ris'n a-gain; Now he lives and lives to reign."
Hail, our Prince of life a-dored! Help and save us, gra-cious Lord!

Text: *Victimae Paschali Laudes*, attr. to Wipo of Burgundy, 10th C.; tr. by Elizabeth Leeson, 1809-1881, and others, Henry Fornby's *Catholic Hymns*, 1851, alt; st. 3, rev. by Ralph Wright, OSB, b.1938, © 1989, GIA Publications, Inc.
Tune: VICTIMAE PASCHALI, 77 77 D; *Catholic Youth's Hymn Book*, 1871; rev. melody, Wuerth's *Katholisches Gesangbuch*, 1859

Love's Redeeming Work Is Done* 122

1. Love's re-deem-ing work is done, Fought the fight, the
2. Lives a-gain our glo-rious King; Where, O death, is
3. Soar we now where Christ has led, Fol-l'wing our ex-

bat - tle won. Death in vain for-bids him rise;
now thy sting? Once he died our souls to save,
alt - ed head; Made like him, like him we rise,

Christ has o-pened par-a-dise. Al - le - lu - ia!
Where thy vic-to-ry, O grave? Al - le - lu - ia!
Ours the cross, the grave, the skies. Al - le - lu - ia!

This hymn may also be sung to RESURREXIT.

* *N.B. This is the same as no. 120, without the first stanza, "Christ the Lord is risen today," but with a different tune and arrangement of alleluias.*

Text : Charles Wesley, 1707-1788, alt.
Tune : ORIENTIS PARTIBUS, 7 7 7 7 with alleluia; attr. to Pierre de Corbeil, d.1222, *Office de la Circomcision*, Sens, early 13th C.; harm. by Ralph Vaughan Williams, 1872-1958, *English Praise*, © Oxford University Press

123 Come and Let Us Drink of That New River

1. Come and let us drink of that new riv - er,
2. Now the world has bright il - lu - mi - na - tion,

Not from bar - ren rock di - vine - ly poured,
Heav - en and all things up - on the earth:

But the fount of life that springs for ev - er
Ris - en is the God of all cre - a - tion,

From the sa - cred bod - y of our Lord.
Christ the Lord who gave cre - a - tion birth.

3. Yes - ter - day with you in bur - ial ly - ing,
Now with you in tri - umph I a - rise,
Yes - ter - day, the part - ner of your dy - ing,
Raise me with you far be - yond the skies.

Text : John of Damascus, c.675-749; tr. by John Mason Neale, 1818-1866; adapt. by Anthony G. Petti, © 1971, Faber Music Ltd.
Tune : NEW RIVER, 10 9 10 9; Kenneth D. Smith, ©

124 Good Christian Friends, Rejoice and Sing!

1. Good Chris-tian friends, re - joice and sing! Now is the
2. The Lord of life is ris'n this day; O wreathe in
3. Praise we in songs of vic - to - ry That love, that
4. Your name we bless, O ris - en Lord, And sing to -

tri - umph of our King! To all the world glad news we bring:
song his glo-rious way; Let all the world re - joice and say:
life which can-not die, And sing with hearts up - lift-ed high:
day with one ac - cord, The life laid down, the life re - stored:

Al - le - lu - ia, al - le - lu - ia, al - le - lu - ia!

Text: Cyril A. Alington, 1872-1955, alt., © 1958, 1986, Hope Publishing Co.
Tune: GELOBT SEI GOTT, 8 8 8 with alleluias; Vulpius' *Ein Schön geistlich Gesangbuch*, 1609; harm. *The Pilgrim Hymnal*, 1958, © The Pilgrim Press

Alternate harmonization

Tune : GELOBT SEI GOTT, 8 8 8 with alleluias; Melchior Vulpius, c.1570-1615; harm. © 1969, Concordia Publishing House

125   O Son of God, Eternal Love

1. O Son of God, e-ter-nal love, Who came in mer-cy from a-bove To bring to us the Fa-ther's grace And sanc-ti-fy our ran-somed race.

2. Il-lu-mine ev-'ry Chris-tian mind, And grant us through your Word to find The truth that sets the sin-ner free, The ser-vice that is lib-er-ty.

3. To Christ whose blood for us was shed, Who rose vic-to-rious from the dead, Whose glo-ry all the saints a-dore, Be end-less praise for ev-er-more. A-men.

Text: G.B. Timms, © Oxford University Press
Tune: WAHRHAFT, DIES IST DER TAG DES HERRN, LM; Mode II; *Antiphonale zum Stundengebet,* © Vier-Türme-Verlag, Muensterschwarzach, 1979;
   acc. by Samuel Weber, OSB, b.1947, © 1987, Saint Meinrad Archabbey

Praise the Savior, Now and Ever 126

1. Praise the Sav - ior, now and ev - er, Praise him, all be -
2. Day of glad - ness! Gone is sad - ness; Christ has bruised the
3. An - thems glo - rious, hymns vic - to - rious, Raise we to our
4. Earth re - joic - es; all its voic - es Glo - ry to the

neath the skies; Come be - fore him and a - dore him,
ser - pent's head; Death no long - er is the strong - er;
pas - chal King. Bonds are bro - ken, heav'n is o - pen;
Fa - ther sing! Praise the Sav - ior, laud him ev - er,

God's own per - fect sac - ri - fice; Vic - t'ry gain - ing,
Hell it - self is cap - tive led. Christ our Sav - ior
Sing, O ran - somed mor - tals, sing! Christ is ris - en
Son of God, our Lord and King! Praise the Spir - it

life ob - tain - ing, Now in glo - ry see him rise!
lives for ev - er; O'er the tomb his light is shed.
from death's pris - on, Heal - ing in his wings to bring.
we in - her - it That in glo - ry we may sing!

Text: Venantius Honorius Fortunatus, 530-609; tr. *Service Book and Hymnal*, 1958, alt., ©
Tune: UPP, MIN TUNGA, 87 87 87; *Koralpsalmboken*, Stockholm, 1697

127 Sing, Choirs of New Jerusalem

1. Sing, choirs of new Je - ru - sa - lem,
2. How Christ the con - q'ring Li - on came
3. Re - splend - ent in his tri - umph now,
4. And as our joy - ful praise we sing,

Your bright-est notes em - ploy, The pas - chal
And crushed the ser - pent's head, Brought out from
His glo - ry shines on all, While heav'n and
His mer - cy we im - plore, That with our

tri - umph loud - ly hymn With tunes of ho - ly joy.
hell, in heav - en's name, The long im - pris - oned dead.
earth be - fore him bow, O - be - dient to his call.
sav - ing Lord and King We may live ev - er - more.

Text: *Chorus novae Jerusalem,* Fulbertus, Bishop of Chartres, c.1028; tr. by Anthony G. Petti based on Robert Campbell's version. © 1971, Faber Music Ltd.
Tune: NUN DANKET ALL' (GRÄFENBERG), CM; *Praxis pietatis,* 1653

Sing of Christ, Proclaim His Glory   128

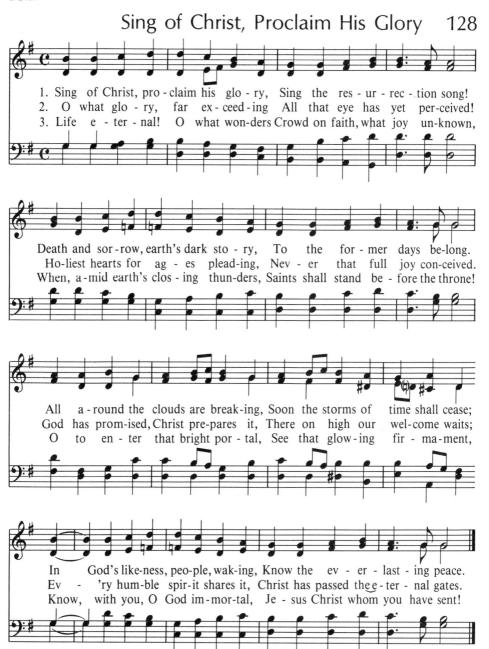

1. Sing of Christ, pro-claim his glo-ry, Sing the res-ur-rec-tion song!
2. O what glo-ry, far ex-ceed-ing All that eye has yet per-ceived!
3. Life e-ter-nal! O what won-ders Crowd on faith, what joy un-known,

Death and sor-row, earth's dark sto-ry, To the for-mer days be-long.
Ho-liest hearts for ag-es plead-ing, Nev-er that full joy con-ceived.
When, a-mid earth's clos-ing thun-ders, Saints shall stand be-fore the throne!

All a-round the clouds are break-ing, Soon the storms of time shall cease;
God has prom-ised, Christ pre-pares it, There on high our wel-come waits;
O to en-ter that bright por-tal, See that glow-ing fir-ma-ment,

In God's like-ness, peo-ple, wak-ing, Know the ev-er-last-ing peace.
Ev-'ry hum-ble spir-it shares it, Christ has passed the e-ter-nal gates.
Know, with you, O God im-mor-tal, Je-sus Christ whom you have sent!

Text : 1 Corinthians 15:20; William Josiah Irons, 1812-1883, *Psalms and Hymns*, 1873, alt.
Tune : HYMN TO JOY, 87 87 D; Ludwig van Beethoven, 1770-1827; adapt. by Edward Hodges, 1796-1867, alt.

129 Tell in Song the Victor's Glory

1. Tell in song the vic-tor's glo-ry, Long to come be-fore his face. Sing of how he tri-umphed strid-ing Through the Red Sea, win-ning peace.

2. Sing of how his flesh was of-fered On the wood a-gainst the sky, Through the dark-ness of his Pas-sion Share in God's e-ter-nal life.

3. Through his blood we find pro-tec-tion From the an-gel's ruth-less sword; Trust-ing him we win new free-dom From the guile of Sa-tan's word.

4. From the tomb he ris-es wak-ing To new cit-a-dels of life, Leads in chains the prince of dark-ness, O-p'ning doors to un-known light.

5. Hear our prayer, al-might-y Fa-ther, Joy-ful in this mys-ter-y; Guide us al-ways through your Spir-it, Be with us e-ter-nal-ly.

Text: Ralph Wright, OSB, b.1938, © 1989, GIA Publications, Inc.
Tune: CHARLESTOWN, 8 7 8 7; American Folk Hymn; *Southern Harmony*, 1835; arr. by Carlton R. Young, © 1965, Abingdon Press

1. Tell in song the vic - tor's glo - ry, Long to
2. Sing of how his flesh was of - fered On the
3. Through his blood we find pro - tec - tion From the
4. From the tomb he ris - es wak - ing To new
5. Hear our prayer, al - might - y Fa - ther, Joy - ful

come be - fore his face. Sing of how he tri-umphed strid - ing
wood a - gainst the sky, Through the dark - ness of his Pas - sion
an - gel's ruth - less sword; Trust - ing him we win new free - dom
cit - a - dels of life, Leads in chains the prince of dark - ness,
in this mys - ter - y; Guide us al - ways through your Spir - it,

Through the Red Sea, win - ning peace.
Share in God's e - ter - nal life.
From the guile of Sa - tan's word.
O - p'ning doors to un - known light.
Be with us e - ter - nal - ly. A - men.

Text: Ralph Wright, OSB, b.1938, © 1989, GIA Publications, Inc.
Tune: HELPING GIFTS, 8 7 8 7; Mode III; Columba Kelly, OSB, b.1930; acc. by Samuel Weber, OSB, b.1947, © 1987, Saint Meinrad Archabbey

130 The Day of Resurrection

1. The day of res - ur - rec - tion! Earth spread the news a - broad;
2. Our hearts be free from e - vil That we may see a - right
3. Now let the heav'ns be joy - ful, And earth her song be - gin,

The Pas - chal feast of glad - ness, the Pas - chal feast of God.
The sav - ior res - ur - rect - ed In his e - ter - nal light;
The whole world keep high tri - umph And all that is there - in;

From death to life e - ter - nal, From earth to heav-en's height
And hear the mes - sage plain - ly, De - liv - ered calm and clear:
Let all things in cre - a - tion Their notes of glad - ness blend,

Our sav - ior Christ has brought us, The glo - rious Lord of light.
"Re - joice with me in tri - umph, Be glad and do not fear"
For Christ the Lord has ris - en, Our joy that has no end.

Text : John of Damascus, c.675-749; tr. by John Mason Neale, 1818-1866; adapt. by Anthony G. Petti, © 1971, Faber Music Ltd.
Tune : ELLACOMBE, 76 76 D; *Würtemberg Gesangbuch*, 1784

The Strife Is O'er, the Battle Done 131

Al - le - lu - ia! Al - le - lu - ia! Al - le - lu - ia! *

1. The strife is o'er, the bat - tle done, The vic - to -
2. The pow'rs of death have done their worst, But Christ their
3. On the third morn he rose a - gain Glo - rious in
4. He closed the yawn - ing gates of hell, The bars from
5. Lord, by your death on Cal - va - ry, From death's dread

ry of life is won; The song of tri - umph
le - gions has dis - persed: Let shouts of praise and
maj - es - ty to reign; O let us swell the
heav'n's high por - tals fell; Let hymns of praise his
sting your peo - ple free, That we may live e -

has be - gun: Al - le - lu - ia!
joy out - burst: Al - le - lu - ia!
joy - ful strain: Al - le - lu - ia!
tri - umphs tell: Al - le - lu - ia!
ter - nal - ly: Al - le - lu - ia!

N.B. This sung only at the beginning and at the end of the stanzas.

Text : *Finita jam sunt proelia*, Latin, *Symphonia Serena Selectarum*, Cologne, 1695; tr. by Francis Pott, 1832-1909, *Hymns Fitted to the Order of Common Prayer*, 1861, alt.
Tune : VICTORY, 888 with alleluias; Giovanni Pierluigi da Palestrina, c. 1525-1594, *Magnificat Tertii Toni*, 1591, adapt. with "Alleluias" by William Henry Monk, 1823-1889, *Hymns Ancient and Modern*, 1861

132 This Day Our Risen Savior Reigns

1. This day our ris - en Sav - ior reigns, Cre - a - tion's un - de - feat - ed King, While an - gels in re - splend - ent light With might - y voice his tri - umph sing.

2. This day the Lord has made his own, Who broke from his con - fin - ing grave. His liv - ing pres - ence fills the world That by his cross he came to save.

3. To God the Fa - ther glo - ry give For Je - sus Christ his death - less Son, Who with the Ho - ly Spir - it lives Im - mor - tal, and for ev - er one.

Text : *The Stanbrook Abbey Hymnal*, rev. ed., © 1974, Stanbrook Abbey Music
Tune : SOLEMNIS HAEC FESTIVITAS, LM; *Graduale*, 1685

SECOND TUNE – 132

1. This day our ris-en Sav-ior reigns, Cre-a-tion's un-de-feat-ed King, While an-gels in re-splend-ent light With might-y voice his tri-umph sing.

2. This day the Lord has made his own, Who broke from his con-fin-ing grave. His liv-ing pres-ence fills the world That by his cross he came to save.

3. To God the Fa-ther glo-ry give For Je-sus Christ his death-less Son, Who with the Ho-ly Spir-it lives Im-mor-tal, and for ev-er one. A - men.

Text: *The Stanbrook Abbey Hymnal*, rev. ed., © 1974, Stanbrook Abbey Music
Tune: AETERNAE RERUM CONDITOR, LM; Ambrosian Chant; acc. by Samuel Weber, OSB, b.1947, © 1987, Saint Meinrad Archabbey

133 This Joyful Eastertide

1. This joy - ful East - er - tide A - way with sin and
2. My flesh in hope shall rest And for a sea - son
3. Death's flood has lost its chill Since Je - sus crossed the

sor - row! My love, the Cru - ci - fied,
slum - ber Till trump from east to west
riv - er; Lov - er of souls, from ill

Has sprung to life this mor - row:
Shall wake the dead in num - ber:
My pass - ing soul de - liv - er:

Had Christ, who once was slain, Not burst his three-day pris - on,

Our faith had been in vain: But now has Christ a - ris - en, a -

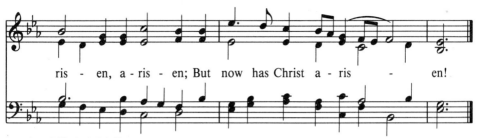

ris - en, a - ris - en; But now has Christ a - ris - en!

Text : George R. Woodward, 1848-1934
Tune : VRUECHTEN, 6 7 6 7 D; Oudaen's *David's Psalmen,* 1685; harm. by Paul G. Bunjes, b.1914, *Lutheran Worship,* © 1969, Concordia Publishing House

134 This Is the Day the Lord Has Made

1. This is the day the Lord has made; He calls the hours his own; Let heav'n re - joice, let earth be glad, And praise sur - round the throne.

2. To - day Christ rose and left the dead, And Sa - tan's em - pire fell; to - day the saints his tri - umph spread And all his won - ders tell.

3. Ho - san - na to the a - noint - ed king, To Da - vid's ho - ly Son! Help us, O Lord; de - scend and bring Sal - va - tion from the throne.

4. Blest be the Lord, who comes to all With mes - sag - es of grace; Who comes in God the Fa - ther's name To save our sin - ful race.

5. O give all praise this ho - ly day To God, the Three in One, To Fa - ther, Son, and Spir - it blest, Who reign while ag - es run.

O Christ, Our Hope 135

1. O Christ, our hope, our hearts' de - sire, Re - demp-tion's on - ly
2. How vast the mer - cy and the love Which led you to the
3. But now the bonds of death are burst, The ran - som has been
4. O may your might - y love pre - vail our sin - ful souls to

spring; Cre - a - tor of the world are you, Its
tree, And on this cross you died for us To
paid; And you are on your Fa - ther's throne In
spare, O may we come be - fore your throne And

Sav - ior and its King, Its Sav - ior and its King.
set your peo - ple free, To set your peo - ple free.
maj - es - ty ar - rayed, In maj - es - ty ar - rayed.
find ac - cep - tance there, And find ac - cep - tance there.

5. Christ Jesus, be our present joy,
   Our future great reward;
   Our only glory may it be
   To glory in the Lord,
   To glory in the Lord!

6. All praise to you, ascended Lord;
   All glory ever be
   To Father, Son and Spirit blest
   Through all eternity,
   Through all eternity.

Text: *Jesu, nostra redemptio*, Latin hymn, c.8th C.; tr. by John Chandler, 1806-1876, *Hymns of the Primitive Church*, 1837, alt.
Tune: HERMANN (LOBT GOTT, IHR CHRISTEN), 86 866; Nikolaus Hermann, c.1485-1561, alt.

136 A Hymn of Glory Let Us Sing!

1. A hymn of glo-ry let us sing! New hymns through-out the world shall ring: Al-le-lu-ia! Al-le-lu-ia! Christ, by a road be-fore un-trod, As-cends un-to the throne of God. Al-le-lu-ia, al-le-lu-ia,

2. The ho-ly ap-os-tol-ic band Up-on the Mount of Ol-ives stand. Al-le-lu-ia! Al-le-lu-ia! And with the vir-gin moth-er see Their Lord as-cend in maj-es-ty. Al-le-lu-ia, al-le-lu-ia,

3. To whom the shin-ing an-gels cry, "Why stand and gaze up-on the sky? Al-le-lu-ia! Al-le-lu-ia! This is the Sav-ior!" thus they say, "This is his glo-rious tri-umph day!" Al-le-lu-ia, al-le-lu-ia,

4. "You see him now, as-cend-ing high Up to the por-tals of the sky. Al-le-lu-ia! Al-le-lu-ia! Here-af-ter Je-sus you shall see Re-turn-ing in great maj-es-ty." Al-le-lu-ia, al-le-lu-ia,

5. O Lord, our home-ward path-way, bend, That our un-wea-ried hearts as-cend. Al-le-lu-ia! Al-le-lu-ia! Where, seat-ed on your Fa-ther's throne, You reign as King of kings a-lone. Al-le-lu-ia, al-le-lu-ia,

al-le-lu - ia, al-le-lu - ia, al-le-lu - ia!

6. Give us your joy on earth, O Lord,
   In heav'n to be our great reward,
   When, throned with you for ever, we
   Shall praise your name eternally.

7. O risen Christ, ascended Lord,
   All praise to you let earth accord:
   You are, while endless ages run,
   With Father and with Spirit one.

Text : *Hymnum canamus Domino (gloriae)*, the Venerable Bede, 673-735; tr. *Lutheran Book of Worship*, © 1978
Tune : LASST UNS ERFREUEN (VIGILES ET SANCTI), LM with alleluias; *Ausserlesne Katolische Geistliche Kirchengesange*, Cologne, 1623; harm. by Ralph
Vaughan Williams, 1872-1958, *English Hymnal*, © Oxford University Press

137 At the Name of Jesus

1. At the name of Je - sus Ev - 'ry knee shall bow,
2. Hum-bled for a sea - son To re - ceive a name
3. Bore it up tri - um - phant With its hu - man light,
4. Name him, Chris-tians, name him— Strong your love as death—
5. In your hearts en - throne him; There let him sub - due

Ev - 'ry tongue pro - claim him King of glo - ry now;
From the lips of sin - ners Un - to whom he came,
Through all ranks of crea - tures To the cen - tral height,
But with awe and won - der And with bait - ed breath;
All that is not ho - ly, All that is not true:

'Tis the Fa - ther's pleas - ure We should call him Lord,
Faith-ful - ly Christ bore it Spot - less to the last,
To the throne of God - head, To the Fa - ther's breast;
He is God the Sav - ior, He is Christ the Lord:
He is your strong ref - uge In temp - ta - tion's hour;

Who from the be - gin - ning Was the might - y Word.
Brought it back vic - to - rious When through death he passed.
Filled it with the glo - ry Of that per - fect rest.
Ev - er to be wor-shipped, Trust - ed, and a - dored.
Let his will en - fold you In its light and pow'r.

6. Christians, this Lord Jesus
   Shall return again
   In his Father's glory
   O'er the earth to reign;
   For all wreaths of empire
   Meet upon his brow,
   And our hearts confess him
   King of glory now.

7. Glory then to Jesus,
   Who, the prince of light,
   To a world in darkness
   Brought the gift of sight;
   Praise to God the Father;
   In the Spirit's love
   Praise we all together
   God who reigns above.

Text : Caroline Maria Noel, 1817-1877, and others
Tune : KING'S WESTON, 65 65 D; Ralph Vaughan Williams, 1872-1958, alt., © Oxford University Press

138 O Jesus, Savior, Lord of All

1. O Jesus, savior, Lord of all, What mind will ever span The measure of your mighty love, O Savior, Son of Man.
2. What loving mercy held your heart That you should bear our sin? Should let yourself be crushed by death That our life might begin?
3. You broke the pow'r of sin and death, You tore the gateway wide, And all who welcomed you were led Back to the Father's side.
4. May this same love surround us now To free us from all harm, That we may soon meet face to face With in our Father's home.
5. O Jesus, be our joy this day, Our comfort in this place, May this your risen life be ours That we may know your peace.

Text: *Jesu nostra redemptio;* tr. by Ralph Wright, OSB, b.1938, © 1989, GIA Publications, Inc.
Tune: DETROIT, CM; Supplement to *Kentucky Harmony,* 1830; harm. by Gerald H. Knight, 1908-1979, © Executor of G.H. Knight

Praise Him As He Mounts the Skies   139

1. Praise him as he mounts the skies,
2. Now at last he takes his throne,
3. Hands and feet and side re - veal,
4. Chris-tians, raise your eyes a - bove!

Al - le - lu - ia!

Christ, the Lord of par - a - dise.
From all ag - es his a - lone.
Wounds of love, high priest-hood's seal!
He will come a - gain in love,

Al - le - lu - ia!

Cry ho - san - na in the height,
With his praise cre - a - tion rings:
Ad - vo - cate for us he pleads;
On that great and won - drous day,

Al - le - lu - ia!

As he ris - es out of sight.
"Lord of lords and King of kings!"
Heav'n-ly priest, he in - ter - cedes!
When this world will pass a - way!

Al - le - lu - ia!

Text : James Quinn, SJ, b.1919, ©
Tune : LLANFAIR, 77 77 with alleluias; Robert Williams, 1781-1821; harm. by John Roberts, 1822-1877

140 Come Down, O Love Divine

1. Come down, O love divine,
2. O let it free - ly burn,
3. Let ho - ly char - i - ty
4. And so the yearn - ing strong,

Seek out this heart of
Till earth-ly pas - sions
My sim-ple ves - ture
With which my soul will

mine, And vis - it it with your own ar - dor glow - ing;
turn To dust and ash - es, in its heat con - sum - ing;
be, And low - li - ness be - come my dai - ly cloth - ing:
long, Shall far out-pass the pow'r of hu - man tell - ing;

Great com-fort - er, draw near, With - in my heart ap -
And let your glo - rious light Shine ev - er on my
True low-li - ness of heart, Which takes the hum - bler
For I'll not know this grace, Till I be - come the

pear, And kin - dle it, your ho - ly flame be - stow - ing.
sight, And clothe me round, the while my path il - lum - ing.
part, And on its own short - com-ings weeps with loath - ing.
place In which the Spir - it glad - ly will be dwell - ing.

Text: *Discendi amor santo*, Bianco da Siena, d.1434; tr. by R.F. Littledale, 1833-1890; st. 1-3, adapt. by Anthony G. Petti, © 1971, Faber Music Ltd.; st. 4, Ralph Wright, OSB, b.1938, © 1989, GIA Publications, Inc.
Tune: DOWN AMPNEY, 66 11 D; Ralph Vaughan Williams, 1872-1958, *English Hymnal*, © Oxford University Press

Spirit of the Lord, Come Down 141

1. Spir-it of the Lord, come down, Spread-ing your pro-tect-ing wing
2. Come in storm-wind, cleans-ing fire, Sweep-ing through a world un-clean;
3. Fa-ther of the poor, come down, In your sight our sins lie bare;
4. Ho-ly Spir-it, bless-ed light, Guide and strength-en mind and will.
5. Through the Fa-ther and the Son, By whose blood our life was bought,

O-ver all that you have made, O-ver ev-'ry liv-ing thing.
Come in ev-'ry gen-tle breeze: Breath of God, un-heard, un-seen.
What is na-ked, clothe with love, That your like-ness we may wear.
Com-fort ev-'ry griev-ing heart, And our in-most be-ing fill.
Fill our emp-ty hands with gifts: Come with grace un-earned, un-sought.

Text: *The Stanbrook Abbey Hymnal*, rev. ed., © 1974 Stanbrook Abbey Music
Tune: SONG 13, 7 7 7 7; melody and bass by Orlando Gibbons; rhythm simplified

142 Creating Spirit, Holy Lord

1. Cre - at - ing Spir - it, ho - ly Lord, The gen - tle
2. O com - fort - er of all who toil, Gift from the
3. O mold - er of our free - dom strong And gen - tle
4. A - lert our sens - es, touch our hearts And fire us
5. Drive far in - to their dark - ness all Who shun your

breeze, the might - y wind, With warmth and pow'r and
foun - tain - head of light, O Spir - it of all
fin - ger of God's hand, Come lead our words with -
with your gift of love, That proud and fall - en,
liv - ing gifts of peace; Pro - tect us deep with -

gra - cious - ness In grace re - fash - ion heart and mind.
love and fire, A - noint - ing chri - sm of all might.
in the paths That wis - dom in your love has planned.
weak and blind, Your light may lead us from a - bove.
in your calm And keep us safe till dan - gers cease.

After last verse:

A - men! Al - le - lu - ia!

6. Through you may we in silence find
   A deeper knowledge of God's Son;
   Through you we know the Father's love
   And live by faith till night is gone.

7. All glory to the Father's Son
   Who from the grave has ris'n on high;
   His Spirit makes us sing with joy
   And praise our God eternally.

Text: *Veni, creator spiritus;* tr. by Ralph Wright, OSB, b.1938
Tune: CREATING SPIRIT, LM; Margaret Daly
© 1989, GIA Publications, Inc.

143 Hail This Joyful Day's Return

1. Hail this joy - ful day's re - turn, Hail the
2. Like to clo - ven tongues of flame On the
3. Lord, to you your peo - ple bend; Un - to
4. You who did our fore - bears guide, With their

Pen - te - cos - tal morn, Morn when our as -
twelve the Spir - it came— Tongues, that earth may
us your Spir - it send; Bless - ings of this
chil - dren still a - bide; Grant us par - don,

cend - ed Lord On his Church his Spir - it poured! Al - le - lu - ia!
hear their call, Fire, that love may burn in all. Al - le - lu - ia!
sa - cred day Grant us, dear - est Lord, we pray. Al - le - lu - ia!
grant us peace, Till our earth - ly wan - d'rings cease. Al - le - lu - ia!

Text: Attr. to Hilary of Poitiers, 4th C.; tr. by Robert Campbell, 1824-1868, alt.
Tune: SONNE DER GERECHTIGKEIT, 7 7 7 7 with alleluia; *Bohemian Brethren Kirchengesang*, 1566

Holy Spirit, God of Light 144

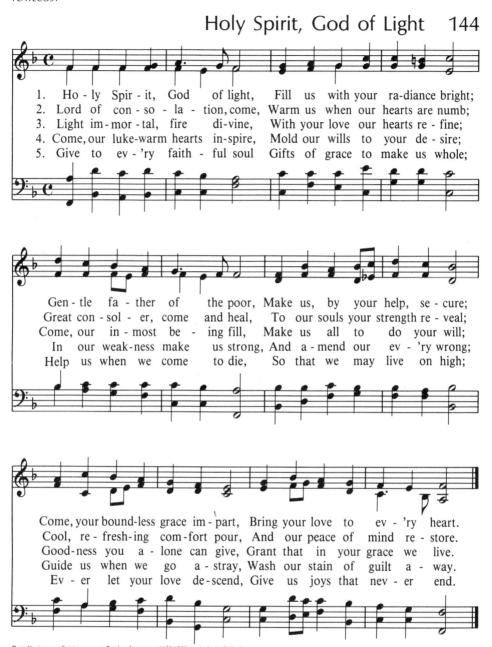

1. Ho - ly Spir - it, God of light, Fill us with your ra-diance bright;
2. Lord of con - so - la - tion, come, Warm us when our hearts are numb;
3. Light im - mor - tal, fire di-vine, With your love our hearts re - fine;
4. Come, our luke-warm hearts in-spire, Mold our wills to your de - sire;
5. Give to ev - 'ry faith - ful soul Gifts of grace to make us whole;

Gen - tle fa - ther of the poor, Make us, by your help, se - cure;
Great con - sol - er, come and heal, To our souls your strength re - veal;
Come, our in - most be - ing fill, Make us all to do your will;
In our weak-ness make us strong, And a - mend our ev - 'ry wrong;
Help us when we come to die, So that we may live on high;

Come, your bound-less grace im - part, Bring your love to ev - 'ry heart.
Cool, re - fresh-ing com-fort pour, And our peace of mind re - store.
Good-ness you a - lone can give, Grant that in your grace we live.
Guide us when we go a - stray, Wash our stain of guilt a - way.
Ev - er let your love de - scend, Give us joys that nev - er end.

Text: *Veni, sancte Spiritus*, ascr. to Stephen Langton, c.1150-1228; tr. Anthony G. Petti
Tune: VENI SANCTE SPIRITUS, 777 D; Samuel Weber, 1740-1816, alt.; adapt. by Geoffrey Laycock
© 1971, Faber Music Ltd.

145 O Holy Spirit, by Whose Breath

1. O Ho-ly Spir-it, by whose breath Life ris-es vib-rant out of death: Come to cre-ate, re-new, in-spire; Come, kin-dle in our hearts your fire.

2. You are the seek-er's sure re-source, Of burn-ing love the liv-ing source, Pro-tec-tor in the midst of strife, The giv-er and the Lord of life.

3. In you God's en-er-gy is shown, To us your var-ied gifts made known. Teach us to speak; teach us to hear; Yours is the tongue and yours the ear.

4. Flood our dull sens-es with your light; In mu-tual love our hearts u-nite. Your pow'r the whole cre-a-tion fills; Con-firm our weak un-cer-tain wills.

5. From inner strife grant us release;
Turn nations to the ways of peace.
To fuller life your people bring
That as one body we may sing:

6. Praise to the Father, Christ his Word,
And to the Spirit, God the Lord;
To whom all honor, glory be
Both now and for eternity.

Text : *Veni, Creator Spiritus*, attr. to Rabanus Maurus, 776-865, tr. by John W. Grant b.1919, ©
Tune : VENI CREATOR SPIRITUS, LM; Mode VIII; setting by Richard J. Wojcik, b.1923, © 1975, GIA Publications, Inc.

Blessing and Honor and Glory and Power 146

1. Bless - ing and hon - or and glo - ry and pow'r,
2. Hear through the heav - ens the sound of God's name,
3. Ev - er as - cend - ing the song and the prayer;
4. Let us give glo - ry and praise to the Lamb,

Wis - dom and rich - es and strength ev - er - more,
While rings the earth with God's glo - ry and fame;
Ev - er de - scend - ing the love that we share;
Tak - ing the robe and the harp and the palm;

Give we to God who our bat - tles has won,
O - cean and moun - tain, stream, for - est, and flow'r
Bless - ing and hon - or and glo - ry and praise —
Sing - ing the song of the Lamb that was slain,

Whose are the king - dom, the crown and the throne.
Ech - o God's prais - es and tell of God's pow'r.
This is the theme of the hymn that we raise.
Dy - ing in weak - ness, but ris - ing to reign.

Text : Horatius Bonar, 1808-1889, alt.
Tune : O QUANTA QUALIA, 10 10 10 10; *Paris Antiphoner*, 1681; harm. by John Bacchus Dykes, 1823-1876

147 Now Fades All Earthly Splendor

1. Now fades all earth-ly splen-dor, The shades of night de-
2. The sil-ver notes of morn-ing Will greet the ris-ing
3. So will the new cre-a-tion Rise from the old re-

scend; The dy-ing of the day-light Fore-tells cre-a-tion's
sun, As once the East-er glo-ry Shone round the Ris-en
born To splen-dor in Christ's glo-ry And ev-er-last-ing

end. Though noon give place to sun-set, Yet dark gives place to
One. So will the night of dy-ing Give place to heav-en's
morn. All dark-ness will be end-ed As faith gives place to

light: The prom-ise of to-mor-row With dawn's new hope is bright.
day, And hope of heav-en's vis-ion Will light our pil-grim way.
sight Of Fa-ther, Son and Spir-it, One God, in heav-en's light.

Text : James Quinn, SJ, b.1919, ©
Tune : CRUGER, 7 6 7 6 D; Johann Cruger's *Neues Volkomliches Gesangbuch,* 1640; adapt. by William Henry Monk, 1823-1889

O Lord, Creator of All Things 148

1. O Lord, Cre-a-tor of all things, The source of day and night,
2. Un-to your courts may we ap-proach, The prize of life to win;

You fash-ioned first of all your works The dawn of ra-diant light.
A-void-ing ev-'ry e-vil path, O keep us free from sin.

By your com-mand the day was named— From dawn to dusk its span.
O lov-ing Fa-ther, hear our prayer, Through Christ, your on-ly Son,

As dark-ness falls we place our lives With-in your gra-cious hand.
Who with the Spir-it ev-er lives, Three per-sons, God-head one.

Text: *Lucis Creator optime*, 7th-8th C.; tr. by Frank C. Quinn, OP, b.1932, alt.,© 1989, GIA Publications, Inc.
Tune: KINGSFOLD, CMD; English Folk Tune, *English Hymnal*, © Oxford University Press; harm. *Lutheran Book of Worship*, © 1978

149 O Lord of Light

1. O Lord of light, who with one word Once formed the seeth-
2. Who poised the struc-ture of the hours From ris-ing dawn
3. Let not our hearts weighed down by guilt Dis-card your liv-
4. But rath-er raise our thoughts on high To grasp your light,
5. Most ho-ly Fa-ther, grant our prayer Through Je-sus Christ,

ing star of day And from its mol-ten heat de-
to tum-bling night, We of-fer prayer as dark-ness
ing gift of grace By feed-ing on the wild de-
your Word re-vealed, Re-ject-ing ha-tred may we
your on-ly Son, That in your Spir-it we may

creed Should come this cool-ing world of clay,
grows And blind-ness greets the death of light.
sires That steal from us your gift of peace,
win The prize re-deem-ing love has sealed.
live And praise your glo-ry ev-er one. A - men.

Text: *Lucis Creator optime*, 7th-8th C.; tr. by Ralph Wright, OSB, b.1938, © 1989, GIA Publications, Inc.
Tune: IAM LUCIS ORTO SIDERE VIII,LM ; Mode VIII; *Antiphonale Monasticum pro Diurnis Horis*, Rome, 1934, alt.; acc. by Samuel Weber, OSB, b.1947,
© 1987, Saint Meinrad Archabbey

O Splendor of Eternal Light   150

1. O splen-dor of e - ter-nal light, Who in full glo - ry dwell on high!
2. Up - on the twi-light cha - os played Your Wis-dom form-ing night and day.
3. For-give the sins we can-not bear, Lest, o-ver-whelmed by earth- ly care,
4. Let heav-en's Spir - it pulse with-in To purge the mem - o - ry of sin;
5. Al-might-y Fa-ther, hear our cry Through Je-sus Christ our Lord most high,

The world be-gan as light from Light, All good-ness in the Fa-ther's sight.
As night de-scends to you we sing To hov - er near on brood-ing wing.
The mind for-get e - ter - nal life, And dwell in ex - ile from its light.
Thus, cast-ing off for - get - ful night, We rise en-robed with first-born light.
Whom in the Spir-it we a - dore, Who reigns with you for ev - er - more.

Text: *Lucis Creator optime*, 7th-8th C.; tr. by Paul Quenon, OCSO, © Abbey of Gethsemani
Tune: TALLIS' CANON, LM; Thomas Tallis, c.1505-1585

150 – SECOND TUNE

1. O splen-dor of e - ter - nal light, Who in full glo - ry
2. Up - on the twi-light cha - os played your Wis-dom form-ing
3. For - give the sins we can - not bear, Lest, o - ver-whelmed by
4. Let heav-en's Spir - it pulse with - in To purge the mem - o -
5. Al - might - y Fa - ther, hear our cry Through Je - sus Christ our

dwell on high! The world be - gan as light from Light,
night and day. As night de - scends to you we sing
earth - ly care, The mind for - get e - ter - nal life,
ry of sin; Thus, cast - ing off for - get - ful night,
Lord most high, Whom in the Spir - it we a - dore,

All good-ness in the Fa - ther's sight.
To hov - er near on brood - ing wing.
And dwell in ex - ile from its light.
We rise en-robed with first - born light.
Who reigns with you for ev - er-more. A - men.

Text: *Lucis Creator optime*, 7th-8th C.; tr. by Paul Quenon, OCSO, © Abbey of Gethsemani
Tune: LUCIS CREATOR OPTIME II, LM; Mode II; acc. by Samuel Weber, OSB, b.1947, © 1987, Saint Meinrad Archabbey

The Molder of the Turning World   151

1. The Mold-er of the turning world Whose pow'r no
2. The sky is fash-ioned for the clouds, The earth is
3. Good Fa-ther, send in time of need The calm-ing
4. In this great dark-ness make our faith A light to
5. Most ho-ly Fa-ther, grant our prayer Through Je-sus

mor-tal mind can know   Dis - pel-ling cha-os
veined with myr-iad streams,   To   staunch the sun's cor-
gift of si-lent grace,   Lest   in our hearts de-
be our con-stant guide   That   we may choose the
Christ, your on-ly Son,   That   in your Spir-it

holds a-part   The   swirl-ing wa-ters' mas-sive flow.
ro-sive heat   And   cool the harsh-ness of her flames.
ceit should tear   The   qui-et fab-ric of your peace.
nar-row way   And   not the way of wound-ed pride.
we may live   And   praise your glo-ry ev-er one.

Text: *Immense Caeli*; tr. by Ralph Wright, OSB, b.1938, © 1989, GIA Publications, Inc.
Tune: CHRISTE, DER DU BIST TAG UND LICHT, LM; J. Klug, *Geistliche Lieder*, 1533; harm. © Evan. Gesangbuch- und Choralbuchverlag

151 – SECOND TUNE

1. The Mold-er of the turn-ing world Whose pow'r no mor-tal
2. The sky is fash-ioned for the clouds, The earth is veined with
3. Good Fa-ther, send in time of need The calm-ing gift of
4. In this great dark-ness make our faith A light to be our
5. Most ho-ly Fa-ther, grant our prayer Through Je-sus Christ, your

mind can know Dis-pel-ling cha-os holds a-
myr-iad streams, To staunch the sun's cor-ro-sive
si-lent grace, Lest in our hearts de-ceit should
con-stant guide That we may choose the nar-row
on-ly Son, That in your Spir-it we may

part The swirl-ing wa-ters' mas-sive flow.
heat And cool the harsh-ness of her flames.
tear The qui-et fab-ric of your peace.
way And not the way of wound-ed pride.
live And praise your glo-ry ev-er one. A-men.

Text: *Immense Caeli;* tr. by Ralph Wright, OSB, b.1938, © 1989, GIA Publications, Inc.
Tune: LUCIS CREATOR OPTIME VIII. LM; Mode VIII; acc. by Samuel Weber, OSB, b.1947, © 1987, Saint Meinrad Archabbey

The Boundless Maker of the World   152

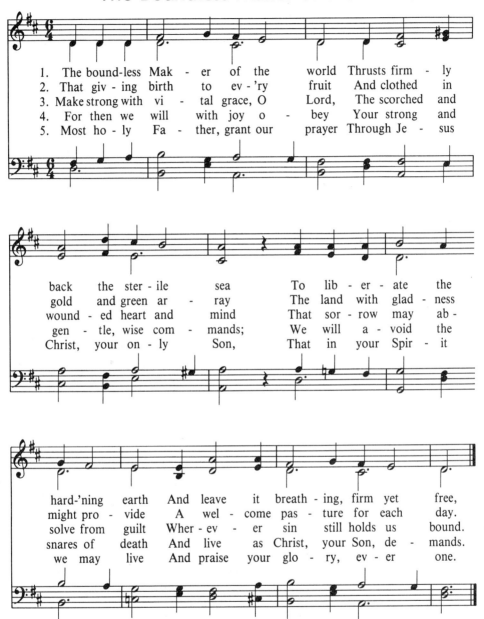

1. The bound-less Mak - er of the world Thrusts firm - ly
2. That giv - ing birth to ev - 'ry fruit And clothed in
3. Make strong with vi - tal grace, O Lord, The scorched and
4. For then we will with joy o - bey Your strong and
5. Most ho - ly Fa - ther, grant our prayer Through Je - sus

back the ster - ile sea To lib - er - ate the
gold and green ar - ray The land with glad - ness
wound - ed heart and mind That sor - row may ab -
gen - tle, wise com - mands; We will a - void the
Christ, your on - ly Son, That in your Spir - it

hard-'ning earth And leave it breath - ing, firm yet free,
might pro - vide A wel - come pas - ture for each day.
solve from guilt Wher - ev - er sin still holds us bound.
snares of death And live as Christ, your Son, de - mands.
we may live And praise your glo - ry, ev - er one.

Text: *Telluris alme*; tr. by Ralph Wright, OSB, b.1938, © 1989, GIA Publications, Inc.
Tune: BEATUS VIR, LM; Samotulsky, *Kancional*, 1561; harm. © 1969, Concordia Publishing House

153   O Master of the Universe

1. O Mas-ter of the u - ni - verse, Cre - a - tor,
2. This mo-ment of cre - a - tion saw Ex - plod - ing
3. For so you would di - vide and keep Each rest - ful
4. Bring light in - to the hearts of all, Di - rect the
5. Most ho - ly Fa - ther, grant our prayer Through Je - sus

source of ev - 'ry light, You poise the dis - tant
in - to mar - v'lous birth, The sun and moon whose
night from each new day And find a meas - ure
force of blind de - sires. O raise the weight of
Christ, your on - ly Son, That in your Spir - it

stars that whirl In si - lence through the blind - ing night.
mo - tions bring Due times and sea - sons to the earth;
for the months And years that swift - ly pass a - way.
sin be - fore The reed is crushed, the spir - it tires!
we may live And praise your glo - ry, ev - er one.

Text: *Caeli, Deus sanctissime;* tr. by Ralph Wright, OSB, b.1938, © 1989, GIA Publications, Inc.
Tune: HERR JESU CHRIST, MEIN. LM; *As Hymnodus Sacer,* Leipzig, 1625

O God of Mastery and Might 154

1. O God of mas - ter - y and might, Who from the
2. That so a myr - iad liv - ing things Might move with
3. Grant that your crea - tures whom the blood Of Je - sus
4. Let not our hearts be crushed by guilt Or raised to
5. Most ho - ly Fa - ther, grant our prayer Through Je - sus

rag - ing deep once raised The life that now still
ease and mul - ti - ply To fill, though fa - thered
Christ has freed from shame May nev - er bear the
heights of vaunt - ing pride, Lest in the dust we
Christ, your on - ly Son, That in your Spir - it

wings the air Or teems be - neath the rest - less wave,
from one source, The emp - ty earth and sea and sky,
lash of sin Or in their weak - ness fall a - gain.
should de - spair Or in our shame at - tempt to hide.
we may live And praise your glo - ry, ev - er one.

Text: *Magnae Deus potentiae;* tr. by Ralph Wright, OSB, b.1938, © 1989, GIA Publications, Inc.
Tune: ICH HEB MEIN AUGEN SEHNLICH AUF, LM; Heinrich Schütz, 1585-1672

154 - SECOND TUNE

1. O God of mas-ter-y and might, Who from the rag-ing
2. That so a myr-iad liv-ing things Might move with ease and
3. Grant that your crea-tures whom the blood Of Je-sus Christ has
4. Let not our hearts be crushed by guilt Or raised to heights of
5. Most ho-ly Fa-ther, grant our prayer Through Je-sus Christ, your

deep once raised The life that now still wings the air
mul-ti-ply To fill, though fa-thered from one source,
freed from shame May nev-er bear the lash of sin
vaunt-ing pride, Lest in the dust we should de-spair
on-ly Son, That in your Spir-it we may live

Or teems be-neath the rest-less wave,
The emp-ty earth and sea and sky,
Or in their weak-ness fall a-gain.
Or in our shame at-tempt to hide.
And praise your glo-ry, ev-er one. A - men.

Text: *Magnae Deus potentiae*; tr. by Ralph Wright, OSB, b.1938, © 1989, GIA Publications, Inc.
Tune: IMMENSE CAELI CONDITOR, LM; Mode VIII; *Antiphonale Monasticum pro Diurnis Horis*, Rome, 1934; acc. by Samuel Weber, OSB, b.1947.
© 1987, Saint Meinrad Archabbey

Jesus, We Greet You,
Source of Life and Goodness 155

1. Je - sus, we greet you, source of life and good - ness, Foun-
2. Pour out your love, Lord, flood our souls with mer - cy; Give
3. May praise and hon - or e - qual - ly be giv - en To

tain of mer - cy, peace and joy un - end - ing. Vic - tim for sin-ners,
us re-newed faith, share your light e - ter - nal. Send forth your Spir-it,
God the Fa - ther and the ris - en Sav - ior, And may the glo-ry

by your cross and pas - sion From death you saved us.
make us prompt and will - ing Al - ways to serve you.
of the Ho - ly Spir - it Spread through the whole world.

Text: Tr. by Roger Schoenbechler, OSB, *The Book of Prayer,* © 1975, The Order of St. Benedict, Inc.
Tune: HERZLIEBSTER JESU, 11 11 11 5; Johann Crüger, 1598-1662; harm. adapt. from Johann Sebastian Bach, 1685-1750

156 The Artist Speaks

1. The Art - ist speaks and var - ied beasts Per - vade the for - ests
2. His Word de - signed their form and gave The per - fect paths for
3. Keep far from all your chil - dren, Lord, The sub - tle charm of
4. O give us bless-ings, give us joy, Give us the gen - tle
5. Most ho - ly Fa - ther, grant our prayer Through Je - sus Christ, your

of the land, Where Ad - am and his part - ner,
liv - ing breath, That they might calm - ly live and
e - vil ways, That so our act - ions and our
pow'rs of grace, That cast - ing out the scourge of
on - ly Son, That in your Spir - it we may

Eve, God's mas - ter - piece, are soon to stand.
move And serve in har - mo - ny till death.
thoughts May be this eve - ning filled with praise.
war We may in won - der find your peace.
live And praise your glo - ry, ev - er one.

Text: *Plasmator hominis, Deus,* 7th-8th C.: tr. by Ralph Wright, OSB, b.1938, © 1989, GIA Publications, Inc.
Tune: PROSPECT,.LM; W. Walter, *Southern Harmony,* 1835; harm. *Lutheran Book of Worship,* © 1978

O Blessed Light   157

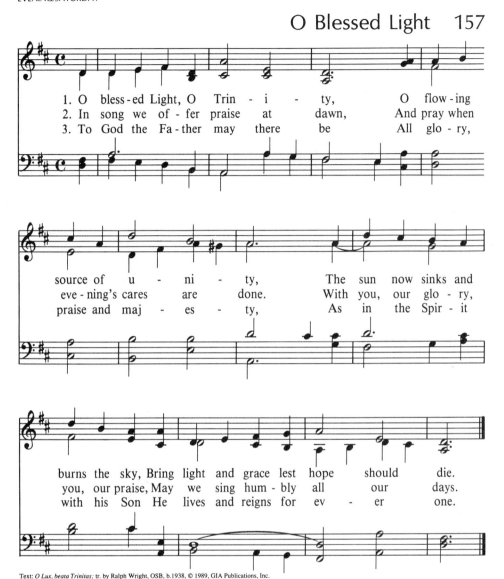

1. O bless-ed Light, O Trin - i - ty,   O flow-ing
2. In song we of - fer praise at   dawn,   And pray when
3. To God the Fa - ther may   there   be   All glo - ry,

source of u - ni - ty,   The sun now sinks and
eve - ning's cares are   done.   With you, our glo - ry,
praise and maj - es - ty,   As   in   the Spir - it

burns the sky, Bring light and grace lest hope   should die.
you, our praise, May we sing hum - bly all   our   days.
with his Son He lives and reigns for ev - er   one.

Text: *O Lux, beata Trinitas;* tr. by Ralph Wright, OSB, b.1938, © 1989, GIA Publications, Inc.
Tune: SOLOTHURN, LM; Swiss, 1826; harm. by Stanley L. Osborne, ©

158 Abide, O Risen Savior

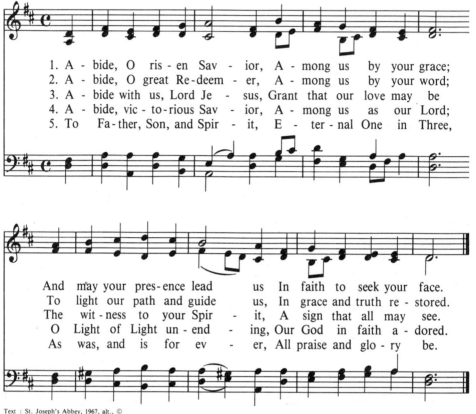

1. A - bide, O ris-en Sav - ior, A - mong us by your grace;
2. A - bide, O great Re-deem - er, A - mong us by your word;
3. A - bide with us, Lord Je - sus, Grant that our love may be
4. A - bide, vic-to-rious Sav - ior, A - mong us as our Lord;
5. To Fa-ther, Son, and Spir - it, E - ter - nal One in Three,

And may your pres-ence lead us In faith to seek your face.
To light our path and guide us, In grace and truth re - stored.
The wit-ness to your Spir - it, A sign that all may see.
O Light of Light un-end - ing, Our God in faith a - dored.
As was, and is for ev - er, All praise and glo-ry be.

Text : St. Joseph's Abbey, 1967, alt., ©
Tune : CHRISTUS, DER IST MEIN LEBEN, 76 76; Melchior Vulpius, 1609

Abide with Me! 159

1. A - bide with me! fast falls the e - ven - tide; The dark-ness
2. Swift to its close ebbs out life's lit - tle day; Earth's joys grow
3. I need your pres-ence ev - 'ry pass-ing hour, What but your
4. I fear no foe, with you at hand to bless; Ills have no
5. Hold then your cross be - fore my clos-ing eyes; Shine through the

deep - ens, Lord with me a - bide; When oth - er help - ers
dim; its glo - ries pass a - way; Change and de - cay in
grace can foil the tempt-er's pow'r? Who like your - self my
weight, and tears no bit - ter - ness: Where is death's sting? Where,
gloom, and point me to the skies: Heav'n's morn-ing breaks, and

fail, and com-forts flee, Help of the help-less, oh, a - bide with me!
all a-round I see; O God, the change-less one, a - bide with me!
guide and stay can be? Through cloud and sun-shine, Lord, a - bide with me!
grace, your vic - to - ry? I tri-umph still, if you a - bide with me!
earth's vain shad-ows flee; In life, in death, O Lord, a - bide with me!

Text : Henry Francis Lyte, 1793-1847, *Remains*, 1850, alt.
Tune : EVENTIDE 10 10 10 10; William Henry Monk, 1823-1889, *Hymns Ancient and Modern*, 1861

160 Christ Be beside Me

1. Christ be be-side me, Christ be be-fore me, Christ be be-hind me, King of my heart.
2. Christ on my right hand, Christ on my left hand, Christ all a-round me, Shield in the strife.
3. Christ be in all hearts Think-ing a-bout me, Christ be on all tongues Tell-ing of me.

Christ be with-in me, Christ be be-low me, Christ be a-bove me, Nev-er to part.
Christ in my sleep-ing, Christ in my sit-ting, Christ in my ris-ing, Light of my heart.
Christ be the vi-sion In eyes that see me, In ears that hear me Christ ev-er be.

Text : Based on *St. Patrick's Breastplate*, 8th C. or later; adapt. by James Quinn, SJ, b.1919, *New Hymns for All Seasons*, ©
Tune : BUNESSAN, 55 54 55 54; Scots Gaelic Melody; harm. by David Evans, 1874-1948, *Revised Church Hymnary 1927*, © Oxford University Press

Christ Mighty Savior 161

1. Christ, might-y Sav-ior, light of all cre-a-tion, You make the
2. Now comes the day's end as the sun is set-ting, Mir-ror of
3. There-fore we come now, eve-ning rites to of-fer, Joy-ful-ly
4. Give heed, we pray you, to our sup-pli-ca-tion: That you may
5. Though bod-ies slum-ber, hearts shall keep their vig-il. For ev-er

day-time ra-diant with the sun-light And to the night give
day-break, pledge of res-ur-rec-tion; While in the heav-ens
chant-ing ho-ly hymns to praise you, With all cre-a-tion
grant us par-don for of-fens-es, Strength for our weak hearts,
rest-ing in the peace of Je-sus, In light or dark-ness

glit-ter-ing a-dorn-ment, Stars in the heav-ens.
choirs of stars ap-pear-ing Hal-low the night-fall.
join-ing hearts and voic-es Sing-ing your glo-ry.
rest for ach-ing bod-ies, Sooth-ing the wea-ry.
wor-ship-ing our Sav-ior Now and for ev-er.

Text : *Christe, lux mundi;* Mozarabic Rite, 10th C.; tr. by Alan G. McDougall, 1895-1964; rev. by Anne K. LeCroy, b. 1930, and others, ©
Tune : MIGHTY SAVIOR, 11 11 11 5; David Hurd, b.1950, © 1985, GIA Publications, Inc.

162 Day Is Done

1. Day is done, but Love un-fail-ing Dwells ev-er here;
2. Dark de-scends, but Light un-end-ing Shines through our night;
3. Eyes will close, but you, un-sleep-ing, Watch by our side;

Shad-dows fall, but hope, pre-vail-ing, Calms ev-'ry fear.
You are with us, ev-er lend-ing New strength to sight;
Death may come: in Love's safe keep-ing Still we a-bide.

Lov-ing Fa-ther, none for-sak-ing, Take our hearts, of Love's own
One in love, your truth con-fess-ing, One in hope of heav-en's
God of love, all e-vil quell-ing, Sin for-giv-ing, fear dis-

mak-ing, Watch our sleep-ing, guard our wak-ing, Be al-ways near!
bless-ing, May we see, in love's pos-sess-ing, Love's end-less light!
pell-ing, Stay with us, our hearts in-dwell-ing, This e-ven-tide!

Text : James Quinn, SJ, b.1919, *New Hymns for All Seasons,* © 1969
Tune : AR HYD Y NOS, 84 84 88 84; Welsh Traditional Melody

For the Beauty of the Earth   163

1. For the beau-ty of the earth, For the beau-ty of the skies,
2. For the beau-ty of each hour Of the day and of the night,
3. For the joy of ear and eye, For the heart and mind's de-light,
4. For the joy of hu-man love, Broth-er, sis-ter, par-ent, child,
5. For the church that ev-er-more Lifts her ho-ly hands a-bove,

For the love which from our birth O-ver and a-round us lies,
Hill and vale, and tree and flow'r, Sun and moon and stars of light,
For the mys-tic har-mo-ny Link-ing sense to sound and sight,
Friends on earth and friends a-bove, For all gen-tle thoughts and mild,
Of-f'ring up on ev-'ry shore Her pure sac-ri-fice of love,

Christ, our God, to you we raise This our hymn of thank-ful praise.

Text : Folliot Sandford Pierpoint, 1835-1917, in Orby Shipley's *Lyra Eucharstica*, 1864, alt.
Tune : DIX, 7 7 7 7 with refrain; from a chorale, *Treuer Heiland*, Conrad Kocher, 1786-1872, *Stimmen aus dem Reiche Gottes*, 1838; arr. by William Henry Monk, 1823-1889

164 Jesus Our Mighty Lord

1. Je - sus our might - y Lord, our strength in sad - ness,
2. Good shep - herd of your sheep, your own de - fend - ing,
3. Glo - rious their life who sing, with glad thanks-giv - ing,

The Fa-ther's con-qu'ring Word, true source of glad-ness;
In love your chil - dren keep to life un - end - ing.
True hymns to Christ the King in all their liv - ing:

Your name we glo - ri - fy, O Je - sus, throned on
You are your-self the Way: lead us then day by
All who con-fess his Name, come then with hearts a -

high; You gave your-self to die for our sal - va - tion.
day In your own steps, we pray, O Lord most ho - ly.
flame; The God of peace ac - claim as Lord and Sav-ior.

Text : Clement of Alexandria, 170?-220?; para. F. Bland Tucker, 1895-1984, rev.
Tune : MONK'S GATE, 11 11 12 11; Sussex Folk Melody; adapt. and harm. by Ralph Vaughan Williams, 1872-1958, *English Hymnal,* © Oxford University Press

Light Serene of Holy Glory 165

1. Light se - rene of ho - ly glo - ry From the Im - mor-tal Fa-ther poured,
2. Now we see the sun de - scend-ing, Now de - clines the eve-ning light,
3. Wor-thy, Lord, of end-less prais-es! Christ the Son of God art thou;

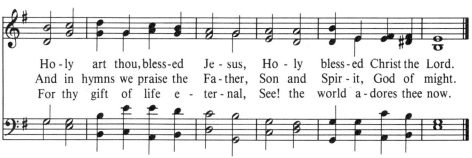

Ho - ly art thou, bless-ed Je - sus, Ho - ly bless-ed Christ the Lord.
And in hymns we praise the Fa-ther, Son and Spir - it, God of might.
For thy gift of life e - ter-nal, See! the world a-dores thee now.

Text : *Phos hilaron;* tr. John Brownlie, 1857-1925
Tune : HERR ICH HABE MISGEHANDELT, 8 7 8 7; Johann Crüger, 1598-1662

166 Lord Jesus Christ, Abide with Us

1. Lord Je - sus Christ, a - bide with us, Now that the sun has run its course; Let hope not be ob - scured by night But may faith's dark - ness be as light.

2. Lord Je - sus Christ, grant us your peace, And when the trials of earth shall cease; Grant us the morn - ing light of grace, The ra - diant splen - dor of your face.

3. Im - mor - tal, Ho - ly Three - fold Light, Yours be the king - dom, pow'r and might; All glo - ry be e - ter - nal - ly To you, life - giv - ing Trin - i - ty!

Text : *Ach bleib uns* or *Mane nobiscum, Domine;* para. by St. Joseph's Abbey, 1968, ©
Tune : OLD HUNDREDTH, LM; Louis Bourgeois, c.1510-1561 *Genevan Psalter*, 1551

1. Lord Je - sus Christ, a - bide with us, Now that the sun
2. Lord Je - sus Christ, grant us your peace, And when the trials
3. Im - mor - tal, Ho - ly Three - fold Light, Yours be the king -

has run its course; Let hope not be ob - scured by night
of earth shall cease; Grant us the morn - ing light of grace,
dom, pow'r and might; All glo - ry be e - ter - nal - ly

But may faith's dark - ness be as light.
The ra - diant splen - dor of your face.
To you, life - giv - ing Trin - i - ty! A - men.

Text: *Ach bleib uns* or *Mane nobiscum, Domine;* para. by St. Joseph;s Abbey, 1968, ©
Tune: BEVOR DES TAGES LICHT VERGEHT, LM; Mode VIII; *Deutsches Psalterium für die Sonntage und Wochentage des Kirchenjahres (Deutsche Antiphonale I),*
Muensterschwarzach; acc. by Samuel Weber, OSB, b.1947, © 1987, Saint Meinrad Archabbey

167 O Blest Creator

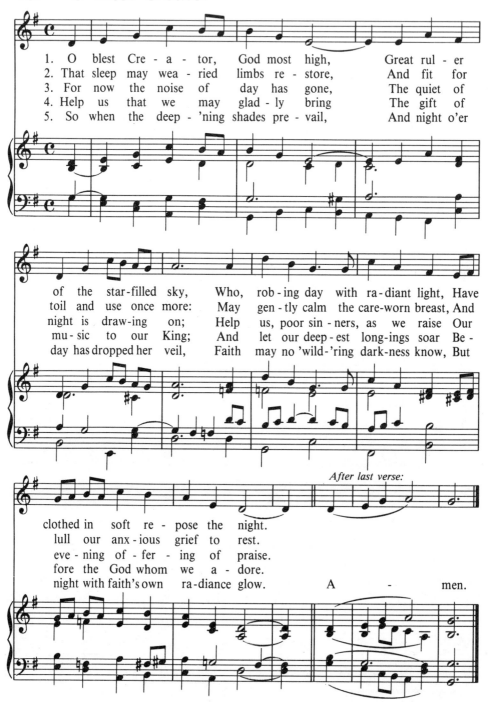

1. O blest Cre-a-tor, God most high, Great rul-er of the star-filled sky, Who, rob-ing day with ra-diant light, Have clothed in soft re-pose the night.

2. That sleep may wea-ried limbs re-store, And fit for toil and use once more: May gen-tly calm the care-worn breast, And lull our anx-ious grief to rest.

3. For now the noise of day has gone, The quiet of night is draw-ing on; Help us, poor sin-ners, as we raise Our eve-ning of-fer-ing of praise.

4. Help us that we may glad-ly bring The gift of mu-sic to our King; And let our deep-est long-ings soar Be-fore the God whom we a-dore.

5. So when the deep-'ning shades pre-vail, And night o'er day has dropped her veil, Faith may no 'wild-'ring dark-ness know, But night with faith's own ra-diance glow.

After last verse: A - men.

6. From ev'ry wrongful passion free,
Our hearts in you protected be;
Nor let our envious foe draw near,
To break our rest with any fear.

7. Christ, with the Father ever one;
Spirit, of Father and of Son;
God, over all, whom all obey,
Shield us, great Trinity, we pray.

Text: *Deus, creator omnium,* Ambrose of Milan, 340-397; tr. by John David Chambers, 1805-1893; alt.by Ralph Wright, OSB, b.1938, © 1989, GIA Publications, Inc.
Tune: GONFALON ROYAL, LM; Percy C. Buck, 1871-1947, © Oxford University Press

O Gladsome Light   168

1. O glad-some light of the Fa - ther im - mor - tal And of the ce-
2. Now to the sun - set a - gain you have brought us, And, see-ing the
3. Fa - ther om - nip - o - tent! Son, our life - giv - er! Spir - it, our

les - tial,   Sa - cred, and bless - ed   Je - sus, our Sav - ior!
eve - ning   Twi - light, we bless   you,   praise you, a - dore you!
com-fort-er!   Wor - thy at   all   times of   wor - ship and won - der.

Text : *Phos Hilaron,* 3rd C.; tr. by Henry W. Longfellow, 1807-1882, alt.
Tune : ELIZABETH, 11 6 10; Allan Mahnke, b. 1944; harm. *Lutheran Book of Worship,* © 1978

169 O God, Our Help in Ages Past

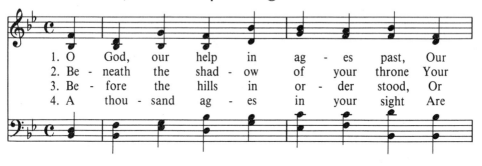

1. O God, our help in ag - es past, Our
2. Be - neath the shad - ow of your throne Your
3. Be - fore the hills in or - der stood, Or
4. A thou - sand ag - es in your sight Are

hope for years to come, Our shel - ter from the
saints have dwelt se - cure, Suf - fi - cient is your
earth re - ceived her frame, From ev - er - last - ing
like an eve - ing gone, Short as the watch that

storm - y blast, And our e - ter - nal home;
arm a - lone, And our de - fense is sure.
you are God, To end - less years the same.
ends the night Be - fore the ris - ing sun.

5. Time, like an ever rolling stream,
   Bears all our lives away;
   They fly, forgotten, as a dream
   Dies at the break of day.

6. O God, our help in ages past,
   Our hope for years to come,
   Be now our guard while troubles last,
   And our eternal home.

Text : Based on Psalm 90; Isaac Watts, 1674-1748, *Psalms of David...*, 1719, alt.
Tune : ST. ANNE, CM; later form of melody (rhythm adapted), attr. to William Croft, 1678-1727, *A Supplement to the New Version of Psalms*, 1708

O Radiant Light 170

1. O ra - diant Light, O sun di - vine Of God the
2. O Son of God, the source of life, Praise is your
3. Lord Je - sus Christ, as day - light fades, As shine the

Fa - ther's death-less face, O Im - age of the light sub -
due by night and day: Our hap - py lips must raise the
lights of e - ven - tide, We praise the Fa - ther with the

lime That fills the heav'n - ly dwell - ing place.
strain Of your es - teemed and splen - did name.
Son, The Spir - it blest and with them one.

Text : *Phos Hilaron*, Greek, 3rd C.; tr. by William G. Storey, b. 1923, ©
Tune : JESU, DULCIS MEMORIA, LM; Mode I; acc. by Richard Proulx, b.1937, © 1975, GIA Publications, Inc.

171 The Day You Gave Us, Lord, Is Ended

1. The day you gave us, Lord, is end - ed, the dark - ness
2. We thank you that your Church, un - sleep-ing While earth rolls
3. A - cross each con - ti - nent and is - land As dawn leads
4. The sun that bids us rest is wak - ing Your peo - ple
5. So be it, Lord; your throne shall nev - er Like earth's proud

falls at your be - hest; To you our morn - ing
on - ward in - to light, Through all the world her
on an - oth - er day, The voice of prayer is
'neath the west - ern sky, And hour by hour new
em - pires, pass a - way: Your king - dom stands, and

hymns as - cend - ed, Your praise shall sanc - ti - fy our rest.
watch is keep-ing, And rests not now by day or night.
nev - er si - lent, Nor dies the strain of praise a - way.
lips are mak-ing Your won - drous do - ings heard on high.
grows for ev - er, Till all your crea - tures own your sway.

Text: John Ellerton, 1826-1893, *A Liturgy for Missionary Meetings*, 1879, and *Church Hymns*. 1871, alt.
Tune: ST. CLEMENT, 9 8 9 8; Clement Cotterill Scholefield. 1839-1904, SPCK *Church Hymns with Tunes*, 1874

The Setting Sun Now Dies Away 172

1. The set-ting sun now dies a-way, and dark-ness
2. We praise your name with joy this night; O watch and
3. To God the Fa-ther, God the Son, And Ho-ly

comes at close of day; Your ra-diant hope, O
guide us till the light That we may rest with-
Spir - it, Three in One, Trin - i - ty blest, whom

Lord, im - part To ev - 'ry mind and ev - 'ry heart.
in your grace And know the calm that is your peace.
we a - dore, Be praise and glo - ry ev - er - more.

Text: *Jam so recedit ibneus;* tr. by Geoffrey Laycock, based on *Primer*, 1706, © 1971, Faber Music Ltd.; adapt. by Ralph Wright, OSB, b.1938, © 1989, GIA Publications, Inc.
Tune: ANGELUS, LM; Georg Joseph, 1657; arr. *Cantica Spirtualia*, 1847; adapt. by Geoffrey Laycock, © 1971, Faber Music Ltd.

173 We Praise You, O God

1. We praise you, O God, our Re-deem-er, Cre-a-tor,
2. We wor-ship you, God of all ag-es, we bless you;
3. With voic-es u-nit-ed our prais-es we of-fer,

In grate-ful de-vo-tion our trib-ute we bring.
Through life's storm and tem-pest our guide you have been.
And glad-ly our songs of true wor-ship we raise.

We lay it be-fore you, we kneel and a-dore you,
When per-ils o'er-take us, you will not for-sake us,
Our sins now con-fess-ing, we pray for your bless-ing;

We bless your ho-ly name, glad prais-es we sing.
O help us, gra-cious Lord, life's bat-tles to win.
To you, our great Re-deem-er, for ev-er be praise!

Text : Julia Cady Cory, 1882-1963, alt.
Tune : PLIMMER, 12 11 12 11; Keith Landis, b.1922; harm. by David N. Johnson, © 1977, Praise Publications, Inc.

All Your Glory, God Almighty   174

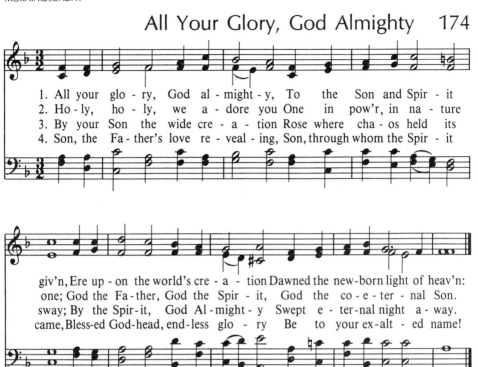

1. All your glo - ry, God al - might - y, To   the   Son and Spir - it
2. Ho - ly, ho - ly, we a - dore you One   in   pow'r, in na - ture
3. By your Son the wide cre - a - tion Rose where cha - os held   its
4. Son, the Fa - ther's love re - veal - ing, Son, through whom the Spir - it

giv'n, Ere up - on the world's cre - a - tion Dawned the new-born light of heav'n:
one; God the Fa - ther, God the Spir - it, God   the   co - e - ter - nal Son.
sway; By the Spir - it, God Al - might - y Swept e - ter - nal night a - way.
came, Bless-ed God-head, end-less glo - ry Be   to your ex - alt - ed name!

Text : Hymn from the Russian Church; tr. by John Brownlie, 1857-1925, alt.
Tune : OMNIE DIE, 87 87; David Gregor Corner's *Gesangbuch*, Nüremburg, 1631; arr. William Smith Rockstro, 1823-1895

175 Eternal Master, Lord of All

1. E - ter - nal Mas - ter, Lord of all, Who rule in
2. The her - ald of the day now sounds While all a -
3. So let us hear his call and rise With ea - ger -
4. O Je - sus, look on us with love And watch us

turn both day and night, You stem the drudg - er - y of
round is dark and still. Be - fore the night suc - cumbs to
ness to greet the dawn. His crow - ing sounds with - in our
when we fall or stray; If you but glance we are re -

time With sea - sons blend - ing dark and light.
dawn He wakes the trav - 'ler by his skill.
ears And bids all lin - g'ring sleep be gone.
stored And tears will wash all guilt a - way.

5. O shine within our heart and mind
   And cast the sleep of night away,
   That gladly we may make your name
   In song the word to greet the day.

6. Most holy Father, grant our prayer
   Through Jesus Christ, your only Son,
   That in your Spirit we may live
   And praise your glory, ever one.

Text: *Aeterne rerum conditor*; tr. by Ralph Wright, OSB, b.1938, © 1989, GIA Publications, Inc.
Tune: DANBY, LM; Traditional English; acc. by Arthur Hutchings, © 1981, ICEL

1. E - ter - nal Mas - ter, Lord of all, Who rule in turn both
2. The her - ald of the day now sounds While all a - round is
3. So let us hear his call and rise With ea - ger - ness to
4. O Je - sus, look on us with love And watch us when we

day and night, You stem the drudg - er - y of time
dark and still. Be - fore the night suc - cumbs to dawn
greet the dawn. His crow - ing sounds with - in our ears
fall or stray; If you but glance we are re - stored

With sea - sons blend - ing dark and light.
He wakes the trav - 'ler by his skill.
And bids all lin - g'ring sleep be gone.
And tears will wash all guilt a - way. A - men.

5. O shine within our heart and mind
And cast the sleep of night away,
That gladly we may make your name
In song the word to greet the day.

6. Most holy Father, grant our prayer
Through Jesus Christ, your only Son,
That in your Spirit we may live
And praise your glory, ever one.

Text: *Aeterne rerum conditor;* tr. by Ralph Wright, OSB, b.1938, © 1989, GIA Publications, Inc.
Tune: SPLENDOR PATERNAE GLORIAE, LM; Mode I; *Antiphonale Monasticum pro Diurnis Horis,* Rome, 1934; acc. by Samuel Weber, OSB, b.1947,
© 1987, Saint Meinrad Archabbey

176 From All Who Dwell below the Skies

1. From all who dwell be-low the skies,
Let the Cre - a - tor's

2. E - ter - nal are your mer-cies, Lord,
E - ter - nal truth at -

praise a - rise;
Al -le - lu - ia! Al -le - lu - ia! Let

tends your word:
Al -le - lu - ia! Al -le - lu - ia! Your

the Re -deem-er's name be sung,
Through ev -'ry land, by ev -'ry

praise shall sound from shore to shore,
Till suns shall rise and set no

tongue.
Al -le - lu - ia! Al -le - lu - ia! Al -le-

more.
Al -le - lu - ia! Al -le - lu - ia! Al -le-

lu - ia! Al -le - lu - ia! Al -le - lu - ia!

lu - ia! Al -le - lu - ia! Al -le - lu - ia!

Text: Isaac Watts, 1674-1748
Tune: LASST UNS ERFREUEN, 88 88 and alleluias; *Geistliche Kirchengesäng*, Cologne, 1623; arr. and harm. by Ralph Vaughan Williams, 1872-1958, *English Hymnal*,
© Oxford University Press

It Is a Wondrous Thing 177

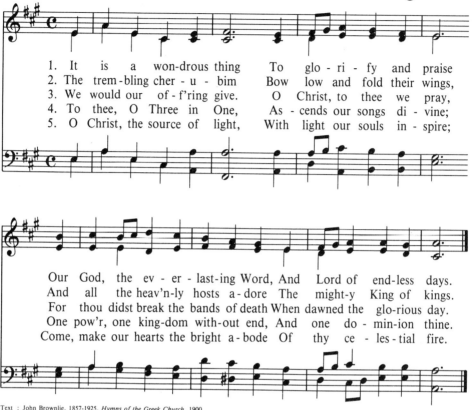

1. It is a won-drous thing   To glo - ri - fy and praise
2. The trem-bling cher - u - bim   Bow low and fold their wings,
3. We would our of - f'ring give.   O Christ, to thee we pray,
4. To thee, O Three in One,   As - cends our songs di - vine;
5. O Christ, the source of light,   With light our souls in - spire;

Our God, the ev - er - last-ing Word, And Lord of end-less days.
And all the heav'n-ly hosts a - dore The might-y King of kings.
For thou didst break the bands of death When dawned the glo-rious day.
One pow'r, one king-dom with-out end, And one do - min-ion thine.
Come, make our hearts the bright a - bode Of thy ce - les-tial fire.

Text : John Brownlie, 1857-1925, *Hymns of the Greek Church*, 1900
Tune : FESTAL SONG, SM; William H. Walter, 1894

178 O Come and Let Us Worship Christ

1. O come and let us wor - ship Christ! All peo - ple, bow
2. The stone was sealed up - on the tomb, And sol - diers guard
3. The morn - ing star shone in the east, The hills with light
4. Where-fore from high - est heav'n the hosts Their songs of vic -

be - fore him Who from the dead a Vic - tor rose:
were keep - ing, Where in the cold em - brace of death
were glow - ing; The Christ a - rose, up - on the world
t'ry blend - ing, Give glo - ry to the might - y Lord,

Sing prais - es and a - dore him
The Christ of God was sleep - ing
His light and life be - stow - ing
And sing his reign un - end - ing A - men.

Text : *Tou lithou sphragisthentos;* tr. by John Brownlie, 1857-1925, *Hymns of the Greek Church,* 1900
Tune : AETERNAE RERUM CONDITOR I, LM adapted to 87 87 for this text; Mode I; acc. by Samuel Weber, OSC, b.1947,
© 1987, Saint Meinrad Archabbey

On This Day the First of Days 179

1. On this day, the first of days,
2. On this day the e - ter - nal Son
3. Word - made - flesh, all prais - es be!
4. Ho - ly Spir - it, you im - part
5. God, the bless - ed Three in One,

God the mak - er's name we praise; Who, cre - a - tion's
O - ver death his tri - umph won; On this day the
You from sin have set us free; And with you we
Gifts of love to ev - 'ry heart; Give us light and
May your ho - ly will be done; In your word our

Lord and spring, Did the world from dark - ness bring.
Spir - it came With its gifts of liv - ing flame.
die and rise Un - to God in sac - ri - fice.
grace, we pray, Fill our hearts this ho - ly day.
souls are free, As we praise the Trin - i - ty.

Text : *Die parente temporum; Carcassone Breviary,* 1745; tr. by Henry William Baker, 1821-1877, *Hymns Ancient and Modern,* alt.
Tune : LUBECK, 77 77; adapt. from a chorale in Johann Anastasius Freylinghausen's *Geistreiches Gesangbuch,* Halle, 1704

180 The First Day of Creation

1. The first day of cre - a - tion Is
2. Yet God is re - cre - at - ing More
3. All life in Christ is com - passed By

dawn - ing in the soul, Up - on the deep God
than our in - ner world: Look up be - yond the
that trans - form - ing grace Which spins new worlds and

hov - ers Where fear and cha - os roll. The
plan - ets Where gal - ax - ies are swirled. Look
won - ders In ev - 'ry time and place. O ·

in - ward dark is part - ing, The seas make
out and see how of - ten Sur - pris - ing
Twirl - er of the star - dust, O Light no

room for land. Great shore - lines are e -
love is shown. Christ is at work re -
dark - ness rims, Your new cre - a - tion

merg - ing, A new world is at hand!
shap - ing Both stars and hearts of stone.
pul - ses With wor - ship, praise, and hymns.

Text: Based on II Corinthians 5:6-10, 14-17; Thomas H. Troeger, b.1945
Tune: NEW CREATION, 7 6 7 6 D; Carol Doran, b.1936
© 1985, Oxford University Press, Inc.

181 Rejoice, the Lord Is King

1. Re - joice the Lord is King; Your Lord and King a -
2. Je - sus the Sav - ior reigns, The God of truth and
3. His king - dom can - not fail; He rules o'er earth and
4. He sits at God's right hand Till all his foes sub -
5. Re - joice in glo - rious hope; Je - sus, the Judge, shall

dore; Re - joice, give thanks and sing And tri - umph
love; When he had purged our stains, He took his
heavn; The keys of death and hell Are to our
mit, And bow to his com - mand, And fall be -
come And take his ser - vants up To their e -

ev - er - more: Lift up your heart, lift
seat a - bove: Lift up your heart, lift
Je - sus giv'n: Lift up your heart, lift
neath his feet: Lift up your heart, lift
ter - nal home: We soon shall hear the arch -

up your voice; Re - joice! A - gain I say: Re - joice!
up your voice; Re - joice! A - gain I say: Re - joice!
up your voice; Re - joice! A - gain I say: Re - joice!
up your voice; Re - joice! A - gain I say: Re - joice!
an - gel's voice; The trump of God shall sound: Re - joice!

Text: Charles Wesley 1707-1788
Tune: DARWALL'S 148th, 6 6 6 6 8 8; John Darwall, 1731-1789, Aaron Williams' *New Universal Psalmodist*, 1770

Come, Father, As We Rise from Sleep 182

1. Come, Fa-ther, as we rise from sleep With strength and hope re-stored,
2. In - spire the words that leave our lips And fire each heart and mind,
3. Bring us your light, re-deem-ing Lord, To guide and to pro-claim,
4. Most ho - ly Fa - ther, grant our prayer Through Christ your on - ly Son,

Be pres-ent for we raise in song Your liv-ing two-edged sword.
That ho - li - ness may touch with pow'r The hands that you de - signed.
That ev - 'ry ac - tion of this day May glo - ri - fy your name.
That in your Spir - it we may live And praise you ev - er one.

Text: Ralph Wright, OSB, b.1938, © 1989, GIA Publications, Inc.
Tune: YORK, CM; *Scottish Psalter*, 1615, harm. by S. Stubbs and John Milton, 1621

183 The Herald of the Newborn Day

1. The her-ald of the new-born day Now sings of grow-ing light.
2. "Dis - pel the cling-ing web of sleep For I am near," he calls.
3. O come, Lord Je - sus, we im - plore With cries of joy or grief.
4. So come, Lord, ban-ish sleep, de - stroy The fet - ters that re - main,
5. Most ho - ly Fa-ther, grant our prayer Through Christ your on - ly Son

Christ stirs our hearts and bids us seize The pass - ing cup of life.
"Love jus - tice; keep a con-stant watch; O - bey my guid-ing laws."
We long to pray with vig - il - ance But we are tired and weak.
Then with your gift of light re - move The dark - ness of our shame.
That in your Spir - it we may live And praise you ev - er one.

Text: Ralph Wright, OSB, b.1938, © 1989, GIA Publications, Inc.
Tune: GLENLUCE, CM; *Scottish Psalter*, 1635

We Bless You, Father, Lord of Life 184

1. We bless you, Fa - ther, Lord of life, To whom all
2. We give you thanks, Re - deem - ing Christ, Who bore our
3. Come, Ho - ly Spir - it, search - ing fire, Whose flame all
4. We praise you, Trin - i - ty in One, Sub - lime in

liv - ing be - ings tend, The source of ho - li - ness and
weight of sin and shame; In dark de - feat, you con - quered
e - vil burns a - way, With light and love come down to
maj - es - ty and might, Who reign for ev - er, Lord of

grace, Our first be - gin - ning and our end.
sin, And death, by dy - ing, o - ver - came.
us In si - lence and in peace to stay.
all, In splen - dor and un - end - ing Light.

Text : *The Stanbrook Abbey Hymnal*, rev. ed., 1974, © Stanbrook Abbey Music
Tune : QUEBEC, LM; Henry Baker, 1854

184 – SECOND TUNE

1. We bless you, Fa-ther, Lord of life, To whom all liv-ing
2. We give you thanks, Re-deem-ing Christ, Who bore our weight of
3. Come, Ho-ly Spir-it, search-ing fire, Whose flame all e-vil
4. We praise you, Trin-i-ty in One, Sub-lime in maj-es-

be - ings tend, The source of ho - li - ness and grace,
sin and shame; In dark de - feat, you con-quered sin,
burns a - way, With light and love come down to us
ty and might, Who reign for ev - er, Lord of all,

Our first be - gin - ning and our end.
And death, by dy - ing, o - ver - came.
In si - lence and in peace to stay.
In splen - dor and un - end - ing Light. A - men.

Text: *The Stanbrook Abbey Hymnal*, rev. ed., 1974, © Stanbrook Abbey Music
Tune: SPLENDOR PATERNAE GLORIAE I, LM; Mode I; *Antiphonale Monasticum Diurnis Horis*, Rome, 1934; acc. by Samuel Weber, OSB, b.1947,
    © 1987, Saint Meinrad Archabbey

Christ the Glory of the Sky 185

1. Christ the glo - ry of the sky, Christ of earth the hope se - cure,
2. Help us now your praise to sing, Praise for this re - turn - ing day,
3. Pur - est Light, with - in us dwell, Nev - er from our souls de - part;
4. Faith in Christ whose name we bear In our heart of hearts a - bound;
5. Praise the Fa - ther, praise the Son; Spir - it, blest, to you be praise;

On - ly Son of God most high, Off - spring of a maid - en pure.
Light and life let morn - ing bring, Clouds and dark - ness flee a - way.
Come, the shades of earth dis - pel, Fill and pu - ri - fy the heart.
Hope, your bright - est torch pre - pare; All with ho - ly love be crowned.
To thee - ter - nal Three in One, Glo - ry be through end - less days.

Text : *Aeterna Christi gloria*, 5th C.; tr. Robert Campbell, 1814-1868, alt.
Tune : CULBACH, 77 77; Johann Scheffler, 1624-1677

186 All Creatures of Our God and King

1. All crea-tures of our God and King,
2. Great rush-ing winds and breez-es soft,
3. Swift flow-ing wa-ter, pure and clear,
4. Dear moth-er earth, who day by day
5. All you with mer-cy in your heart,

Lift up your
You clouds that
Make mu-sic
Un-fold your
For-giv-ing

voic-es, let us sing; Al-le-lu-ia, al-le-lu-ia!
ride the heav'ns a-loft, Sing your prais-es, al-le-lu-ia!
for your Lord to hear, Al-le-lu-ia, al-le-lu-ia!
bless-ings on our way, Sing your prais-es, al-le-lu-ia!
oth-ers, take your part, O sing now: al-le-lu-ia!

Bright burn-ing sun with gold-en beams,
Fair ris-ing morn, with praise re-joice,
Fire, so in-tense and fierce-ly bright,
All flow'rs and fruits that in you grow,
All you that pain and sor-row bear,

Pale sil-ver
Stars night-ly
You give to
Let them God's
Sing praise, and

moon that gen-tly gleams,
shin-ing, find a voice,
us both warmth and light,   God, we praise you. God, we praise you. Al-le -
glo-ry al - so show:
cast on God your care:

lu - ia, al - le - lu - ia, al - le - lu - ia.

6. And even you, most gentle death,
Waiting to hush our final breath,
Sing your praises, alleluia!
You lead back home the child of God,
For Christ our Lord that way has trod:
God, we praise you. God, we praise you.
Alleluia, alleluia, alleluia.

7. Let all things their creator bless,
And worship God in humbleness,
Sing your praises, alleluia!
Praise God the Father, praise the Son
And praise the Spirit, Three in One:
God, we praise you. God, we prase you.
Alleluia, alleluia, alleluia.

Text : Francis of Assisi, 1182-1226; tr. William H. Draper, 1855-1933, alt.
Tune : LASST UNS ERFREUEN, 8 8 4 4 8 8 with refrain; *Auserlesene Catholische Kirchengesang,* 1623; adapt. and harm. by Ralph Vaughan Williams, 1872-1958,
English Praise, © Oxford University Press

187 Eternal, Unchanging

1. E - ter - nal, Un - chang - ing, we sing now your praise:
2. A - gain we re - joice in the world you have made,
3. We praise you for Je - sus, our Mas - ter and Lord,

Your mer - cies are end - less, and right - eous your ways,
Your might - y cre - a - tion in beau - ty ar - rayed,
The might of his Spir - it, the truth of his word,

Your ser - vants pro - claim the re - nown of your name
We thank you for life and we praise you for joy,
His com - fort in sor - row, his pa - tience in pain,

Who, though Lord of crea - tures, are ev - er the same.
For love and for hope that no pow'r can de - stroy.
The faith sure and stead - fast that Je - sus shall reign.

Text: Robert B.Y. Scott, b. 1899, alt., © Emmanuel College, University of Toronto
Tune: NORMANDY, 11 11 11 11; Traditional French Melody; harm. by David Kingsley, ©

Father, We Praise You   188

1. Fa - ther, we praise you, Now that night is o - ver;
2. Fa - ther of all things, Form us for your dwell - ing;
3. All ho - ly Fa - ther, Son, and Ho - ly Spir - it,

Ac - tive and watch - ful, Here we stand be - fore you. Sing - ing, we
Ban - ish our weak - ness, Health and whole - ness send - ing. Bring us to
Trin - i - ty bless - ed, Send us your sal - va - tion. Yours is the

of - fer prayer and med - i - ta - tion: Thus we a - dore you.
heav - en, with your saints u - nit - ed: Joy with - out end - ing.
king - dom, pow - er, and the glo - ry: Through all cre - a - tion.

Text : *Nocte surgentes*, ascr. to St. Gregory the Great, 540-604; tr. by Percy Dearmer, 1867-1936, alt.
Tune : DIVA SERVATRIX, 11 11 11 5; *Bayeux Antiphoner, 1739*

188 – SECOND TUNE

1. Fa - ther, we praise you, Now that night is o - ver; Ac - tive
2. Fa - ther of all things, Form us for your dwell - ing; Ban - ish
3. All ho - ly Fa - ther, Son, and Ho - ly Spir - it, Trin - i -

and watch-ful, Here we stand be - fore you. Sing - ing, we of - fer
our weak-ness, Health and whole-ness send-ing. Bring us to heav - en,
ty bless - ed, Send us your sal - va - tion. Yours is the king-dom,

prayer and med - i - ta - tion: Thus we a - dore you.
with your saints u - nit - ed: Joy with - out end - ing.
pow - er, and the glo - ry: Through all cre - a - tion. A - men.

Text: *Nocte surgentes*, ascr. to St. Gregory the Great, 540-604; tr. by Percy Dearmer, 1867-1936, alt.
Tune: NOCTE SURGENTES, 11 11 11 5; Mode VI; acc. by Samuel Weber, OSB, b.1947, © 1987, Saint Meinrad Archabbey

Firm through the Endless Years  189

1. Firm through the end - less years, Your king-dom stands se - cure,
2. For, from the Par - a - clete, O Word, you came to earth
3. You came as Light from Light With - in our world to shine
4. Now ev - 'ry - thing that breathes Brings hom-age to the Word;
5. O Sav - ior, God most high, In - car-nate Word of Light,

And your do - min - ion ev - er-more, Through ag - es shall en - dure.
And, Christ our God, you hum-bly stooped To share our low - ly birth.
And brought in - to the dark-est heart The hope of light di - vine.
The glo-ry of al - might-y God Is seen in Christ the Lord.
Be mer - ci - ful and save us all From sin's e - ter - nal night.

Text : *N basileia sou*, Anatolios, 9th C.; tr. by John Brownlie, *Hymns of the Holy Eastern Church*, 1902; alt. by Ralph Wright, OSB. b. 1938, ©
Tune : BOYLESTON, SM; Lowell Mason, 1832

190 God, Whose Almighty Word

1. God, whose al - might - y word, Cha - os and dark - ness heard,
2. Sav - ior, who came to give Those who in dark - ness live
3. Spir - it of truth and love, Life - giv - ing ho - ly dove,
4. Ho - ly and bless - ed Three, Glo - ri - ous Trin - i - ty,

And took their flight, Hear us, we hum - bly pray, And where the
Heal - ing and sight, Help those who seek to find, Heal those whose
Speed forth your flight; Move on the wa - ters' face, Bear - ing the
Wis-dom, Love, Might; Bound-less as o - cean's tide Roll - ing in

Gos - pel - day Sheds not its glo - rious ray, Let there be light!
hearts are blind, And in each hum - ble mind Let there be light!
lamp of grace And in earth's dark - est place Let there be light!
full - est pride, Through the earth far and wide Let there be light!

Text : John Marriott, 1780-1825, *Evangelical Magazine*, June, 1825, alt.
Tune : MOSCOW, 664 6664; Felice de Giardini, 1716-1796; adapt. in Martin Madan's *Collection of Psalm and Hymn Tunes*, 1769

Great Lord of Splendor 191

1. Great Lord of splen-dor, Source of Light, Your gen - tle rays dis-
2. Lord Je - sus, Day Star from on high, Your ris - ing her - alds
3. More ra - diant than ten thou-sand suns, True Light en - light-'ning
4. The Fa - ther spoke: Let light shine forth: And light was born, God's
5. Yours is the realm of truth and life, Of jus - tice, peace and

pel the night Whose reign of dark - ness yields to dawn,
in the dawn; True Morn - ing Star which nev - er sets,
ev - 'ry one, Shine in the dark - ness of our hearts;
pur - est gift. Un - less your light burn in our heart,
ho - li - ness: Then yours be glo - ry, Christ, true King,

Then dies in blaze of ris - ing sun.
Come, shed your light on hu - man-kind.
Come with your heal - ing grace and truth.
Cha - os re - turns, and form - less void.
With Fa - ther and with Par - a - clete. A - men.

Text : *Lucis largitor splendide*, 9th C.; tr. Gethsemani Abbey, alt., © 1975
Tune : SPLENDOR PATERNAE GLORIAE IVa, LM; Mode IV; *Antiphonale Monasticum pro Diurnis Horis*, Rome, 1934; adapt. by Columba Kelly, OSB, b.1930 acc. by Samuel Weber, OSB, b.1947, © 1987, Saint Meinrad Archabbey

192 I Sing As I Arise Today

1. I sing as I a - rise to - day! I call up - on the
2. The word of God to be my speech, The hand of God to
3. Al - le - lu - ia, al - le - lu - ia, Al - le - lu - ia, al -

Fa - ther's might: The will of God to be my
be my stay,   The shield of God to be my
le - lu - ia,   Al - le - lu - ia, al - le - lu -

guide,   The eye of God to be
strength,   The path of God to be
ia,   Al - le - lu - ia, al - le -

1,2.
my sight,
my way.
lu -

3.
ia.

Text : Ascr. to St. Patrick, 372-466; tr. anonymous
Tune : KING, LM; David Hurd, b.1950, © 1983, GIA Publications, Inc.

193 Immortal, Invisible, God Only Wise

1. Im - mor - tal, in - vis - i - ble, God on - ly wise, In
2. Un - rest - ing, un - hast - ing, and si - lent as light, Nor
3. Life - giv - ing Cre - a - tor, of both great and small; Of
4. Great Fa - ther of glo - ry, pure Fa - ther of light, Your

light in - ac - ces - si - ble hid from our eyes, Most
want - ing, nor wast - ing, you rule day and night; Your
all life the mak - er, the true life of all; We
an - gels a - dor - ing, all veil - ing their sight; We

bless - ed, most glo - rious, the An - cient of Days, Al -
jus - tice like moun - tains high soar - ing a - bove, Your
blos - som, then with - er as leaves on a tree, But
too, God in - vis - i - ble, of - fer our praise; O

might - y, vic - to - rious, your great name we praise.
clouds which are foun - tains of good - ness and love.
you live for ev - er, who is and will be.
light in - ac - ces - si - ble, An - cient of Days!

Text: Based on 1 Timothy 1:17, Walter Chalmers Smith, 1824-1908, *Hymns of Christ and the Christian Life*, 1867, alt.
Tune: ST. DENIO, 11 11 11 11; Welsh Melody, John Roberts' *Canaidau y Cyssegr*, 1839

Lord God of Morning and of Night 194

1. Lord God of morn - ing and of night,
   We thank you for your gifts of light;
   As in the dawn the shad - ows fly,
   We seem to find you now more nigh.

2. Fresh hopes have wak - ened in the heart,
   Fresh force to do our dai - ly part;
   In peace - ful sleep our strength re - store,
   Through - out the day to serve you more.

3. O Lord of light, your love a - lone
   Can make our hu - man hearts your own;
   Be ev - er with us, Lord, that we
   Your bless - ed face one day may see.

4. Praise God, our mak - er and our friend;
   Praise God through time, till time shall end;
   Till psalm and song God's name a - dore,
   Through heav'n's great day of ev - er - more.

Text : Francis Turner Palgrave, 1824-1897, Sir R. Palmer's *Book of Praise*, 1862, alt.
Tune : FULDA (WALTON), LM; attr. to William Gardiner, 1770-1853, *Sacred Melodies*, Vol. II, 1815

195 Lord, in Your Name Your People Meet

1. Lord, in your name your peo - ple meet All thanks to your
2. At - tend when un - to you we pray; Each si - lent sup -
3. To all your faith - ful peo - ple grant Rich bless - ings from
4. Give ear to us this morn - ing hour And heark - en to
5. May all who love your ho - ly Name Sing praise to you

a - bun - dant grace! With rev - 'rent fear we wor - ship you
pli - ca - tion heed; O God and King, hear our ap - peal
your bound - less store. Lord, with your mer - cy gird us round;
our fer - vent cry. Our needs are told, and now we wait
with glad - some voice; Let all who build their trust on you

In this your cho - sen dwell - ing place.
And aid us in our time of need.
Your fa - vor shield us ev - er - more.
Your gra - cious an - swer from on high.
Now mag - ni - fy you, and re - joice. A - men.

Text: Based on Psalm 5; *The Scottish Metrical Psalter*, 1650, alt., © T. & T. Clark
Tune: IAM LUCIS ORTO SIDERE II, LM; Mode II; acc. by Samuel Weber, OSB, b.1947, © 1987, Saint Meinrad Archabbey

Lord of All Being, Throned Afar 196

1. Lord of all be - ing, throned a - far, Your glo - ry flames from sun and star; Cen - ter and soul of ev - 'ry sphere, And yet to lov - ing hearts how near.
2. Sun of our life, your liv - ing ray Sheds on our path the glow of day; Star of our hope, your gen - tle light Shall ev - er cheer the long - est night.
3. Lord of all life, be - low, a - bove, Whose light is truth, whose warmth is love; Be - fore the bril - liance of your throne We ask no lus - ter of our own.
4. Give us your grace to make us true, And kin - dling hearts that burn for you, Till all your liv - ing al - tars claim One ho - ly light, one heav'n - ly flame.

Text: Oliver Wendell Holmes, 1809-1894
Tune: UFFINGHAM, LM; Jeremiah Clarke, c.1659-1707

197 Lord of Creation, to You Be All Praise

1. Lord of cre - a - tion, to you be all praise! Most might-y your working, most won-drous your ways! Your glo - ry and might are be-yond us to tell, And yet in the heart of the hum - ble you dwell.

2. Lord of all pow-er, I give you my will, In joy-ful o - be-dience your tasks to ful - fill. Your bond - age is free-dom; your ser-vice is song; And, held in your keep-ing, our weak-ness is strong.

3. Lord of all wis-dom, I give you my mind, Rich truth that sur - pass - es all knowl-edge to find; What eye has not seen and what ear has not heard Is taught by your Spir-it and shines from your word.

4. Lord of all boun-ty, I give you my heart; I praise and a - dore you for all you im - part, Your love to in - spire me, your coun-sel to guide, Your pres-ence to shield me, what - ev - er be - tide.

5. Lord of all be-ing, I give you my all; If e'er I dis - own you, I stum-ble and fall; But, led in your ser - vice your word to o - bey, I'll walk in your free-dom to the end of the way.

Text : Jack Copley Winslow, 1882-1974, alt.; © Mrs. J. Tyrell
Tune : SLANE, 10 11 11 11; Irish Traditional Melody; harm. by Erik Reginald Routley, 1917-1982, © 1985, Hope Publishing Co.

Now That the Daylight Fills the Sky 198

1. Now that the day - light fills the sky, We lift our
2. O Lord, re - strain our tongues from strife, From wrath and
3. O may our in - most hearts be pure, From thoughts of
4. So we, when this day's work is o'er, And shades of
5. All praise to God the Fa - ther be, And praise the

hearts to God on high, that God in all we
an - ger shield our life; And guard with watch - ful
fol - ly kept se - cure, And all our pow'rs de -
night re - turn once more, Our path of tri - al
Son e - ter - nal - ly, Whom with the Spir - it

do or say, Would keep us free from harm to - day.
care our eyes That we will choose from all that's wise.
vot - ed be To deeds of love, that keep us free.
safe - ly trod, Shall give the glo - ry to our God.
we a - dore, One God a - lone, for ev - er more.

Text : *Jam lucis orto sidere*, Latin, 8th C.; tr. by John Mason Neale, 1818-1866, and others, *Hymnal Noted*, 1852, alt.
Tune : SURREXIT CHRISTUS, LM; 14th C.; acc. by Arthur Hutchings, © 1981, ICEL.

199 O God beyond All Praising

1. O God be-yond all prais-ing, We wor-ship you to - day
2. Then hear, O gra-cious Sav - ior, Ac - cept the love we bring,

And sing the love a - maz-ing That songs can-not re - pay;
That we who know your fa - vor May serve you as our king;

For we can on - ly won - der At ev - 'ry gift you send,
And wheth - er our to - mor-rows Be filled with good or ill,

At bless-ings with-out num-ber And mer-cies with-out end:
We'll tri-umph through our sor-rows And rise to bless you still:

We lift our hearts be-fore you And wait up-on your word,
To mar-vel at your beau-ty And glo-ry in your ways,

We hon-or and a-dore you, Our great and might-y Lord.
And make a joy-ful du-ty Our sac-ri-fice of praise.

Text : Michael Perry, b.1942, © 1982, Hope Publishing Co.
Tune : THAXTED, 13 13 13 13 13 13; Gustav Holst, 1874-1934

200 O Christ the Light of Heaven

1. O Christ, the Light of heav - en And of the world true Light,
2. May what is false with - in us Be - fore your truth give way,
3. May stead-fast faith sus - tain us And hope made firm in you;
4. Blest Trin - i - ty we praise you In whom our quest will cease;

You come in all your ra - diance To cleave the web of night.
That we may live un - trou - bled, With qui - et hearts this day.
The love that we have wast - ed, O God of love, re - new.
Keep us with you for ev - er In hap - pi - ness and peace.

Text: *The Stanbrook Abbey Hymnal*, rev. ed., 1974, © Stanbrook Abbey Music
Tune: SPLENDOR PATERNAE GLORIAE, 7 6 7 6; Mode IV; alt. and acc. by Frank Quinn, OP, b.1932, © 1989, GIA Publications, Inc.

O Worship the King 201

1. O wor-ship the King All glo-rious a-bove,
2. O tell of his might And sing of his grace,
3. The earth with its store Of won-ders un-told,
4. O mea-sure-less Might, O won-der-ful Love!

And grate-ful-ly sing His pow'r and his love,
Whose robe is the light, Whose can-o-py space;
Al-might-y, your pow'r Has found-ed of old,
While an-gels de-light To hymn you a-bove,

Our Shield and De-fend-er, The An-cient of Days,
His char-iots of wrath the Deep thun-der-clouds form,
Es-tab-lished it fast by A change-less de-cree,
Your hum-bler cre-a-tion, Though weak be their song,

Pa-vil-ioned in splen-dor And gird-ed with praise.
And dark is his path on The wings of the storm.
And round it has cast, like A man-tle, the sea.
Shall praise and ex-tol you, To whom they be-long.

Text: Based on Psalm 104; Robert Grant, 1779-1838; alt. by Frank Quinn, OP, b.1932. © 1989, GIA Publications, Inc.
Tune: HANOVER, 55 55 65 65; attr. to William Croft, 1678-1727

202 Pax Domini

Cantor:

1. Pax Do-mi-ni sit no - bis, Lux Do-mi-ni: To bring your
2. Pax Do-mi-ni sit no - bis, Lux Do-mi-ni: That all may
3. Pax Do-mi-ni sit no - bis, Lux Do-mi-ni: That dawn may

Choir:

light   to mind and   heart,   To bind to-geth - er and im -
see   and un-der - stand   That truth and love   lie   in your
break the long night sky,   That truth may grow and er - ror

part   A love that none   may rend a - part:
hand   And that your peace   a - lone may stand:
die,   That war may end, Lord, hear our cry:

All:

Da

Pax Do-mi-ni sit no - bis. A - men! A -

men!

Text: Ralph Wright, OSB, b.1938, © 1989, GIA Publications, Inc.
Tune: PAX DOMINI, 11 8 8 8 with refrain; Margaret Daly; © Irish Institute of Pastoral Liturgy

Sing Praise to God Who Reigns Above 203

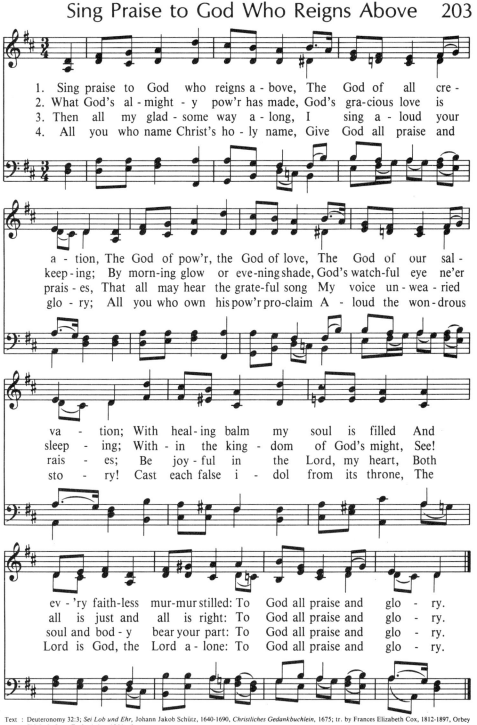

1. Sing praise to God who reigns a-bove, The God of all cre-
2. What God's al-might-y pow'r has made, God's gra-cious love is
3. Then all my glad-some way a-long, I sing a-loud your
4. All you who name Christ's ho-ly name, Give God all praise and

a-tion, The God of pow'r, the God of love, The God of our sal-
keep-ing; By morn-ing glow or eve-ning shade, God's watch-ful eye ne'er
prais-es, That all may hear the grate-ful song My voice un-wea-ried
glo-ry; All you who own his pow'r pro-claim A-loud the won-drous

va-tion; With heal-ing balm my soul is filled And
sleep-ing; With-in the king-dom of God's might, See!
rais-es; Be joy-ful in the Lord, my heart, Both
sto-ry! Cast each false i-dol from its throne, The

ev-'ry faith-less mur-mur stilled: To God all praise and glo-ry.
all is just and all is right: To God all praise and glo-ry.
soul and bod-y bear your part: To God all praise and glo-ry.
Lord is God, the Lord a-lone: To God all praise and glo-ry.

Text : Deuteronomy 32:3; *Sei Lob und Ehr,* Johann Jakob Schütz, 1640-1690, *Christliches Gedankbuchlein,* 1675; tr. by Frances Elizabeth Cox, 1812-1897, Orbey
  Shipley's *Lyra Eucharistica,* 1864, alt.
Tune : MIT FREUDEN ZART, 8 7 8 7 88 7; *Kirchengeseng,* 1566; orig. rhythm adapt.

204 The Dark of Night Is Fading

1. The dark of night is fad - ing As sun - light wakes the
2. With - hold our tongues from an - ger Lest bit - ter words re -
3. Make pure our hearts with - in us, Let wis - dom be our
4. That when the day is dy - ing And eve - ning shad-ows
5. Give glo - ry to the Fa - ther, To Je - sus Christ his

dawn, We turn in prayer to you, Lord, O
sound, Pre - vent our eyes from ling - 'ring, Where
guide; By gov - ern - ing our pas - sions, May
fall, Pro - tect - ed from de - file - ment, We
Son, In un - ion with the Spir - it They

keep us clear from harm, O keep us clear from harm.
lust or greed are found, Where lust or greed are found.
we sub-due our pride, May we sub-due our pride.
may give praise for all, We may give praise for all.
reign for ev - er one, They reign for ev - er one.

Text: Ralph Wright, OSB, b.1938, © 1989, GIA Publications, Inc.
Tune: PROTECTOR, 7 6 7 6; Der Sieg, Franz Schubert, 1797-1820; adapt. by Geoffrey Laycock, b.1927, © 1971, Faber Music Ltd.

1. The dark of night is fad - ing As sun - light wakes the dawn, We turn in prayer to you, Lord, O keep us clear from harm.
2. With-hold our tongues from an - ger Lest bit - ter words re - sound, Pre - vent our eyes from ling - 'ring, Where lust or greed are found.
3. Make pure our hearts with - in us, Let wis - dom be our guide; By gov - ern - ing our pas - sions, May we sub - due our pride.
4. That when the day is dy - ing And eve - ning shad - ows fall, Pro - tect - ed from de - file - ment, We may give praise for all.
5. Give glo - ry to the Fa - ther, To Je - sus Christ his Son, In un - ion with the Spir - it They reign for ev - er one. A - men.

Text: Ralph Wright, OSB, b.1938, © 1989, GIA Publications, Inc.
Tune: HEAVENLY LIGHT, 7 6 7 6; Mode IV; Columba Kelly, OSB, b. 1930; acc. by Samuel Weber, OSB, b.1947, © 1987, Saint Meinrad Archabbey

205 This Day God Gives Me

1. This day God gives me Strength of high heav - en, Sun and moon
2. This day God sends me Strength as my guard - ian, Might to up -
3. God's way is my way, God's shield is round me, God's host de -
4. Ris - ing, I thank you, Might - y and strong One, King of cre -

shin - ing, Flame in my hearth, Flash - ing of light - ning,
hold me, Wis - dom as guide. Your eyes are watch - ful,
fends me, Sav - ing from ill. An - gels of heav - en,
a - tion, Giv - er of rest, Firm - ly con - fess - ing

Wind in its swift - ness, Deeps of the o - cean, Firm - ness of earth.
Your ears are list - 'ning, Your lips are speak - ing, Friend at my side.
Drive from me al - ways All that would harm me, Stand by me still.
Three-ness of Per - sons, One-ness of God - head, Trin - i - ty blest.

Text : *St. Patrick's Breastplate*, 8th C. or later; adapt. by James Quinn, SJ, © 1968
Tune : BUNESSAN, 555 4 D; Scots Gaelic Melody; arr. and harm., by Martin Shaw, 1875-1958, *Enlarged Songs of Praise*, © Oxford University Press

Thy Strong Word Did Cleave the Darkness 206

1. Thy strong word did cleave the dark-ness; At thy speak-ing it was done;
2. Lo, on those who dwelt in dark-ness, Dark as night and deep as death,
3. Thy strong word be-speaks us right-eous; Bright with thine own ho - li-ness,
4. God the Fa-ther, Light-Cre - a - tor, To thee laud and hon - or be;

For cre - at - ed light we thank thee, While thine or-dered sea-sons run:
Broke the light of thy sal - va-tion, Breathed thine own life - giv-ing breath:
Glo-rious now, we press toward glo - ry, And our lives our hopes con-fess:
To thee, Light of Light be - got - ten, Praise be sung e - ter - nal-ly;

Al - le - lu - ia, al - le - lu - ia! Praise to thee who light dost send!
Al - le - lu - ia, al - le - lu - ia! Praise to thee who light dost send!
Al - le - lu - ia, al - le - lu - ia! Praise to thee who light dost send!
Ho - ly Spir-it, Light-Re - veal - er, Glo - ry, glo - ry be to thee;

Al - le - lu - ia, al - le - lu - ia! Al - le - lu - ia with-out end!
Al - le - lu - ia, al - le - lu - ia! Al - le - lu - ia with-out end!
Al - le - lu - ia, al - le - lu - ia! Al - le - lu - ia with-out end!
Mor-tals, an-gels, now and ev - er Praise the Ho - ly Trin - i - ty.

Text : Martin H. Franzmann, 1907-1976, *Worship Supplement,* © 1969, Concordia Publishing House
Tune : EBENEZER (TON-Y-BOTEL), 8 7 8 7 D; Thomas John Williams, 1869-1944

207 When Morning Fills the Sky

1. When morn-ing fills the sky, Our hearts a-wak-ing cry: May
2. To God, the word on high The hosts of an-gels cry: May
3. Let earth's wide cir-cle round In joy-ful notes re-sound: May
4. Be this when day is past Of all our thoughts the last: May
5. Then let us join to sing, To Christ our lov-ing King: May

Je-sus Christ be praised! In all our work and prayer, We
Je-sus Christ be praised! Let mor-tals, too, up-raise Their
Je-sus Christ be praised! Let air, and sea, and sky, From
Je-sus Christ be praised! The night be-comes as day, When
Je-sus Christ be praised! Be this thee-ter-nal song Through

ask his lov-ing care: May Je - sus Christ be praised!
voice in hymns of praise: May Je - sus Christ be praised!
depth to height re - ply: May Je - sus Christ be praised!
from the heart we say: May Je - sus Christ be praised!
all the ag - es long: May Je - sus Christ be praised!

Text : *Beim fruehen Morgenlicht*, anon., Wurzburg *Katolisches Gesangbuch*, 1828; tr. by Edward Caswall, 1814-1878, et al., *Masque of Mary*, 1858, alt.
Tune : LAUDES DOMINI, 66 6 D; Joseph Barnby, 1838-1896, *Hymns Ancient and Modern*, 1868

Blessed Jesus, at Your Word 208

1. Bless-ed Je - sus, at your word We are gath-ered all to hear you; Let our hearts and minds be stirred Now to seek and love and fear you; By your gos - pel, pure and ho - ly, Teach us, Lord, to love you sole - ly.

2. All our knowl-edge, sense, and sight Lie in deep - est dark - ness shroud - ed, Till your Spir - it breaks the night, Fill - ing us with light un - cloud - ed. All good thoughts and all good liv - ing Come but by your gra-cious giv - ing.

3. Glo-rious Lord, your - self im - part, Light of light, from God pro - ceed - ing; O - pen now our ears and hearts, Help us by your Spir - it's plead - ing; Hear the cry your church now rais - es, Lord, ac - cept our prayers and prais - es.

4. Fa - ther, Son and Spir - it blest, Praise to you and ad - o - ra - tion! Grant that we your Word may trust And ob - tain true con - so - la - tion While we here on earth a - wait you, Till in heav'n with praise we greet you.

Text : *Liebster Jesu, wir sing hier*, Tobias Clausnitzer, 1619-1684, *Altdorffisches Gesang-Buchlein*, 1663; tr. by Catherine Winkworth, 1827-1878, *Lyra Germanica II*, 1858, alt.
Tune : LIEBSTER JESU, 7 8 7 8 88; Johann Rudolph Ahle, 1625-1673, Darmstadt *Grosee Cantional*, 1687, alt.; harm. by George H. Palmer, 1846-1926

209 Bright as Fire in Darkness

1. Bright as fire in dark - ness, Sharp - er than a sword,
2. Fa - ther, Son, and Spir - it, Trin - i - ty of might,

Lives through-out the ag - es, God's e - ter - nal word.
Com - passed in your glo - ry, Give the world your light.

Text : *The Stanbrook Abbey Hymnal*, rev. ed., 1974, © Stanbrook Abbey Music
Tune : WEM IN LEIDEN STAGEN, 6 5 6 5; Friedrich Filtz, 1804-1876

210 Christ, Your Eyes of Mercy

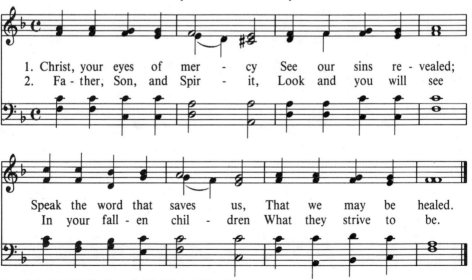

1. Christ, your eyes of mer - cy See our sins re - vealed;
2. Fa - ther, Son, and Spir - it, Look and you will see

Speak the word that saves us, That we may be healed.
In your fall - en chil - dren What they strive to be.

Text : *The Stanbrook Abbey Hymnal*, rev. ed., 1974, © Stanbrook Abbey Music
Tune : WEM IN LEIDEN STAGEN, 6 5 6 5; Friedrich Filtz, 1804-1876

Help Us, O Lord, to Learn 211

1. Help us, O Lord, to learn The truths your word im - parts: To
2. Help us, O Lord, to live The faith which we pro - claim, That
3. Help us, O Lord, to teach The beau - ty of your ways, That

stu - dy that your laws may be In - scribed up - on our hearts.
all our thoughts and words and deeds May glo - ri - fy your name.
yearn - ing souls may find the Christ, And make a life of praise.

Text: William Watkins Reid, b.1923, © 1959, 1987, The Hymn Society of America
Tune: DAY OF PRAISE, 66 86; Charles Steggall, 1826-1905

212   O God of Truth

1. O God of truth, pre - pare our minds To hear and
2. Al - might - y Fa - ther, with your Son And bless - ed

heed your ho - ly word; Fill ev - 'ry heart that longs
Spir - it, hear our prayer: Teach us to love e - ter -

for you With your mys - te - rious pres - ence, Lord.
nal truth And seek its free - dom ev - 'ry - where.

Text : *The Stanbrook Abbey Hymnal*, rev. ed. 1974, © Stanbrook Abbey Music
Tune : ST. BARTHOLOMEW, LM; Henry Duncalf, 1762

O God, You Are the Father   213

1. O God, you are the Fa - ther Of all who have be - lieved;
2. O God you are the mak - er Of all cre - at - ed things;

From whom all choirs of an - gels Have life and pow'r re - ceived.
The u - ni - verse is in your hands, O might - y King of kings.

Now to the meek and low - ly Your King - dom you un - fold,
I walk se - cure and bless - ed, In God who strength-ens me,

Your sav - ing plan u - nites in Christ All things both new and old.
The Fa - ther, Son and Spir - it, One God e - ter - nal - ly.

Text : St. Columba; tr. anonymous, alt.
Tune : FITZWILLIAM, 7 6 7 6 D; *Augsburg Gesangbuch*, 1609, and *Fitzwilliam Virginal Book*, c.1622, adapt.

214 Send Down Your Truth, O God

1. Send down your truth, O God, Too long the shad - ows frown, Too long the dark - ened way we've trod. Your truth, O Lord, send down.

2. Send down your Spir - it free, Till wil - der - ness and town One tem - ple for your wor - ship be. Your Spir - it, Lord, send down.

3. Send down your love, your life, Our less - er lives to crown, And cleanse them of their hate and strife. Your liv - ing love send down.

4. Send down your peace, O Lord; Earth's bit - ter voic - es drown, In one deep o - cean of ac - cord. Your peace, O God, send down.

Text : *The Hermitage*, 1867, Edward Rowland Sill, 1841-1887, alt.
Tune : ST. THOMAS, SM; Aaron Williams, 1731-1776; abbr. form of tune from Isaac Smith's *Collection of Psalm Tunes*, c.1770

The Mystery of the Hidden Plan   215

1. The mys-t'ry of the hid-den plan That long was kept con-cealed
2. For when we killed the Fa-ther's Son And left him in the grave,
3. Then sent the Ho-ly Spir-it down To live with-in our hearts,

The great-ness of the Fa-ther's love Is now in Christ re-vealed.
God raised him from the grip of death And out of love for-gave;
That pu-ri-fied we might pro-claim The pow'r that faith im-parts.

He came to save us from our sins, He spoke, he healed, he died.
For-gave our lack of faith, our doubt, Our ha-tred and our lust;
The pow'r to praise the Fa-ther's love Re-vealed in Christ our Lord,

He proved that God's own love for us Is great-er than our pride.
For-gave the self-ish-ness that taints And then cor-rodes our trust.
The pow'r to live in him and be On earth his liv-ing word.

Text: Ralph Wright, OSB, b.1938, © 1989, GIA Publications, Inc.
Tune: SALVATION, CMD; attr. to R. Boyd, *Kentucky Harmony*, 1816

216 You Are the Way

1. You are the way; to you a - lone From
2. You are the truth; your word a - lone True
3. You are the life; the rend - ing tomb Pro -
4. You are the way, the truth, the life; Grant

sin and death we flee; And all who would the
wis - dom can im - part; You on - ly can in -
claims your con-qu'ring arm; And those who put their
us that way to know, That truth to keep, that

Fa - ther seek Must seek you faith - ful - ly.
form the mind And pu - ri - fy the heart.
trust in you Not death nor hell shall harm.
life to win, Whose joys e - ter - nal flow.

Text : George Washington Doane, 1799-1859, *Verses for 1851 in Commemoration of the 3rd Jubilee of SPG*, alt.
Tune : DUNDEE (FRENCH), CM; *The Scottish Psalter*, Edinburgh, 1615; harm. by Thomas Ravenscroft, c.1590-1633, *Psalmes*, 1621

Your Saving Word Was Spoken, Lord   217

1. Your sav - ing word was spok - en, Lord, Up - on the moun - tain, in the plain; O may your voice once more be heard And won - der touch our hearts a - gain.

2. We all have se - cret fears to face, Our minds and mo - tives to a - mend; We seek your truth, we need your grace, Our liv - ing Lord and pres - ent Friend.

3. The Gos - pel speaks; and we re - ceive Your light, your love, your own com-mand. O help us live what we be - lieve In dai - ly work of heart and hand.

Text: H.C.A. Gaunt, b.1902, © Oxford University Press, alt.
Tune: CERNE ABBAS, LM; Cyril Taylor, b.1907, © 1989, Hope Publishing Co.

218 Your Words to Me Are Life and Health

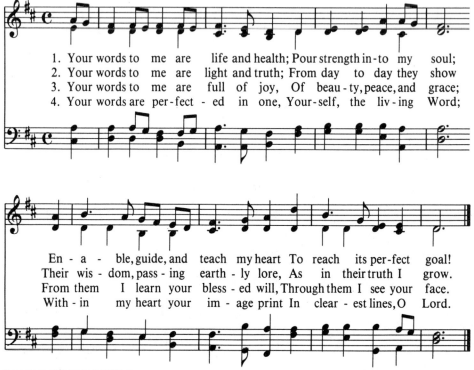

1. Your words to me are life and health; Pour strength in-to my soul;
2. Your words to me are light and truth; From day to day they show
3. Your words to me are full of joy, Of beau-ty, peace, and grace;
4. Your words are per-fect-ed in one, Your-self, the liv-ing Word;

En - a - ble, guide, and teach my heart To reach its per-fect goal!
Their wis - dom, pass - ing earth - ly lore, As in their truth I grow.
From them I learn your bless - ed will, Through them I see your face.
With - in my heart your im - age print In clear - est lines, O Lord.

Text : George Currie Martin, 1865-1937, alt.
Tune : CAPEL, 86 86; English Traditional Melody; coll. by Lucy Broadwood, 1858-1929; harm. and arr. by Ralph Vaughan Williams, 1872-1958, *English Hymnal*,
© Oxford University Press

Awake, Be Lifted Up, O Heart 219

1. A - wake, be lift - ed up, O heart, And
2. All praise to you who safe have kept And
3. Lord, we our vows to you re - new; Dis -
4. Di - rect, con - trol, sug - gest, this day, All
5. Praise God, from whom all bless - ings flow, Praise

with the an - gels bear your part, Who all night long un -
have re - freshed us while we slept; Grant, Lord, when we from
perse our sins as morn - ing dew; Guard our first springs of
we de - sign, or do, or say; That all our pow'rs, with
God all crea - tures here be - low; Praise God a - bove, you

wea - ried sing High praise to the e - ter - nal king.
death shall wake, We may of end - less light par - take.
thought and will, And with your - self our spir - its fill.
all their might, In your sole glo - ry may u - nite.
heav'n - ly host: Praise Fa - ther, Son, and Ho - ly Ghost.

Text : Thomas Ken, 1637-1711, alt.
Tune : OLD HUNDREDTH, LM; *Geneval Psalter*, Louis Bourgeois, 1510-1561

220 From the Calm of Sleep Awaking

1. From the calm of sleep a - wak - ing, Fall we now be -
2. From the night of rest up - ris - ing In my soul with
3. When the Judge shall come for judg - ment And our deeds are

fore your feet, And with an - gel hymns a - dor - ing,
bright - ness shine, O - pen now my lips to praise you,
brought to light, Fear - ful we shall lift our voic - es

God al - might - y we would greet:
Bless - ed Trin - i - ty Di - vine: Ho - ly, ho - ly,
In the mid - dle of the night:

ho - ly Lord, bless us, save us by your Word.

Text : Tr. by J. Brownlie, 1857-1925, alt.
Tune : UNSER HERRSCHER, 8 7 8 7 7 7; Joachim Neander, 1650-1680

Father, We Praise You 221

1. Fa - ther, we praise you, night is near - ly o - ver;
2. Mak - er of all things, fit us for your man - sions;
3. All - ho - ly Fa - ther, Son and e - qual Spir - it,

Ac - tive and watch - ful, stand we all be - fore you;
Ban - ish our weak - ness, health and whole-ness send - ing;
Trin - i - ty bless - ed, send us your sal - va - tion;

Sing - ing we of - fer prayer and med - i - ta - tion:
Bring us to heav - en, where your saints, u - nit - ed,
Yours is the glo - ry, ra - diant and re - sound - ing

[1,2.]
Thus we a - dore you.
Joy with - out end - ing.

[3.]
Through all cre - a - tion.

Text : *Nocte surgentes*, attr. to St. Gregory the Great, 540-604; tr. by Percy Dearmer, 1867-1936
Tune : AD TUUM NOMEN 11 11 11 5; *Chartres Antiphoner*, 1784

221– SECOND TUNE

1. Fa - ther, we praise you, night is near - ly o - ver;
2. Mak - er of all things, fit us for your man - sions;
3. All - ho - ly Fa - ther, Son and e - qual Spir - it,

Ac - tive and watch - ful, stand we all be - fore you;
Ban - ish our weak - ness, health and whole-ness send - ing;
Trin - i - ty bless - ed, send us your sal - va - tion;

Sing - ing we of - fer prayer and med - i -
Bring us to heav - en, where your saints, u -
Yours is the glo - ry, ra - diant and re -

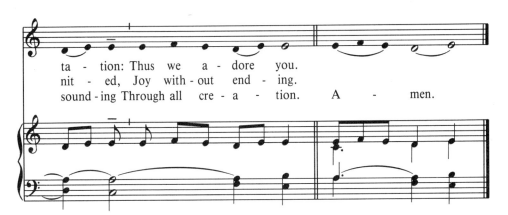

ta - tion: Thus we a - dore you.
nit - ed, Joy with - out end - ing.
sound - ing Through all cre - a - tion. A - men.

Text: *Nocte surgentes*, attr. to St. Gregory the Great, 540-604; tr. by Percy Dearmer, 1867-1936
Tune: ECCE IAM NOCTIS, 11 11 11 5; Mode IV; *Antiphonale Monasticum pro Diurnis Horis*, Rome, 1934; acc. by Samuel Weber, OSB, b.1947, © 1987, Saint
   Meinrad Archabbey

222 Almighty Ruler, God of Truth

1. Al - migh - ty Rul - er, God of Truth Who guide and
2. O quench the fires of ha - tred, Lord, Of an - ger
3. Most ho - ly Fa - ther, grant our prayer Through Christ your

mas - ter all; The rays with which you gild the dawn
and of strife; Bring health to ev - 'ry mind and heart
on - ly Son That in your Spir - it we may live

With noon - day heat now fall.
That peace may en - ter life.
And praise you ev - er one. A - men.

Text: Ralph Wright, OSB, b.1938, © 1989, GIA Publications, Inc.
Tune: POPE'S WOOD; CM; Prinknash Tone, © Trustees of Prinknash Abbey; acc. by Br. Ashenden, ©

Eternal Living Lord of All 223

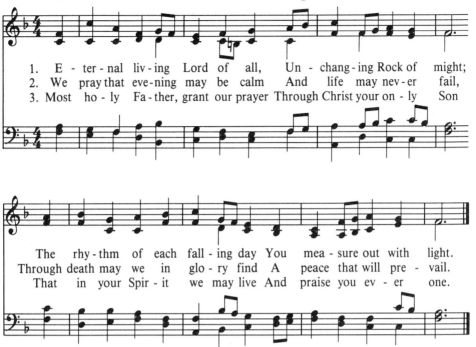

1. E - ter - nal liv - ing Lord of all, Un - chang - ing Rock of might;
2. We pray that eve - ning may be calm And life may nev - er fail,
3. Most ho - ly Fa - ther, grant our prayer Through Christ your on - ly Son

The rhy - thm of each fall - ing day You mea - sure out with light.
Through death may we in glo - ry find A peace that will pre - vail.
That in your Spir - it we may live And praise you ev - er one.

Text: *Rerum, Deus, tenax vigor;* attr. to St. Ambrose, 340-397; tr. by Ralph Wright, OSB, b.1938, © 1989, GIA Publications, Inc.
Tune: ST. STEPHEN (NEWINGTON), CM; William Jones, 1789

224 Glory to Christ on High!

1. Glo - ry to Christ on high! Let heav'n and earth re - ply:
2. Je - sus our Lord and King! Through earth and heav'n shall ring
3. Let all the hosts a - bove Join in one song of love,

Praised be his name! His love and grace a - dore, Who
Praise to his name! Tell what his arm has done, How
Prais - ing his name! To Christ for ev - er be Through

all our sor - rows bore; Loud - ly sing ev - er - more: Wor - thy the Lamb!
he the Fa - ther's Son For us the vic - t'ry won: Wor - thy the Lamb!
all e - ter - ni - ty Hon - or and ma - je - sty: Wor - thy the Lamb!

Text : James Allen, 1734-1804, et al., alt.
Tune : DENBIGH, 664 666 4; Welsh Traditional Melody; arr. *English Hymnal*, © Oxford University Press

Into the Silence of Our Hearts 225

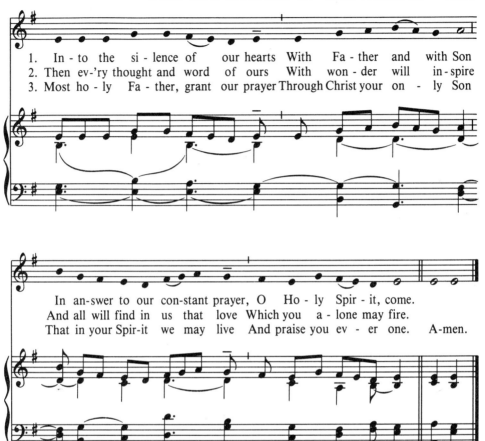

1. In - to the si - lence of our hearts With Fa - ther and with Son
2. Then ev-'ry thought and word of ours With won - der will in - spire
3. Most ho - ly Fa - ther, grant our prayer Through Christ your on - ly Son

In an-swer to our con-stant prayer, O Ho - ly Spir - it, come.
And all will find in us that love Which you a - lone may fire.
That in your Spir-it we may live And praise you ev - er one. A-men.

Text: *Nunc Sancte nobis Spiritus;* ascr. to St. Ambrose, 340;397; tr. by Ralph Wright, OSB, b.1938, © 1989, GIA Publications, Inc.
Tune: PRINKNASH PARK, CM; Prinknash Tone, © Trustees of Prinknash Abbey; acc. by Br. Ashenden, ©

226 Lord of All Hopefulness

1. Lord of all hope-ful-ness, Lord of all joy, Whose trust, ev - er
child-like, no cares can de - stroy: Be there at our wak - ing and
give us, we pray, Your bliss in our hearts, Lord, at the break of the day.

2. Lord of all ea - ger-ness, Lord of all faith, Whose strong hands were
skilled at the plane and the lathe: Be there at our la - bors, and
give us, we pray, Your strength in our hearts, Lord, at the noon of the day.

3. Lord of all kind - li - ness, Lord of all grace, Your hands swift to
wel - come, your arms to em - brace: Be there at our hom - ing, and
give us, we pray, Your love in our hearts, Lord, at the eve of the day.

4. Lord of all gen - tle - ness, Lord of all calm, Whose voice is con -
tent-ment, whose pres - ence is balm: Be there at our sleep - ing, and
give us, we pray, Your peace in our hearts, Lord, at the end of the day.

Text: Jan Struther, 1901-1953, *Enlarged Songs of Praise*, © Oxford University Press
Tune: SLANE, 10 11 11 12; Gaelic Melody; harm. by Carlton R. Young, *The Book of Hymns*, © 1964, Abingdon Press

Now, Holy Spirit, Ever One 227

1. Now, Ho - ly Spir - it, ev - er One With God the Fa - ther and the Son, Pour forth in - to our hearts, we pray, The full - ness of your grace to - day.

2. Let mouth and tongue, mind, sense, and strength God's might - y ac - tions tell at length; Let love in flames of liv - ing fire The hearts of all the world in - spire.

3. Al - might - y Fa - ther, hear our cry Through Je - sus Christ, our Lord Most High, Whom with the Spir - it we a - dore For ev - er and for ev - er - more.

Text: *Nunc Sancte nobis Spiritus;* ascr. to St. Ambrose, 340-397; ver. *The Hymnal 1982,* © 1985, Church Pension Fund; st. 3, James Waring McCrady, b.1938, © 1982
Tune: NUNC SANCTE NOBIS SPIRITUS, LM; Mode V; Verona MS., 12th C.; acc. by Gerard Farrell, OSB, b.1919, © 1984

228 O God of Truth

1. O God of truth and Lord of pow'r, With or-der ru-ling time and change, Whose splen-dor shines in morn-ing-light, Whose glo-ry burns in mid-day fire.

2. Ex-tin-guish ev-'ry flame of strife And ban-ish ev-'ry wrong de-sire, Grant health of bod-y and of mind, Cre-ate in us true peace of heart.

3. To God the Fa-ther glo-ry be, All glo-ry to the on-ly Son And to the Spi-rit, Par-a-clete, In time and in e-ter-ni-ty. A-men.

Text: *Rector potens, verax Deus;* ascr. to St. Ambrose, 340-397; tr. Benedictine Nuns of St. Mary' Abbey, West Malling, Kent, ©
Tune: SEVERN VIEWS,LM; Prinknash Tone, © Trustees of Prinknash Abbey; acc. by Br. Ashenden, ©

Your Kingdom Come, O Father 229

1. Your king - dom come, O Fa-ther, To earth's re - mot-est shore.
2. On all who lift your ban-ner, Your bless - ing, Lord, be - stow;
3. Your love with - in us quick-en; In - crease it day by day.
4. The des - ert, as you prom-ised, Shall blos - som far and near;

Your ho - ly fire en - kin - dle And let it flame the more.
Let all, your cross be - hold-ing, In hum - ble faith bend low.
That all, our - selves de - ny - ing, May find in you the way.
And through earth's mists and shad-ows The sun's mild rays ap - pear.

Your ser - vants send to la - bor Where liv - ing har - vests grow,
Oh, make your Church, dear Sav - ior, A wit - ness true and clear,
You once left all, O Sav - ior, A thorn - y path to tread;
For that blest day we wait, Lord, When, doubts and dark-ness gone,

That all, your truth re - ceiv - ing, Your sav - ing grace may know.
Your sav - ing death pro - claim-ing, That all the world may hear.
Help us to fol - low glad - ly, Wher - ev - er you may lead.
We wit - ness earth's re - demp-tion, And sum - mer morn shall dawn.

Text : Kauko-Veikko Tamminem, 1882-1946; tr. by Ernest E. Ryden, b.1886, alt., *Laudamus*, © 1970, Lutheran World Federation
Tune : NOORMARKKU, 7 6 7 6 D; Finnish Folk Tune; harm. *Lutheran Book of Worship*, © 1978

230 All Praise to You, O God, This Night

1. All praise to you, O God, this night, For all the
2. For-give us, Lord, through Christ your Son What-ev - er
3. En - light - en us, O bless - ed Light, And give us

bless - ings of the light; Keep us, we pray, O
wrong this day we've done; Your peace give to the
rest through - out this night. O strength - en us, that

King of kings, Be - neath your own al - might - y wings.
world, O Lord, That all might live in one ac - cord.
for your sake, We all may serve you when we wake.

Text : Thomas Ken, 1637-1711, alt.
Tune : TALLIS' CANON, LM; Thomas Tallis, c.1515-1585, Thomas Ravenscroft's *Psalmes*, 1621

Be Thou My Vision 231

1. Be thou my vi - sion, O Lord of my heart,
2. Be thou my wis - dom, be thou my true word,
3. Be thou my breast-plate, my sword for the fight;
4. Rich - es I heed not, nor all the world's praise:
5. High King of heav - en, thou heav - en's bright Sun.

Be all else but naught to me, save that thou art;
Be thou ev - er with me, and I with thee, Lord:
Be thou my whole ar - mor, be thou my true might;
Be thou my in - her - i - tance, now and al - ways;
O grant me its joys af - ter vic - t'ry is won;

Be thou my best thought in the day and the night,
Be thou my great Fa - ther, and I thy true heir;
Be thou my soul's shel - ter, be thou my strong tow'r:
Be thou and thou on - ly the first in my heart:
Great Heart of my own heart, what - ev - er be - fall,

Both wak - ing and sleep - ing, thy pres - ence my light.
Be thou in me dwell - ing, and I in thy care.
O raise thou me heav'n-ward, great Pow'r of my pow'r.
O Sov - 'reign of heav - en, my trea - sure thou art.
Still be thou my vi - sion, O Ru - ler of all.

Text: Irish, 5th C.; tr. by Mary Byrne, 1880-1931; versified by Eleanor Hull, 1860-1935, © Chatto and Windus, Ltd., alt.
Tune: SLANE, 10 11 11 11; Gaelic Melody; harm. by Erik Reginald Routley, 1917-1982, © 1985, Hope Publishing Co.

232   Before the Light of Evening Fades

1. Be - fore the light of eve - ning fades We pray, O Lord of all,
2. Re - pel the ter - rors of the night And Sa - tan's pow'r of guile,
3. Most ho - ly Fa - ther, grant our prayer Through Christ your on - ly Son

That by your love we may be saved From ev - 'ry griev-ous fall.
Im - pose a calm and rest - ful sleep That noth-ing may de - file.
That in your Spir - it we may live And praise you ev - er one.

Text: *Te lucis ante terminum;* tr. by Ralph Wright, OSB, b.1938, © 1989, GIA Publications, Inc.
Tune: BÉVENOT, CM; Laurence Bévenot, *The Office of Compline,* © Ampleforth Abbey Trustees

Before the Light of Evening Fades   233

1. Be - fore the light of eve - ning fades We
2. Re - pel the ter - rors of the night And
3. Most ho - ly Fa - ther, grant our prayer Through

pray, O Lord of all, That by your love
Sa - tan's pow'r of guile, Im - pose a calm
Christ your on - ly Son That in your Spir -

we may be saved From ev - 'ry griev - ous fall.
and rest - ful sleep That noth - ing may de - file.
it we may live And praise you ev - er one.

Text: *Te lucis ante terminum;* tr. by Ralph Wright, OSB, b.1938, © 1989, GIA Publications, Inc.
Tune: ST. COLUMBA, CM; Irish Hymn Melody; harm. by H. Walford Davies, 1923

234 Eternal Light

1. E - ter - nal light, shine in my heart; E - ter - nal
2. E - ter - nal life, raise me from death; E - ter - nal
3. Un - til by your most cost - ly grace, In - vit - ed

hope, lift up my eyes; E - ter - nal pow'r, be
bright - ness, help me see; E - ter - nal Spir - it,
by your ho - ly word, At last I come be -

my sup - port; E - ter - nal wis - dom, make me wise.
give me breath; E - ter - nal Sav - ior, come to me:
fore your face To know you, my e - ter - nal God.

Text: From a prayer of Alcuin, 735?-804; Christopher Idle, b.1938, © 1982, Hope Publishing Co.
Tune: ACH BLEIB BEI UNS, LM; Samuel Scheidt, 1567-1654; harm. by Seth Calvisius, 1556-1615

God Be in My Head 235

Org.

God be in my head, and in my un-der-stand-ing; God be in mine eyes, and in my look-ing; God be in my mouth, and in my speak-ing; God be in my heart, and in my think-ing; God be in mine end, and at my de-part-ing.

Text : *Horae B.V.M.; Sarum Primer*, 1514
Tune : GOD BE IN MY HEAD, 12 10 10 10 10 11; H. Walford Davies, 1869-1941, © Oxford University Press

236 God, Who Made the Earth and Heaven

1. God, who made the earth and heav-en, Dark - ness and light:
2. And when morn a - gain shall call us To run life's way,
3. Guard us wak-ing, guard us sleep-ing, And, when we die,
4. Ho - ly Fa-ther, throned in heav-en, All ho - ly Son,

You the day for work have giv - en, For rest the night.
May we still what-e'er be-fall us, Your will o - bey.
May we in your might - y keep-ing All peace-ful lie.
Ho - ly Spir-it free - ly giv - en, Blest Three in One:

May your an - gel guards de-fend us, Slum-ber sweet your mer - cy send us,
From the pow'r of e - vil hide us, In the nar-row path-way guide us,
When the last dread call shall wake us, Then, O Lord, do not for-sake us,
Grant us grace we now im-plore you, Till we lay our crowns be-fore you

Ho - ly dreams and hopes at-tend us, All through the night.
Nev - er be your smile de-nied us, All through the day.
But to reign in glo - ry take us, With you on high.
And in wor-thier strains a-dore you While ag - es run.

Text : St. 1, Reginald Heber, 1783-1826; st. 2,4, William Mercer, 1811-1873; st. 3, Richard Whately, 1787-1863, alt.
Tune : AR HYD Y NOS, 84 84 88 84; Welsh; *English Hymnal,* © Oxford University Press

Lower key: No. 162

Jesus, Redeemer of the World   237

1. Je - sus, Re - deem - er of the world, Word of the
2. The whole cre - a - tion's ar - chi - tect, You set the
3. You broke the chains of death and hell: Lord, free us
4. Lord, while we live for this short time As mor - tals
5. All glo - ry be to you, Lord Christ, Who, con - q'ring

Fa - ther throned on high, Light from the light in - vis - i -
bounds of night and day; Give to our wea - ried bod - ies
from our an - cient foe And let him nev - er lead a -
clothed in earth - bound frame, Re - fresh us now with rest - ful
death, reign glo - rious - ly With God, Cre - a - tor of all

ble, And watch - ful guard - ian o - ver all:
rest In night's en - fold - ing qui - et - ness.
stray Those you have ran - somed by your blood.
sleep That wak - ing we may watch with you.
things And with the Spir - it, Com - fort - er.

Text: Latin, 10th C.; st. 1-4, version *The Hymnal.1982*, © 1985, Church Pension Fund; st. 5, Anne K. LeCroy, b.1930, © 1982
Tune: JESU NOSTRA REDEMPTIO, LM; Mode VIII; Worchester MS., 13th C.; acc. by Richard Solly, b.1952, © 1984

238 Now, God, Be with Us

1. Now, God, be with us, for the night is clos- ing; The light and dark - ness are of your dis- pos - ing; And 'neath your shad - ow here to rest we yield us, For you will shield us.

2. Let ho - ly thoughts be ours when sleep o'er - takes us; Our ear - liest thought be yours when morn-ing wakes us; All day serve you, in all that we are do - ing Your praise pur - su - ing.

3. We have no ref - uge, none on earth to aid us, Save you, O Fa - ther, who in love has made us; But your dear pres - ence will not leave them lone - ly Who seek you on - ly.

4. Fa - ther, your name be praised, your king - dom giv - en; Your will be done on earth as now in heav - en; Keep us in life, for - give our sins, de - liv - er Us now and ev - er.

Text: *Die Nacht ist kommen,* Petrus Herbert, d. 1571; Bohemian Brethren's *Kirchengesange,* 1566; tr. by Catherine Winkworth, 1827-1878, *Chorale-Book for England,*
1863, alt.
Tune: LOBET DEN HERREN, 11 11 11 5; Johann Crueger, 1598-1662, *Geistliche Lieder und Psalmen,* 1653

O Christ, You Are the Light and Day 239

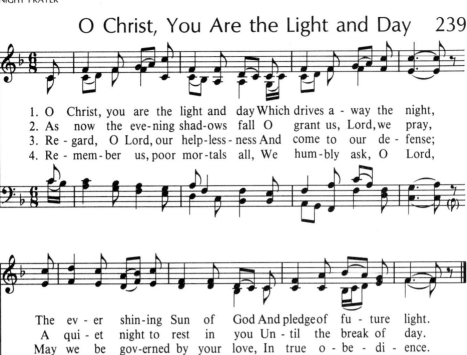

1. O Christ, you are the light and day Which drives a - way the night,
2. As now the eve-ning shad-ows fall O grant us, Lord, we pray,
3. Re - gard, O Lord, our help-less - ness And come to our de - fense;
4. Re - mem - ber us, poor mor-tals all, We hum-bly ask, O Lord,

The ev - er shin-ing Sun of God And pledge of fu - ture light.
A qui - et night to rest in you Un - til the break of day.
May we be gov-erned by your love, In true o - be - di - ence.
And may your pres-ence in our souls Be now our great re - ward.

Text: *Christe qui Lux es et Dies*, c.800; tr. by Frank C. Quinn, OP, b.1932, © 1989, GIA Publications, Inc.
Tune: LAND OF REST, CM; American Folk Melody; arr. by Erik Routley, 1917-1982, © 1976, Hinshaw Music Inc.

240 O Father, Bring Us Back Again

1. O Fa - ther, bring us back a - gain Who on this
2. Give us un - trou - bled heart and mind, So flood - ed
3. We thank you, Fa - ther, source of light, With Christ your

day have strayed from you, That, shel - tered by your
with your tran - quil light, That noth - ing e - vil
Son and Spir - it blest, Who give the mar - vel

lov - ing hand, Our eve - ning prayer we may re - new.
there may hide To take a - way our peace to - night.
of new day, And, with the eve - ning star, give rest.

Text : *The Stanbrook Abbey Hymnal*, rev. ed., 1974, © Stanbrook Abbey Music
Tune : ACK, BLIV HOS OSS, LM; *Koralpsalmboken*, Stockholm, 1697, © Concordia Publishing House

O Love of God, How Strong and True   241

1. O love of God, how strong and true, E - ter - nal,
2. O heav'n - ly love, how pre - cious still In days of
3. O wide - em - brac - ing won - drous love, We read thee
4. We read thee best in him who came And bore for
5. O love of God, our shield and stay Through all the

and yet ev - er new, Un - com - pre - hend - ed and un -
wea - ri - ness and ill, In nights of pain and help - less -
in the sky a - bove; We read thee in the earth be -
us the cross of shame, Sent by the Fa - ther from on
per - ils of our way— E - ter - nal love, in thee we

bought, Be - yond all knowl-edge and all thought!
ness, To heal, to com - fort and to bless!
low, In seas that swell and streams that flow.
high, Our life to live, our death to die.
rest, For ev - er safe, for ev - er blest.

Text: Horatius T. Bonar, 1808-1889
Tune: DUNEDIN, LM; Vernon Griffiths, b.1894-1985, © 1971, Faber Music Ltd.

242 This World,
My God, Is Held within Your Hand

1. This world, my God, is held with-in your hand,
3. From youth-ful con-fi-dence to care-ful age,

we for-get your love and stead-fast might, And
Help us each one to be your lov-ing friend, Re-

in the chang-ing day un-cer-tain stand, Dis-
ward-ed by the faith-ful ser-vant's wage,

*stanza two
next page*

turbed by morn-ing and a-fraid of night.
God in three per-sons, reign-ing with-out end.

2. Grant in the peace of eve-ning we may walk As A-dam in the gar-den that first day, Un-til we come with you in qui-et talk To our e-ter-nal home the straight-est way.

Text: Hamish Swanston, © 1971, Faber Music Ltd.
Tune: IN MANUS TUAS, 10 10 10 10; Herbert Howells, ©

243 We Praise You, Father

1. We praise you, Fa - ther, for your gift Of dusk and
2. With - in your hands we rest se - cure; In qui - et
3. Your glo - ry may we ev - er seek In rest, as

night - fall o - ver earth, Fore - shad - ow - ing the
sleep our strength re - new; Yet give your peo - ple
in ac - tiv - i - ty, Un - til its full - ness

mys - ter - y Of death that leads to end - less day.
hearts that wake In love to you, un - sleep - ing Lord.
is re - vealed, O source of life, O Trin - i - ty.

Text: The Benedictine Nuns of St. Mary's Abbey, West Malling, Kent, ©
Tune: AUCTORITATE SAECULI, LM; Poitiers *Antiphoner*, 1746; harm. by Redmund Shaw, ©

Eternal Trinity of Love 244

1. E - ter - nal Trin - i - ty of love, In peace and maj - es - ty you reign, All things come forth from you a - lone, To you they must re - turn a - gain.

2. Cre - a - tion lives and breathes in you, Sus - tained by your al - might - y will; Grant us to know you, God of truth, In whom the quest - ing mind is still.

3. Our Fa - ther, in the name of Christ, Un - ceas - ing - ly your Spir - it send; Be with us, ev - er - last - ing God: Ful - fill your pur - pose to the end.

4. We praise you, God - head, One in Three, Im - mor - tal Trin - i - ty of light; Un - chang - ing through e - ter - nal days, You live un - moved, se - rene in might.

Text : *The Stanbrook Abbey Hymnal*, rev. ed, 1974, © Stanbrook Abbey Music
Tune : WAREHAM, LM; William Knapp, 1698-1768; harm. *Hymns Ancient and Modern*, 1875, after James Turle, 1802-1882

245 Father Eternal, Lord of the Ages

1. Fa - ther e - ter - nal, Lord of the ag - es, You who have made us, You who have called us, Look on your chil - dren Gath - ered be - fore you, Wor - ship they bring you, Fa - ther of all.

2. Je - sus our Sav - ior, Born of a Vir - gin, Truth from high heav - en You came to teach us; You are the way that Leads to the Fa - ther, Be now our life both Here and a - bove.

3. Spir - it all - ho - ly, Spir - it of mer - cy, Bind us in one with Christ and the Fa - ther, Give us all joy and Peace in be - liev - ing, Firm on the rock of Faith in our God.

4. Fa - ther e - ter - nal, Je - sus, re - deem - er, Spir - it all - ho - ly, Trin - i - ty per - fect, Un - i - ty end - less, Love ev - er - last - ing, Praise ev - er - more we Of - fer to you.

Text : G.B. Timms, b.1910
Tune : GEORGE, 10 10 10 9; Arthur Hutchings, b.1906, © 1975, Oxford University Press

Father in Heaven 246

1. Fa-ther in heav-en, Grant to your chil-dren Mer-cy and
2. Je-sus, Re-deem-er, May we re-mem-ber Your gra-cious
3. Spir-it de-scend-ing Whose is the bless-ing, Strength for the

bless-ing, Songs nev-er ceas-ing, Love to u-nite us, Grace to re-
pas-sion, Your res-ur-rec-tion. Wor-ship we bring you, Praise we shall
wea-ry, Help for the need-y, Fired with com-pas-sion, Yours by a-

deem us— Fa-ther in heav-en, Fa-ther our God.
sing you— Je-sus, Re-deem-er, Je-sus our Lord.
dop-tion— Spir-it de-scend-ing, Spir-it a-dored.

Text: Daniel Thambyrajah Niles, 1908-1970, *CCA Hymnal*, © Christian Conference of Asia; alt. by Ralph Wright, OSB, b.1938, © 1989, GIA Publications, Inc.
Tune: HALAD, 55 55 55 54; Filipino Folk Melody, *Awitan Ta Ang Dyos*, 1962, © Silliman Music Foundation Inc.; arr. by Elena Maquiso, fl. 1961, © L.F. Bartlett

247 O Blessed Light, O Trinity

1. O bless-ed Light, O Trin-i-ty, O source of deep-est u-ni-ty! The sun now sinks and burns the sky; Bring light and peace lest hope should die.

2. In song we of-fer praise at dawn And pray when eve-ning's cares are done. With you our glo-ry, you our praise, May we sing glad-ly all our days. A-men.

Text: Ralph Wright, OSB, b.1938, © 1989, GIA Publications, Inc.
Tune: CHRISTUS, DU LICHT VOM WAHREN LICHT, LM; Mode I; St. Ottilien, 1979; *Antiphonale zum Stundengebet,* © Vier-Türme-Verlag, Muensterschwarzach, 1979;
acc. by Samuel Weber, OSB, b.1947, © 1987, Saint Meinrad Archabbey

O God, Almighty Father 248

1. O God, al-might-y Fa - ther, Cre - a - tor of all things, The
2. O Je - sus, Word in - car - nate, Re - deem-er most a - dored, All
3. O God, the Ho - ly Spir - it, Who lives with - in our soul, Send

heav-ens stand in won - der, While earth your glo - ry sings.
glo - ry, praise, and hon - or Be yours, O sov-'reign Lord.
forth your light and lead us To our e - ter - nal goal.

O most ho - ly Trin - i - ty, Un - di - vid - ed u - ni - ty,

Ho - ly God, might - y God, God im - mor - tal be a - dored!

Text: *Gott Vater sei gepriesen;* Anon.; tr. by Irvin Udulutsch, OFM Cap., alt., © 1959, 1977, The Order of St. Benedict, Inc.
Tune: GOTT VATER SEI GEPRIESEN, 76 76 with refrain; *Limburg Gesangbuch,* 1838; harm. by Healey Willan, 1880-1968, © 1958, Willis Music Co.

249 O Jesus, Joy of Loving Hearts

1. O Je - sus, joy of lov - ing hearts, The fount of
2. Your truth un-changed has ev - er stood; You save all
3. For you our rest - less spir - its yearn Wher - e'er our
4. O Je - sus, ev - er with us stay; Make all our

life and our true light, We seek the peace your
those who heed your call; To those who seek you,
chang - ing lot is cast; Glad, when your pres - ence
mo - ments calm and bright; Oh, chase the night of

love im - parts And stand re - joic - ing in your sight.
you are good, To those who find you all in all.
we dis - cern, Blest, when our faith can hold you fast.
sin a - way, Shed o'er the world your ho - ly light.

Text : *Jesu, dulcis memoria*, Anon., sometimes attr. to St. Bernard of Clairvaux, 1091-1153; tr. and para. by Ray Palmer, 1808-1887, *Sabbath Hymn Book*, 1858, alt.
Tune : JESU DULCIS MEMORIA, LM; Mode II; acc. by Richard Proulx, b.1937, © 1975, GIA Publications, Inc.

1. O Je - sus, joy of lov - ing hearts, The fount of
2. Your truth un - changed has ev - er stood; You save all
3. For you our rest - less spir - its yearn Wher - e'er our
4. O Je - sus, ev - er with us stay; Make all our

life and our true light, We seek the peace your
those who heed your call; To those who seek you,
chang - ing lot is cast; Glad, when your pres - ence
mo - ments calm and bright; Oh, chase the night of

love im - parts And stand re - joic - ing in your sight.
you are good, To those who find you all in all.
we dis - cern, Blest, when our faith can hold you fast.
sin a - way, Shed o'er the world your ho - ly light.

Text: *Jesu, dulcis memoria*, Anon.; sometimes attr. to St. Bernard of Clairvaux, 1091-1153; tr. and para. by Ray Palmer, 1808-1887, *Sabbath Hymn Book*, 1858, alt.
Tune: O JESU CHRIST, MEINS LEBENS LICHT, LM; *As Hymnodus Sacer*, Leipaiz, 1625, adapt.

250 Weave a Song within the Silence

1. Weave a song with-in the si - lence That these mys - ter -
2. Mar - y bore him, sin - less Vir - gin, When to this our
3. While re - clin - ing that last eve - ning Tak - ing sup - per
4. See the won - der of this mo - ment! Watch with awe what

ies cre - ate Of the Bod - y of the Sav - ior
world he came To walk free - ly through the fur - rows
with his friends When the pas - chal meal was end - ed
comes to be! He, the Word made flesh, has spo - ken

Who was tor-tured for our sake And the Blood that left
Scat - ter - ing his Fa - ther's grain Till he end - ed his
With the rites the Law de - mands He gave them as bread
And the bread and wine per - ceived Are now tru - ly his

his	bod - y	Sav - ing	sin - ners	from their fate.
brief	vis - it	With a	har - vest	reaped in pain.
his	bod - y,	Bro - ken	in his	sa - cred hands.
own	bod - y	Feed - ing	all who	will be - lieve. A - men.

5. Humbly we bow down before him
And in awe we do proclaim
This his presence on our altar
Glorified beyond all pain.
What our senses cannot master
By our faith we now acclaim.

6. Honor, praise and thanks be given
To the Father and the Son.
Sing with joy in their own Spirit
Who alone can make us one,
And from heaven now with power
Gently to our hearts has come.

Text: *Pange lingua*, Saint Thomas Aquinas, c.1225-1274; tr. by Ralph Wright, OSB, b.1938, © 1989, GIA Publications, Inc.
Tune: PANGE LINGUA, 8 7 8 7 8 7; Mode III

251 All You Who Seek a Comfort Sure

1. All you who seek a com-fort sure In sad-ness and dis - tress,
2. Now hear him as he speaks to us Those words for ev - er blest:

What - ev - er sor - row bur-dens you, What - ev - er griefs op - press:
"All you who la - bor, come to me, And I will give you rest."

When Je - sus gave him - self for us And died up - on the tree,
O heart a - dored by saints on high, And hope of sin - ners here,

His heart was pierced for love of us; He died to set us free.
We place our ev - 'ry trust in you And lift to you our prayer.

Text: *Quicumque certum quaeritis;* Latin. 18th C.; tr. by Edward Caswall, 1814-1878. alt.
Tune: KINGSFOLD, CMD; English Traditional; harm. by Ralph Vaughan Williams, 1872-1958. © Oxford University Press

See How the Legion of Our Sin 252

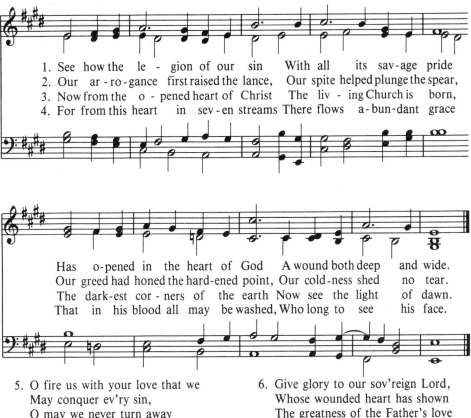

1. See how the le - gion of our sin   With all   its sav-age pride
2. Our ar - ro-gance first raised the lance,   Our spite helped plunge the spear,
3. Now from the o - pened heart of Christ   The liv - ing Church is   born,
4. For from this heart   in sev - en streams There flows   a - bun-dant grace

Has   o-pened in the heart of God   A wound both deep   and wide.
Our greed had honed the hard-ened point, Our cold-ness shed   no   tear.
The dark-est cor - ners of   the earth Now see the light   of dawn.
That   in his blood all may   be washed, Who long to   see   his face.

5. O fire us with your love that we
    May conquer ev'ry sin,
    O may we never turn away
    Or wound your heart again.

6. Give glory to our sov'reign Lord,
    Whose wounded heart has shown
    The greatness of the Father's love
    Revealed within his own.

Text: *En ut superba criminum*, tr. by Ralph Wright, OSB, b.1938, © 1989, GIA Publications, Inc.
Tune: SPRINGDALE, CM; Erik Routley, 1917-1982, Hope Publishing Co.

253 Jesus Shall Reign

1. Je - sus shall reign wher - e'er the sun Does its suc-
2. For him shall end - less prayer be made, And prais-es
3. Bless - ings a - bound wher - e'er he reigns: The pris-'ner
4. Let ev - 'ry crea - ture rise and bring Their spe - cial

ces - sive jour - neys run; His king-dom stretch from
throng to crown his head; His name like sweet per -
leaps to lose his chains: The wea - ry find e -
hon - ors to our King, An - gels de - scend with

shore to shore, Till moons shall wax and wane no more,
fume shall rise With ev - 'ry morn - ing sac - ri - fice.
ter - nal rest: All chil-dren of the poor are blest.
songs a - gain, And earth re - peat the long a - men.

Text : Based on Psalm 72, Isaac Watts 1674-1748
Tune : DUKE STREET, LM; John Hatton, c.1710-1793

O Jesus, Mighty Prince of Peace 254

1. O Je - sus, might - y Prince of Peace, Take war from
each re - bel - lious heart. U - nite with - in one
com - mon fold All those whom sin still keeps a - part.

2. It was for this you o - pened wide Your arms in
wel - come on the tree, Re - veal - ing in your
shat - tered heart The kind of love that keeps us free.

3. All whom the dross of sin be - guiles Re - fuse to
wel - come this your reign. But Christ as Lord and
King of all In tri - umph glad - ly we pro - claim.

4. We praise you might - y Lord of all, O Je - sus,
come! O Christ, O King! O Fa - ther, come! O
Spir - it, come! Re - ceive the hom - age that we bring.

Text: *Te saeculorum principem*, tr. by Ralph Wright, OSB, b.1938
Tune: GLENCAIRN, LM; Margaret Daly
© 1989, GIA Publications, Inc.

255 A Light from Heaven

1. A light from heav - en shone a - round, And in that light a voice was heard. Then Saul fell, blind - ed, to the ground And cried a - loud: "Who are you, Lord?"
2. It was the bless - ed Son come down To save him from his fear - ful ways And free him from the bonds of sin, A sin - ner saved by Je - sus' grace.
3. Saint Paul was changed by God's free love. The scales fell from his eyes, he saw The love of God, the cos - mos move In time with grace, be - yond the law.
4. Re - new us with your love, O Lord. Your new cre - a - tion let us be; Re - deemed for ev - er and re - stored, With Paul's new vi - sion, let us see.

Text : Gracia Grindal, b.1943, alt., © 1980
Tune : CORNISH, LM; M. Lee Suitor, b.1942, © 1984

O Gently Blinding Glorious Light 256

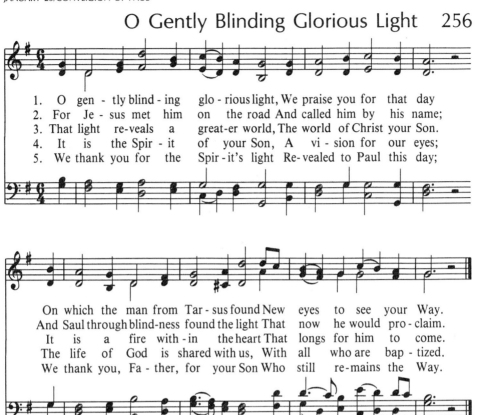

1. O gen-tly blind-ing glo-rious light, We praise you for that day
2. For Je-sus met him on the road And called him by his name;
3. That light re-veals a great-er world, The world of Christ your Son.
4. It is the Spir-it of your Son, A vi-sion for our eyes;
5. We thank you for the Spir-it's light Re-vealed to Paul this day;

On which the man from Tar-sus found New eyes to see your Way.
And Saul through blind-ness found the light That now he would pro-claim.
It is a fire with-in the heart That longs for him to come.
The life of God is shared with us, With all who are bap-tized.
We thank you, Fa-ther, for your Son Who still re-mains the Way.

Text: Ralph Wright, OSB, b.1938, © 1989, GIA Publications, Inc.
Tune: STROUDWATER, CM; Matthew Wilkin's *Psalmody*, c.1725

257 Blest Are the Pure in Heart

1. Blest are the pure in heart, For they shall see our God; The
2. Give ear, O kings, bow down, You rul-ers of the earth. This,
3. With joy-ful hymns of praise On Si-on's Prince now wait: In
4. The Lord, who left the throne Our life and peace to bring, To

se-cret of the Lord is theirs, Their soul is Christ's a - bode.
this is he; your new-born Priest, Your God and King by birth.
high pro-ces-sion pass-ing on He nears the tem-ple gate.
dwell in low-li-ness with us, Our pat-tern and our King:

5. Still to the lowly soul
   He doth himself impart,
   And for his dwelling and his throne
   Selects the pure in heart.

6. Lord, we thy presence seek;
   May ours this blessing be:
   O give the pure and lowly heart,
   A temple meet for thee.

Text: John Keble, 1819, alt., © Abbey of Gethsemani
Tune: FRANCONIA, SM; Johann Balthasar König, 1691-1758; adapt. by William Henry Havergal, 1793-1870

Hail to the Lord Who Comes 258

1. Hail to the Lord who comes, Comes to his tem-ple gate, Not
2. But borne up-on the throne Of Mar-y's gen-tle breast; Thus
3. The world's true light draws near All dark-ness to dis-pel, The
4. Our bod-ies and our souls Are tem-ples now for him, For
5. O light of all the earth! We light our lives with thee; The

with his an-gel hosts, Not in his roy-al state;
to his Fa-ther's house He comes, a hum-ble guest.
flame of faith is lit And dies the pow'r of hell.
we are born of grace God lights our souls with-in.
chains of dark-ness gone, All heirs of God are free.

Text: John Ellerton, 1826-1893, alt.
Tune: PSALM 32, 66 66; Henry Lawes, 1595-1662; harm. from *Praise the Lord,* © 1972, Geoffrey Chapman Publishers

259 In His Temple Now Behold Him

1. In his tem - ple now be - hold him, See the long ex -
pect - ed Lord; An - cient proph - ets had fore - told him;
God has now ful - filled this word. Now, to praise him,
his re - deem - ed Shall break forth with one ac - cord.

2. In the arms of her who bore him, Vir - gin pure, be -
hold him lie, While his a - ged saints a - dore him
Ere in faith and hope they die. Al - le - lu - ia!
Al - le - lu - ia! Lo, the in - car - nate God most high.

3. Je - sus, by your pre - sen - ta - tion, When they blest you,
weak and poor, Make us see our great sal - va - tion,
Seal us with your prom - ise sure, And pre - sent us
in your glo - ry To your Fa - ther, cleansed and pure.

4. Prince and au - thor of sal - va - tion, Be your bound - less
love our theme! Je - sus, praise to you be giv - en,
By the world you did re - deem, With the Fa - ther
and the Spir - it, Lord of maj - es - ty su - preme!

Text: Luke 2: 22; St. 1-3, Henry John Pye, 1825-1903; st. 4, William Cooke, 1821-1894
Tune: SIEH, HIER BIN ICH, 8 7 8 7 8 7; *Geistreiches Gesang-Buch*, Darmstadt, 1698

We Praise You, Father, in Whose Mighty Wisdom 260

1. We praise you, Fa - ther, in whose might - y wis - dom,
2. We praise you for the fish - er - man you sum - moned
3. "De - part from me, O Lord, I am a sin - ner."
4. We pray for heal - ing for the bro - ken Bod - y,
5. O Fa - ther, hear the prayer of that one Shep - herd,

The world and all the gal - ax - ies of light
To be a Rock for all who would be - lieve,
"If all de - ny you, I will not de - ny."
A u - ni - ty for all who are bap - tized.
Who is your Son, our broth - er and our Lord.

Were ut - tered and re - veal to hu - man vi - sion
For Si - mon Pe - ter in whose hum - ble dark - ness
"I nev - er knew the man. I do not know him."
We pray for great - er love a - mong all Chris - tians;
U - nit - ed in your Spir - it may we hon - or

The maj - es - ty of day suc - ceed - ing night.
The na - ture of your Light could be re - vealed.
"I love you and I need you. Hear my cry."
Let no one in the Bod - y be de - spised.
The one who brought your peace in - to the world.

Text: Ralph Wright, OSB, b.1938, © 1989, GIA Publications, Inc.
Tune: PSALM 12 (DONNE SECOURS), 11 10 11 10; *Genevan Psalter*, 1551

261 We Praise You, Father, for That Man

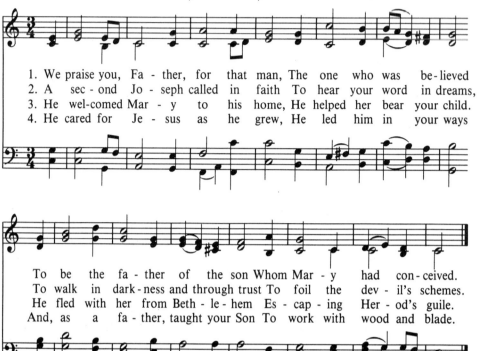

1. We praise you, Fa - ther, for that man, The one who was be - lieved
2. A sec - ond Jo - seph called in faith To hear your word in dreams,
3. He wel-comed Mar - y to his home, He helped her bear your child.
4. He cared for Je - sus as he grew, He led him in your ways

To be the fa - ther of the son Whom Mar - y had con - ceived.
To walk in dark - ness and through trust To foil the dev - il's schemes.
He fled with her from Beth - le - hem Es - cap - ing Her - od's guile.
And, as a fa - ther, taught your Son To work with wood and blade.

5. You called him to that narrow road
   That leads beyond the light,
   To trust, compassion, gentleness,
   And patience through the night.

6. O Father, hear the patient prayers
   Of Joseph, through your Son,
   That in your Spirit we may work
   To see your Kingdom come.

Text: Ralph Wright, OSB, b.1938, © 1989, GIA Publications, Inc.
Tune: WETHERBY, CM: S.S. Westley, 1872

Come, Raise Your Voices, Praise the Lord   262

PART I: MORNING

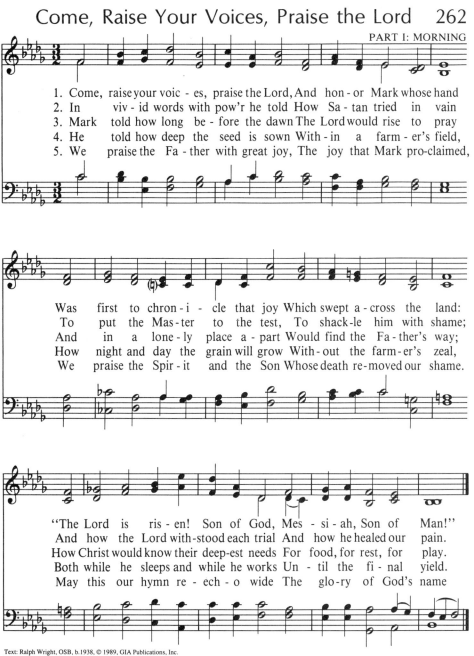

1. Come, raise your voic - es, praise the Lord, And hon - or Mark whose hand
2. In viv - id words with pow'r he told How Sa - tan tried in vain
3. Mark told how long be - fore the dawn The Lord would rise to pray
4. He told how deep the seed is sown With - in a farm - er's field,
5. We praise the Fa - ther with great joy, The joy that Mark pro - claimed,

Was first to chron - i - cle that joy Which swept a - cross the land:
To put the Mas - ter to the test, To shack - le him with shame;
And in a lone - ly place a - part Would find the Fa - ther's way;
How night and day the grain will grow With - out the farm - er's zeal,
We praise the Spir - it and the Son Whose death re - moved our shame.

"The Lord is ris - en! Son of God, Mes - si - ah, Son of Man!"
And how the Lord with-stood each trial And how he healed our pain.
How Christ would know their deep-est needs For food, for rest, for play.
Both while he sleeps and while he works Un - til the fi - nal yield.
May this our hymn re - ech - o wide The glo - ry of God's name

Text: Ralph Wright, OSB, b.1938. © 1989, GIA Publications, Inc.
Tune: NEW HOPE CHURCH, 8 6 8 6 8 6; Henry Bryan Hays, *Swayed Pines*, 1981, © 1981, The Order of St. Benedict, Inc.

PART II: EVENING

1. Come, raise your voic-es, praise the Lord, And hon-or Mark whose hand
2. How Je-sus in the tem-ple healed Up-on a Sab-bath day
3. How on the hill a Ro-man watched The Just One hang in pain;
4. And fi-nal-ly his words re-late How Christ rose from the tomb.
5. We praise the Fa-ther with great joy, The joy that Mark pro-claimed,

Was first to chron-i-cle that joy Which swept a-cross the land:
And an-gri-ly con-front-ed those Who watched him as their prey:
And when he died the sol-dier made A loud and star-tling claim:
He broke the hold of death and came To greet them in their room;
We praise the Spir-it and the Son Whose death re-moved our shame.

"The Lord is ris-en! Son of God, Mes-si-ah, Son of Man!"
For in their hearts and in their eyes Hy-poc-ri-sy held sway.
"In-deed this was the Son of God!" His wit-ness has re-mained.
To chide some with their dis-be-lief, Dis-pel-ling all their gloom.
May this our hymn re-ech-o wide The glo-ry of God's name.

Text: Ralph Wright, OSB, b.1938, © 1989, GIA Publications, Inc.
Tune: NEW HOPE CHURCH, 8 6 8 6 8 6; Henry Bryan Hays, *Swayed Pines*, 1981, © 1981, The Order of St. Benedict, Inc.

The Great Forerunner of the Morn 263

1. The great fore-run-ner of the morn, The her-ald of the Word, is born; And faith-ful hearts shall nev-er fail With thanks and praise his light to hail.
2. With heav'n-ly mes-sage Ga-briel came, That John should be the her-ald's name, And with pro-phet-ic ut-t'rance told His ac-tions great and man-i-fold.
3. John, still un-born, yet gave a-right His wit-ness to the com-ing light; And Christ the sun of all the earth, Ful-filled that wit-ness at his birth.
4. Of wom-an born shall nev-er be A great-er proph-et than was he, Whose might-y deeds ex-alt his fame To great-er than a proph-et's name.
5. All praise to God the Fa-ther be, And to the Son e-ter-nal-ly, Whom with the Spir-it we a-dore For ev-er and for ev-er-more.

Text: *Praecursor altus luminis*, the Venerable Bede, 673-735; John Mason Neale, 1818-1866, *Hymnal Noted*, 1854, slightly alt.
Tune: SEDULIUS, LM; *Nurnbergisches Gesang-Buch*, 1676

264 O Prophet John, O Man of God

1. O proph-et John, O man of God, Your love was pure as
2. The An-gel came and brought the word That soon your moth-er
3. Through un-be-lief his tongue was tied, His voice was si-lent
4. While still with-in your moth - er's womb You leapt to greet the
5. To God the Fa-ther of - fer praise, To Je-sus Christ his

des - ert fire, Ob-tain for us pure hearts that
would con - ceive. Your fa-ther heard your cho-sen
till that day When he de-clared "His name is
hid - den Word. Your moth-er spoke, a-live with
on - ly Son, And in their gra-cious Spir-it

we May sing with voic-es that in - spire.
name But in his heart could not be - lieve.
John!'' And all were filled with deep dis - may.
joy, And Mar - y praised her might - y Lord.
sing Of all that God in love has done.

Text: *Ut queant laxis resonare fibris;* tr. by Ralph Wright, OSB, b.1938, © 1989, GIA Publications, Inc.
Tune: GOD AND KING, LM; Hal H. Hopson, © 1989, Hope Publishing Co.

When Jesus Came to Jordan 265

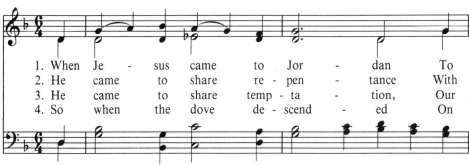

1. When Je - sus came to Jor - dan To
2. He came to share re - pen - tance With
3. He came to share temp - ta - tion, Our
4. So when the dove de - scend - ed On

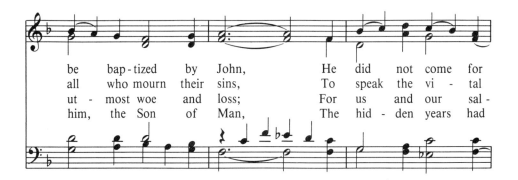

be bap - tized by John, He did not come for
all who mourn their sins, To speak the vi - tal
ut - most woe and loss; For us and our sal -
him, the Son of Man, The hid - den years had

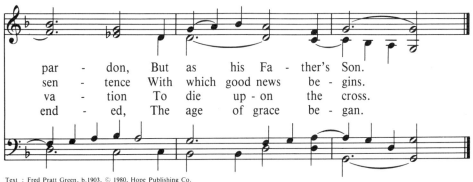

par - don, But as his Fa - ther's Son.
sen - tence With which good news be - gins.
va - tion To die up - on the cross.
end - ed, The age of grace be - gan.

Text : Fred Pratt Green, b.1903, © 1980, Hope Publishing Co.
Tune : DE EERSTEN ZIJN LAATSTEN, 7 6 7 6; Frits Mehrtens, 1922-1975, © Boekencentrum

266 O Light of Lights

1. O Light of lights, what mol-ten blaze Of pur-ple, red and gold
2. Like com-ets in the depth of night These two in bright-ness whirled:
3. This day made re-gal by their blood A-dorns e-ter-nal Rome.

You pour a-cross the wak-ing sky As this great day un-folds!
The keep-er of the gates of heav'n,The teach-er of the world.
Their death wins par-don for our sins And mer-cy from God's throne.

A day which her-alds two great men Who free-ly gave their lives
For Pe-ter through his Mas-ter's cross And Paul be-neath the sword
Give glo-ry, hon-or, thanks and praise To God both one and three

That all might see the love of God With-in them as they died.
Have won their way to vic-to-ry And tri-umphed with their Lord.
Who rules with ev-er-last-ing might All whom the cross sets free.

Text: *Aurea luce et decore roseo;* tr. by Ralph Wright, OSB, b.1938, © 1989, GIA Publications, Inc.
Tune: SALVATION, CMD; attr. to R. Bovdin, *Kentucky Harmony,* 1816

Hail, Redeemer, King Divine   267

1. Hail, Re-deem-er, King di - vine! Priest and Lamb, the throne is thine;
2. Christ, thou King of truth and might, Be to us e - ter - nal light,

King whose reign shall nev - er cease, Prince of ev - er - last - ing peace.
Till in peace each na - tion rings With thy prais - es, King of kings.

An - gels, saints, and na - tions sing: "Praised be Je - sus Christ, our King;
An - gels, saints, and na tions sing: "Praised be Je - sus Christ, our King;

Lord of earth and sky and sea, King of love on Cal - va - ry."
Lord of earth and sky and sea, King of love on Cal - va - ry."

Text : Patrick Brennan, CSSR, 1877-1951, *The Westminster Hymnal*, alt., © Search Press, Ltd.
Tune : ST. GEORGE'S WINDSOR, 7 7 7 7 D; George J. Elvey, 1816-1893

268 Lift High the Cross

Lift high the cross, the love of Christ pro-claim till all the world a-dore his sa-cred name.

1. Come, Chris-tains, fol-low where the Mas-ter trod, Our
2. Led on their way by this tri-um-phant sign, The
3. Each new-born fol-l'wer of the Cru-ci-fied Bears
4. O Lord, once lift-ed on the glo-rious tree, Your
5. So shall our song of tri-umph ev-er be: Praise

King vic-to-rious, Christ, the Son of God.
hosts of God in con-qu'ring ranks com-bine.
on the brow the seal of him who died.
death has bought us life e-ter-nal-ly.
to the Cru-ci-fied for vic-to-ry!

D.C.

Text: 1 Corinthians 1:18; George W. Kitchen, 1827-1912, and Michael R. Newbolt, 1874-1956, alt.
Tune: CRUCIFER, 10 10 with refrain; Sydney H. Nicholson, 1875-1947
© 1974, Hope Publishing, Co.

O Christ, Our Hope 269

1. O Christ, our hope, our hearts' de-sire, Re-demp-tion's on-ly
2. How vast the mer-cy and the love Which led you to the
3. Christ Je-sus, be our pres-ent joy. Our fu-ture great re-
4. All praise to you, as-cend-ed Lord; All glo-ry ev-er

spring; Cre-a-tor of the world are you, Its
tree, And on this cross you died for us To
ward; Our on-ly glo-ry may it be To
be To Fa-ther, Son and Spir-it blest Through

Sav-ior and its King, Its Sav-ior and its King.
set your peo-ple free, To set your peo-ple free.
glo-ry in the Lord, To glo-ry in the Lord!
all e-ter-ni-ty, Through all e-ter-ni-ty.

Text : *Jesu, nostra redemptio*, Latin hymn, c.8th C., tr. by John Chandler, 1806-1876, *Hymns of the Primitive Church*, 1837, alt.
Tune : LOBT GOTT, IHR CHRISTEN, 8 6 8 66; Nikolaus Hermann, c.1485-1561, alt.

270 A Tax Collector, Scorned by All

PART I: MORNING

1. A tax col - lec - tor, scorned by all, A serf of sov-'reign Rome,
2. You found in him a dif - f'rent gold, The treas-ure of the field,
3. We praise you, Fa - ther, Lord of all, We praise you, Christ the Son,

Christ called you, Mat-thew, from your gold To fol - low him a - lone.
The Pearl be - yond all hum - an price, A whole new world re - vealed.
We praise you, Spir - it, for in you We may yet live as one;

For Je - sus passed you by one day, He looked and called your name,
Then in your joy you called your friends To meet the one who saves,
We beg you for that gift of sight To see in each your face,

And in his gaze you knew his love And, leav - ing all, you came.
That in the vine - yard they might work For his e - ter - nal wage.
That e - ven now our world may know The full - ness of your peace.

Text: Ralph Wright, OSB, b.1938, © 1989, GIA Publications, Inc.
Tune: SHEPHERD'S PIPES, CMD; Annabeth McClelland Gay, ©1958, The Pilgrim Press

1. Be with us, Mat-thew, help us now To trump-et forth God's name,
2. For free-ly is his grace be-stowed Like seed up-on the ground,
3. We praise you, Fa-ther, Lord of all, We praise you, Christ the Son,

That all we do may spread a-broad This word that you pro-claimed:
And he is with us e-ven now, While still the weeds a-bound,
We praise you, Spir-it, for in you We may yet live as one;

That Je-sus lives be-side us now, The Word, the Bread, the Vine,
To help us in our dai-ly task Un-til our work is done,
We beg you for that gift of sight To see in each your face,

To be our hope and pow'r and joy Un-til the end of time.
To be his liv-ing word of hope, To let his King-dom come.
That e-ven now our world may know The full-ness of your peace.

Text: Ralph Wright, OSB, b.1938, © 1989, GIA Publications, Inc.
Tune: SHEPHERD'S PIPES, CMD; Annabeth McClelland Gay, ©1958, The Pilgrim Press

271 Jesus, Splendor of the Father

1. Je - sus, splen-dor of the Fa-ther, Heart of light, im - mor - tal blaze,
2. Through these pow'r-ful, friend-ly guard-ians, Christ our King, O drive a - way
3. Let us praise the might-y Fa-ther With the Spir - it and the Son;

Hear the hum-ble prayers we of - fer Where the an - gels sing your praise.
Ev-'ry swift de - ceit of Sa - tan That our frail - ty might o - bey;
May our song win hearts to praise them Who are three but al - so one.

Hear the soar-ing hymn of glo - ry That in mel - o - dy we raise.
Then with hearts made pure to love you In your King-dom we will stay.
May the mu - sic of our voic - es Share their glo - ry all day long.

Text: *Jesu, splendor Patris;* tr. by Ralph Wright, OSB, b.1938, © 1989, GIA Publications, Inc.
Tune: DULCE CARMEN, 8 7 8 7 8 7; *Essay on the Church Plain Chant,* 1782

Come, Raise a Song of Joy This Day 272

PART I: MORNING

1. Come, raise a song of joy this day, Let all the earth ap - plaud
2. In sim - ple words Luke told the world How Je - sus was con - ceived,
3. He showed how in the heart of God Com-pas - sion wins the day;
4. We praise you, Fa - ther, Lord of all, We praise you, Christ the Son,

The one whose gos - pel has re - vealed The gen - tle - ness of God,
How Zach - a - ry had doubt-ed God And Mar - y had be - lieved.
The shep-herd car - ries to the fold The sheep that went a - stray.
We praise you, Spir - it, for in you We may yet live as one;

The gen - tle Luke whose care - ful zeal Probed deep in - to the past
He told how an - gels woke the night And made the si - lence sing,
He shows the joy that floods the sky Each time God's grace has won,
We beg you for that gift of sight To see in each your face,

And won from Mar - y's qui - et mind The mys - t'ries of her heart.
How shep-herds came to Da - vid's town To hon - or Da - vid's King.
And in the Fa - ther's o - pen arms We see the con-trite son.
That e - ven now our world may know The full - ness of your peace.

Text: Ralph Wright, OSB, b.1938, © 1989, GIA Publications, Inc.
Tune: FOREST GREEN, CMD; English Folk Melody; arr. by Ralph Vaughan Williams, 1872-1958, © Oxford University Press

PART II: EVENING

1. Come raise a song of joy this day, Let all the earth ap - plaud
2. Luke told of one who on the road Walked with them to re - veal
3. O good phy-si - cian, pray for us That we may hear his word,
4. We praise you, Fa - ther, Lord of all, We praise you, Christ the Son,

The one whose gos-pel has re - vealed The gen - tle - ness of God,
The na-ture of re - deem - ing love That burns that it may heal;
The word that burns that it may heal, But heals when it is heard;
We praise you, Spir - it, for in you We may yet live as one;

The gen - tle Luke whose care - ful zeal Probed deep in - to the past
Who stayed with them when dark-ness came To be with them and dine;
The Word the Fa - ther sent that we In him might live as one;
We beg you for that gift of sight To see in each your face,

And won from Mar-y's qui - et mind The mys - t'ries of her heart.
Who left them hav - ing bro-ken bread And hav - ing blessed their wine.
The Word the Spir - it speaks in all Who would re - ceive the Son.
That e - ven now our world may know The full - ness of your peace.

Text: Ralph Wright, OSB, b.1938, © 1989, GIA Publications, Inc.
Tune: FOREST GREEN, CMD; English Folk Melody; arr. by Ralph Vaughan Williams, 1872-1958, © Oxford University Press

SECOND TUNE – 272
PART I: MORNING

1. Come, raise a song of joy this day, Let all the earth ap - plaud
2. In sim - ple words Luke told the world How Je - sus was con - ceived,
3. He showed how in the heart of God Com - pas - sion wins the day;
4. We praise you, Fa - ther, Lord of all, We praise you, Christ the Son.

The one whose gos - pel has re-vealed The gen - tle - ness of God,
How Zach - a - ry had doubt-ed God And Mar - y had be - lieved.
The shep - herd car - ries to the fold The sheep that went a - stray.
We praise you, Spir - it, for in you We may yet live as one;

The gen - tle Luke whose care - ful zeal Probed deep in - to the past
He told how an - gels woke the night And made the si - lence sing,
He shows the joy that floods the sky Each time God's grace has won,
We beg you for that gift of sight To see in each your face,

And won from Mar - y's qui - et mind The mys - t'ries of her heart.
How shep-herds came to Da - vid's town to hon - or Da - vid's King.
And in the Fa - ther's o - pen arms We see the con-trite son.
That e - ven now our world may know The full-ness of your peace.

Text: Ralph Wright, OSB, b.1938, © 1989, GIA Publications, Inc.
Tune: MOZART, CMD; Wolfgang A. Mozart, 1756-1791

PART II: EVENING

1. Come raise a song of joy this day, Let all the earth ap - plaud
2. Luke told of one who on the road Walked with them to re - veal
3. O good phy - si - cian, pray for us That we may hear his word
4. We praise you, Fa - ther, Lord of all, We praise you, Christ the Son,

The one whose gos - pel has re - vealed The gen - tle - ness of God.
The na - ture of re - deem - ing love That burns that it may heal;
The word that burns that it may heal, But heals when it is heard;
We praise you, Spir - it, for in you We may yet live as one;

The gen - tle Luke whose care - ful zeal Probed deep in - to the past
Who stayed with them when dark - ness came To be with them and dine;
The Word the Fa - ther sent that we In him might live as one;
We beg you for that gift of sight To see in each your face,

And won from Mar - y's qui - et mind The mys - t'ries of her heart.
Who left them hav - ing bro - ken bread And hav - ing blessed their wine.
The Word the Spir - it speaks in all Who would re - ceive the Son.
That e - ven now our world may know The full - ness of your peace.

Text: Ralph Wright, OSB, b.1938, © 1989, GIA Publications, Inc.
Tune: MOZART, CMD; Wolfgang A. Mozart, 1756-1791

Now from the Heavens Descending 273

1. Now from the heav'ns de-scend-ing, Is seen a glo-rious light,
2. This is the hour of glad-ness for Bride-groom and for Bride.
3. He who is throned in heav-en Takes up his dwell-ing-place
4. See how a new cre-a-tion Is brought at last to birth,

The Bride of Christ in splen-dor, Ar-rayed in pur-est white.
The Lamb's great feast is read-y, His Bride is at his side.
A-mong his cho-sen peo-ple, Who see him face to face.
A new and glo-rious heav-en, A new and glo-rious earth.

She is the ho-ly Cit-y, Whose ra-diance is the grace
How blessed are those in-vit-ed To share his wed-ding feast:
No sound is heard of weep-ing For pain and sor-row cease,
Death's pow'r for ev-er bro-ken, Its em-pire swept a-way,

Of all the saints in glo-ry, From ev-'ry time and place.
The least be-come the great-est, The great-est are the least.
And sin shall reign no long-er, But love and joy and peace.
The prom-ised dawn of glo-ry Be-gins its end-less day.

Text : James Quinn, SJ, b.1919, *New Hymns for All Seasons,* © 1969
Tune : AURELIA, 76 76 D; Samuel S. Wesley, 1810-1876

274 O Savior, Jesus, Lord of All

1. O Sav - ior, Je - sus, Lord of all, Come save us from our sin - ful ways And through your Vir - gin Moth - er's prayers May we her chil - dren sing your praise.

2. We call on you, O sov-'reign Pow'rs, The ar - mies of the Lord of Light, From pres - ent, past and fu - ture sin Pro - tect us in the wars of night.

3. We beg you, Proph-ets of our God, And you, A - pos-tles of the Word, O pray that we may hear that voice And in the Spir - it be re - stored.

4. O pray, you Mar - tyrs of the Lord, Who through your blood pro-claimed God's Son, O pray, all you who spread his reign And quiet - ly lived to see it come.

5. O men and wom - en, vir - gins strong, Who gave what you could not af - ford, Now help us to sur - ren - der all To meet our Bride-groom, Christ the Lord.

6. May all the pow'rs of night be crushed
That people may at last be free
To leap with joy and praise their God
Whose Son was nailed upon the tree.

7. To God the Father who creates
And to his one begotten Son
May songs of glory now be raised
For in their Spirit all are one.

Text: *Christe redemptor omnium;* tr. by Ralph Wright, OSB, b.1938
Tune: SAVIOR JESUS, LM; Margaret Daly
© 1989, GIA Publications, Inc.

275 Ye Watchers and Ye Holy Ones

1. Ye watch-ers and ye, ho - ly ones, Bright ser-aphs, cher-u-
2. O high - er than the cher - u - bim, More glo-rious than the
3. Re - spond, ye souls in end - less rest, Ye pa - tri-archs and
4. O friends, in glad-ness let us sing, Su - per-nal an-thems

bim and thrones, Raise the glad strain: "Al - le - lu - ia!"
ser - a - phim, Lead their prais - es; "Al - le - lu - ia!"
proph - ets blest: "Al - le - lu - ia, Al - le - lu - ia!"
ech - o - ing: "Al - le - lu - ia, Al - le - lu - ia!"

Cry out, do-min-ions, prince-doms, pow'rs, Vir - tues, arch-an-
Thou bear-er of the e-ter - nal Word, Most gra-cious, mag-
Ye ho - ly twelve, ye mar - tyrs strong, All saints tri - um-
To God the Fa-ther, God the Son, And God the Spir-

gels', an - gels' choirs: "Al - le - lu - ia! Al - le - lu - ia!"
ni - fy the Lord:
phant, raise the song:
it, Three in One:

Al - le - lu - ia, al - le - lu - ia, al - le - lu - ia!

Text : J. Athelstan Riley, 1858-1945
Tune : LASST UNS ERFREUEN, 88 44 88 with alleluias; *Geistliche Kirchengesänge*, Köln, 1623, © Oxford University Press

276 Wake the Song of Jubilee

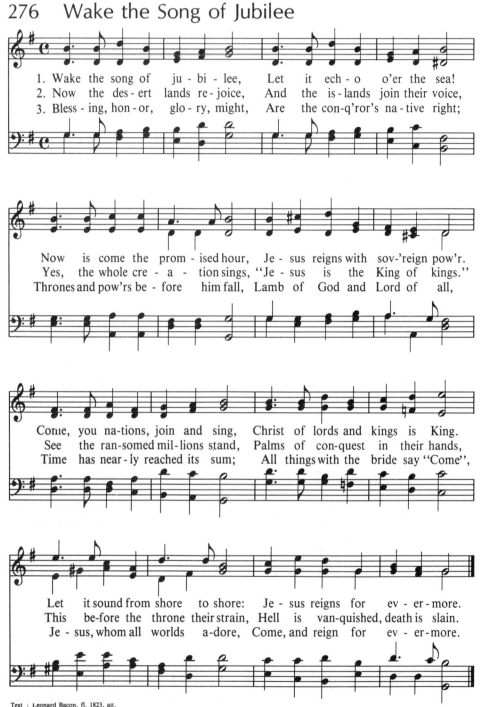

1. Wake the song of ju-bi-lee, Let it ech-o o'er the sea!
2. Now the des-ert lands re-joice, And the is-lands join their voice,
3. Bless-ing, hon-or, glo-ry, might, Are the con-q'ror's na-tive right;

Now is come the prom-ised hour, Je-sus reigns with sov-'reign pow'r.
Yes, the whole cre-a-tion sings, "Je-sus is the King of kings."
Thrones and pow'rs be-fore him fall, Lamb of God and Lord of all,

Come, you na-tions, join and sing, Christ of lords and kings is King.
See the ran-somed mil-lions stand, Palms of con-quest in their hands,
Time has near-ly reached its sum; All things with the bride say "Come",

Let it sound from shore to shore: Je-sus reigns for ev-er-more.
This be-fore the throne their strain, Hell is van-quished, death is slain.
Je-sus, whom all worlds a-dore, Come, and reign for ev-er-more.

Text : Leonard Bacon, fl. 1823, alt.
Tune : ST. GEORGE'S WINDSOR, 77 77 D; George J. Elvey, 1816-1893

Lower key: No. 267

We Sing of That Disciple   277

PART I: MORNING

1. We sing of that dis - ci - ple, Be - lov - ed of the Lord,
2. His words dis - pel the dark - ness And God's own light re - veal:
3. John tells of birth in dark - ness, Of yearn - ing for the Light:
4. O sing of that great ea - gle, The trum - pet - er of Light,
5. We praise you, God our Fa - ther, We praise you, Christ the Lord,

Who, tell - ing all he wit-nessed, Pro-claimed the Fa-ther's Word;
The mys - te - ry of Je - sus, The Word so long con-cealed.
A man born blind a - noint-ed With mud re - ceives his sight.
Who soars be - yond the dark-ness With mas - ter - y of flight.
We praise you, Ho - ly Spir - it, Through whom we know the Word;

John is that tow'r - ing ea - gle Who soars a - loft in flight
He tells of thirst for wat - er: A wom - an by a well;
The proud he shows de - spis - ing The one who gives this sign,
O sing of that dis - ci - ple, Be - lov - ed of the Lord,
We pray with that dis - ci - ple, The one whom Je - sus loved,

And with great ease dis - clos - es The mys - ter - y of Light.
A Bread sent down to feed us That words will nev - er tell.
And those with eyes to see by He shows re - main - ing blind.
Whose heart had learned in Je - sus The el - o - quence of God.
That we may share the vic - t'ry, The vic - t'ry of his blood.

Text: Ralph Wright, OSB, b.1938, © 1989, GIA Publications, Inc.
Tune: MUNICH, 7 6 7 6 D; *Neuvermehrtes Meinigisches Gesangbuch,* 1693; adapt. by Felix Mendelssohn, 1809-1847

PART II: EVENING

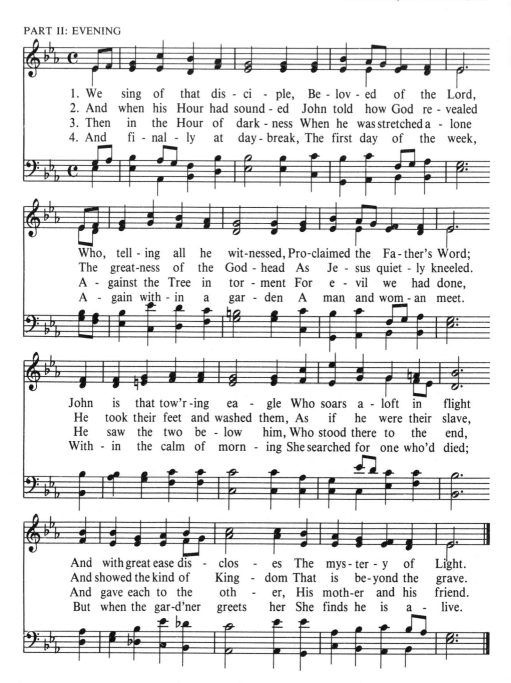

1. We sing of that dis - ci - ple, Be - lov - ed of the Lord,
2. And when his Hour had sound - ed John told how God re - vealed
3. Then in the Hour of dark - ness When he was stretched a - lone
4. And fi - nal - ly at day - break, The first day of the week,

Who, tell - ing all he wit-nessed, Pro-claimed the Fa - ther's Word;
The great-ness of the God - head As Je - sus quiet - ly kneeled.
A - gainst the Tree in tor - ment For e - vil we had done,
A - gain with - in a gar - den A man and wom - an meet.

John is that tow'r - ing ea - gle Who soars a - loft in flight
He took their feet and washed them, As if he were their slave,
He saw the two be - low him, Who stood there to the end,
With - in the calm of morn - ing She searched for one who'd died;

And with great ease dis - clos - es The mys - ter - y of Light.
And showed the kind of King - dom That is be - yond the grave.
And gave each to the oth - er, His moth - er and his friend.
But when the gar - d'ner greets her She finds he is a - live.

5. O sing of that great eagle
The trumpeter of Light,
Who soars beyond the darkness
With mastery of flight.
O sing of that disciple,
Beloved of the Lord,
whose heart had learned in Jesus
The eloquence of God.

6. We praise you, God our Father,
We praise you, Christ the Lord,
We praise you, Holy Spirit,
Through whom we know the Word;
We pray with that disciple,
The one whom Jesus loved,
That we may share the vict'ry,
The vict'ry of Christ's blood.

Text: Ralph Wright, OSB, b.1938, © 1989, GIA Publications, Inc.
Tune: MUNICH, 7 6 7 6 D; *Neuvermehrtes Meinigisches Gesangbuch*, 1693; adapt. by Felix Mendelssohn, 1809-1847

278 In Bethlehem a Newborn Boy

1. In Beth - le - hem a new-born boy Was hailed with songs of
2. sol - diers sought the child in vain: Not yet was he to
3. rage the fires of hate to - day, And in - no-cents the
4. Je - sus, through our night of loss Shines out the won - der
5. that great love our lives con - trol And con - quer hate in

praise and joy. Then warn - ing came of dan - ger near; King
share our pain. But down the ag - es rings the cry Of
price must pay, While ach - ing hearts in ev - 'ry land Cry
of your cross, The love that can - not cease to bear Our
ev - 'ry soul, Till, pledged to build and not de - stroy, We

[1-4]

He - rod's troops would soon ap - pear.
those who saw their chil - dren die.
out: "We can - not un - der - stand."
hu - man an - guish ev - 'ry - where.
share your pain and find your joy.

Final Ending

2. The
3. Still
4. Lord
5. May

Text : Rosamond E. Herklots, b.1905, © Oxford University Press
Tune : IN BETHLEHEM, LM; Wilbur Held, b.1914, © 1983

Christ Became Our Sure Foundation 279

1. Christ be - came our sure foun - da - tion, He is
2. To this tem - ple where we gath - er, Come, O
3. Praise and hon - or to the Fa - ther, Praise and

head and cor - ner - stone, Join - ing both his cho - sen peo - ples,
Lord of hosts, to - day Show to us your lov - ing kind - ness,
hon - or to the Son, Praise and hon - or to the Spir - it,

Bind - ing now his Church in one. May he be our
Hear your peo - ple as they pray; Grant to us your
Ev - er Three and ev - er One: Let our voic - es

help for ev - er, And our con - fi - dence a - lone.
grace for ev - er, May it be for us the way.
sing their glo - ry, While un - end - ing ag - es run.

Text: *Angularis fundamentum*; tr. by John Mason Neale, 1818-1866; rev. by David F. Wright, OP, fl. 1975, © 1989, GIA Publications, Inc.
Tune: LAUDA ANIMA, 87 87 87; J. Goss, 1800-1880

280 Christ the Rock

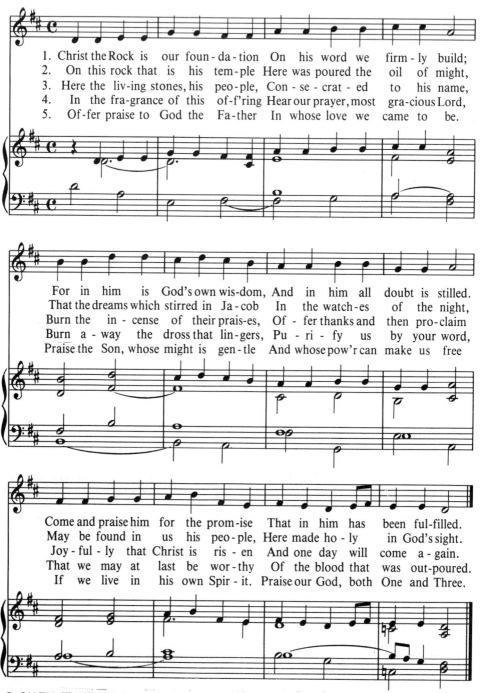

1. Christ the Rock is our foun-da-tion On his word we firm-ly build;
2. On this rock that is his tem-ple Here was poured the oil of might,
3. Here the liv-ing stones, his peo-ple, Con-se-crat-ed to his name,
4. In the fra-grance of this of-f'ring Hear our prayer, most gra-cious Lord,
5. Of-fer praise to God the Fa-ther In whose love we came to be.

For in him is God's own wis-dom, And in him all doubt is stilled.
That the dreams which stirred in Ja-cob In the watch-es of the night,
Burn the in-cense of their prais-es, Of-fer thanks and then pro-claim
Burn a-way the dross that lin-gers, Pu-ri-fy us by your word,
Praise the Son, whose might is gen-tle And whose pow'r can make us free

Come and praise him for the prom-ise That in him has been ful-filled.
May be found in us his peo-ple, Here made ho-ly in God's sight.
Joy-ful-ly that Christ is ris-en And one day will come a-gain.
That we may at last be wor-thy Of the blood that was out-poured.
If we live in his own Spir-it. Praise our God, both One and Three.

Text: Ralph Wright, OSB, b.1938, © 1989, GIA Publications, Inc.
Tune: SUN JOURNEY, 87 87 87; Henry Bryan Hays, *Swayed Pines*, 1981, © 1981, The Order of St. Benedict, Inc.

O Jerusalem, the Blessed 281

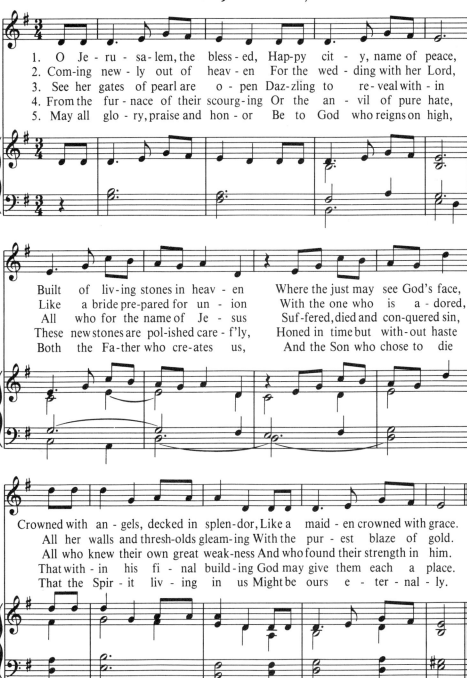

1. O Je - ru - sa - lem, the bless - ed, Hap-py cit - y, name of peace,
2. Com-ing new - ly out of heav - en For the wed - ding with her Lord,
3. See her gates of pearl are o - pen Daz-zling to re - veal with - in
4. From the fur - nace of their scourg-ing Or the an - vil of pure hate,
5. May all glo - ry, praise and hon - or Be to God who reigns on high,

Built of liv-ing stones in heav - en Where the just may see God's face,
Like a bride pre-pared for un - ion With the one who is a - dored,
All who for the name of Je - sus Suf-fered, died and con-quered sin,
These new stones are pol-ished care - f'ly, Honed in time but with-out haste,
Both the Fa-ther who cre-ates us, And the Son who chose to die

Crowned with an - gels, decked in splen-dor, Like a maid - en crowned with grace.
All her walls and thresh-olds gleam-ing With the pur - est blaze of gold.
All who knew their own great weak-ness And who found their strength in him.
That with - in his fi - nal build-ing God may give them each a place.
That the Spir - it liv - ing in us Might be ours e - ter - nal - ly.

Text: *Urbs Jerusalem beata*, Ralph Wright, OSB, b.1938
Tune: LIVING STONES, 87 87 87; Margaret Daly
© 1989, GIA Publications, Inc.

282 The Church's One Foundation

1. The Chur-ch's one foun - da - tion Is Je - sus Christ her Lord: She
2. E - lect from ev - 'ry na - tion Yet one o'er all the earth, Her
3. Through toil and trib - u - la - tion And tu - mult of her war She
4. Yet she on earth has un - ion With God, the Three in One, And

is his new cre - a - tion By wa - ter and the word; From
char - ter of sal - va - tion One Lord, one faith, one birth, One
waits the con - sum - ma - tion Of peace for ev - er - more, Till
mys - tic sweet com - mun - ion With those whose rest is won. O

heav'n he came and sought her To be his ho - ly bride; With
ho - ly name she bless - es, Par - takes one ho - ly food, And
with the vi - sion glo - rious Her long - ing eyes are blest, And
hap - py ones and ho - ly! Lord, give us grace that we Like

his own blood he bought her, And for her life he died.
to one hope she press - es, With ev - 'ry grace en - dued.
the great Church vic - to - rious Shall be the Church at rest.
them, the meek and low - ly, On high may dwell with thee.

Text : Samuel John Stone, 1837-1900, *Lyra Fidelium*, 1866, slightly alt.
Tune : AURELIA, 7 6 7 6 D; Samuel Sebastian Wesley, 1810-1876, Kemble's *Selection of Psalms and Hymns*, 1864

The New Jerusalem, Abode of Joy 283

1. The new Je - ru - sa - lem, a - bode of joy,
2. Her streets and walls are made of pur - est gold;
3. The cor - ner - stone of this bright realm is Christ;
4. Through - out the cit - y songs of joy are heard;
5. O God, be pres - ent in this earth - ly church,

Where peace and love hold un - dis - put - ed sway,
Her gates of pearl bring joy to ev - 'ry eye.
Its cit - i - zens the saints, a priest - ly race,
Its tow - ers ech - o with this lit - ur - gy,
This im - age of our last - ing home a - bove.

De - scend from heav - en like a bride a - dorned
Here en - ter all the faith - ful, called by God,
Ex - ult - ing to pro - claim the Fa - ther's praise,
Re - sound - ing to the far - thest ends of space
Bring all who en - ter here to par - a - dise

And ea - ger for the long a - wait - ed day.
Who, while on earth, had placed their hopes on high.
In ad - o - ra - tion fall be - fore his face.
In praise of God, the ho - ly Trin - i - ty.
That they may wor - ship you in end - less love.

Text: *Urbs Jerusalem beata*, 6th-7th C. ; tr. by Frank C. Quinn, OP, b.1932, © 1989, GIA Publications, Inc.
Tune: TOULON, 10 10 10 10; *Genevan Psalter*, 1551

284 By All Your Saints Still Striving

1. By all your saints still striv - ing, For all your saints at rest,
*2. A - pos - tles, proph-ets, mar - tyrs, And all the no - ble throng
3. Then let us praise the Fa - ther And wor-ship God the Son

Your ho - ly Name, O Je - sus, For ev - er-more be blessed.
Who wear the spot - less rai - ment And raise the cease-less song:
And sing to God the Spir - it, E - ter - nal Three in One,

You rose, our King vic - to - rious, That they might wear the crown
For them and those whose wit - ness Is on - ly known to you
Till all the ran - somed num - ber Who stand be - fore the throne,

And ev - er shine in splen - dor Re - flect - ed from your throne.
By walk - ing in their foot - steps We give you praise a - new.
A - scribe all pow'r and glo - ry And praise to God a - lone.

* This stanza may be replaced by an appropriate stanza taken from the following pages.

January 25: Conversion of Paul

Praise for the light from heaven
    And for the voice of awe:
Praise for the glorious vision
    The persecutor saw.
O Lord, for Paul's conversion,
    We bless your Name today.
Come shine within our darkness
    And guide us in the Way.

February 22: Chair of Peter

We praise you, Lord, for Peter,
    So eager and so bold:
Thrice falling, yet repentant,
    Thrice charged to feed your fold.
Lord, make your pastors faithful
    To guard your flock from harm
And hold them when they waver
    With your almighty arm.

March 19: Joseph, Husband of Mary

All praise, O God, for Joseph,
    The guardian of your Son,
Who saved him from King Herod,
    When safety there was none.
He taught the trade of builder,
    When they to Naz'reth came,
And Joseph's love made "Father"
    To be, for Christ, God's name.

March 25: Annunciation of Our Lord

We sing with joy of Mary
    Whose heart with awe was stirred
When, youthful and unready,
    She heard the angel's word;
Yet she her voice upraises
    God's glory to proclaim,
As once for our salvation
    Your mother she became.

April 25: Mark

For Mark, O Lord, we praise you,
    The weak by grace made strong:
His witness in his Gospel
    Becomes victorious song.
May we, in all our weakness,
    Receive your power divine,
And all, as faithful branches,
    Grow strong in you, the Vine.

May 3: Philip and James

We praise you, Lord, for Philip,
    Blest guide to Greek and Jew,
And for young James the faithful,
    Who heard and followed you,
O grant us grace to know you,
    The victor in the strife,
That we with all your servants
    May wear the crown of life.

May 14: Matthias

For one in place of Judas,
    The apostles sought God's choice:
The lot fell to Matthias
    For whom we now rejoice.
May we like true apostles
    Your holy Church defend,
And not betray our calling
    But serve you to the end.

June 11: Barnabas

For Barnabas we praise you,
    Who kept your law of love
And, leaving earthly treasures,
    Sought riches from above.
O Christ, our Lord and Savior,
    Let gifts of grace descend,
That your true consolation
    May through the world extend.

June 24: Birth of John the Baptist

All praise for John the Baptist,
    Forerunner of the Word,
Our true Elijah, making
    A highway for the Lord.
The last and greatest prophet,
    He saw the dawning ray
Of light that grows in splendor
    Until the perfect day.

June 29: Peter and Paul

We praise you for Saint Peter;
    We praise you for Saint Paul.
They taught both Jew and Gentile
    That Christ is all in all.
To cross and sword they yielded
    And saw the kingdom come:
O God, your two apostles
    Won life through martyrdom.

July 3: Thomas

All praise, O Lord, for Thomas
  Whose short-lived doubtings prove
Your perfect twofold nature,
  The depth of your true love.
To all who live with questions
  A steadfast faith afford;
And grant us grace to know you,
  Made flesh, yet God and Lord.

July 22: Mary Magdalene

All praise for Mary Magdalene,
  Whose wholeness was restored
By you, her faithful Master,
  Her Savior and her Lord.
On Easter morning early,
  A word from you sufficed:
Her faith was first to see you,
  Her Lord, the risen Christ.

July 25: James

O Lord, for James, we praise you,
  Who fell to Herod's sword.
He drank the cup of suff'ring
  And thus fulfilled your word.
Lord, curb our vain impatience
  For glory and for fame,
Equip us for such suff'rings
  As glorify your Name.

August 24: Bartholomew

Praised for your blest apostle
  Surnamed Bartholomew;
We know not his achievements
  But know that he was true,
For he at the Ascension
  Was an apostle still.
May we discern your presence
  And seek, like him, your will.

September 21: Matthew

We praise you, Lord, for Matthew,
  Whose gospel words declare
That, worldly gain forsaking,
  Your path of life we share.
From all unrighteous mammon,
  O raise our eyes anew,
That we, whate'er our station
  May rise and follow you.

October 18: Luke

For Luke, beloved physician,
  All praise; whose Gospel shows
The healer of the nations,
  The one who shares our woes.
Your wine and oil, O Savior,
  Upon our spirits pour,
And with true balm of Gilead
  Anoint us evermore.

October 28: Simon and Jude

Praise, Lord, for your apostles,
  Saint Simon and Saint Jude.
One love, one hope impelled them
  To tread the way, renewed.
May we with zeal as earnest
  The faith of Christ maintain,
Be bound in love together,
  And life eternal gain.

November 30: Andrew

All praise, O Lord, for Andrew,
  The first to follow you;
He witnessed to his brother,
  "This is Messiah true."
You called him from his fishing
  Upon Lake Galilee;
He rose to meet your challenge,
  "Leave all and follow me."

December 26: Stephen

All praise, O Lord, for Stephen
  Who, martyred, saw you stand
To help in time of torment,
  To plead at God's right hand.
Like you, our suff'ring Savior,
  His enemies he blessed,
With "Lord, receive my spirit,"
  His faith, in death, confessed.

December 27: John

For John, your loved disciple,
  Exiled to Patmos' shore,
And for his faithful record,
  We praise you evermore;
Praise for the mystic vision
  His words to us unfold.
Instill in us his longing,
  Your glory to behold.

December 28: Holy Innocents

Praise for your infant martyrs,
  Whom your mysterious love
Called early from life's conflicts
  To share your peace above.
O Rachel, cease your weeping;
  They're free from pain and cares.
Lord, grant us crowns as brilliant
  And lives as pure as theirs.

Text: Horatio Bolton Nelson, 1823-1913; alt. by Jerry D. Godwin, b.1944, © 1982, Church Pension Fund
Tune: KING'S LYNN, 7 6 7 6 D; English Melody; adapt. by Ralph Vaughan Williams, 1872-1958, © Oxford University Press

284 – SECOND TUNE

1. By all your saints still striv - ing, For all your saints at rest,
*2. A - pos-tles, proph-ets, Mar - tyrs, And all the no - ble throng
3. Then let us praise the Fa - ther And wor-ship God the Son

Your ho - ly Name, O Je - sus, For ev - er - more be blessed.
Who wear the spot-less rai - ment And raise the cease-less song:
And sing to God the Spir - it, E - ter - nal Three in One,

You rose, our King vic - to - rious, That they might wear the crown
For them and those whose wit - ness Is on - ly known to you
Till all the ran-somed num - ber Who stand be - fore the throne,

This stanza may be replaced by an appropriate stanza taken from the preceeding pages.

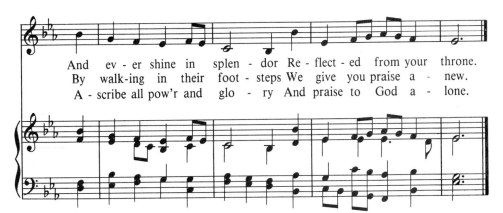

And ev-er shine in splen - dor Re - flect - ed from your throne.
By walk-ing in their foot - steps We give you praise a - new.
A - scribe all pow'r and glo - ry And praise to God a - lone.

Text: Horatio Bolton Nelson, 1823-1913; alt. by Jerry D. Godwin, b.1944, © 1982, Church Pension Fund
Tune: NYLAND, 76 76 D; Finnish Folk Melody; adapt. and harm. by David Evans, 1874-1948, © Oxford University Press

285 All Hail the Power of Jesus' Name

1. All hail the pow'r of Je - sus' name, Be - fore him let us fall;
2. Crown him, you mar - tyrs of our God, Who from his al - tar call;
3. You proph - ets who our free - dom won, Dis - ci - ples great and small;
4. Let ev - 'ry na - tion, ev - 'ry tongue To him their hearts en - thrall;

Bring out the roy - al di - a - dem To crown him Lord of all.
Give praise to him whose path you trod And crown him Lord of all.
By whom the work of truth is done, Now crown him Lord of all.
Raise high the u - ni - ver - sal song, And crown him Lord of all.

Bring out the roy - al di - a - dem To crown him Lord of all.
Give praise to him whose path you trod And crown him Lord of all.
By whom the work of truth is done, Now crown him Lord of all.
Raise high the u - ni - ver - sal song, And crown him Lord of all.

Text : Edward Perronet, 1726-92, adapt. Anthony G. Petti, 1971, alt. © Faber Music, Ltd.
Tune : CORONATION, CM, extended; Oliver Holden, 1793

Christ Is the King! O Friends, Rejoice 286

1. Christ is the King! O friends, re - joice;
2. O mag - ni - fy the Lord, and raise
3. They, with a faith for ev - er new,
4. O Chris - tian wom - en, Chris - tian men,

Broth - ers and sis - ters, with one voice
An - thems of joy and ho - ly praise
Fol - lowed the King, and round him drew
All the world o - ver, seek a - gain

Let na - tions know he is your choice.
For Christ's brave saints of an - cient days.
Thou - sands of faith - ful ones and true.
The way dis - ci - ples fol - lowed then.

Al - le - lu - ia! Al - le - lu - ia! Al - le - lu - ia!

5. Christ through all ages is the same:
   Place the same hope in his great name,
   With the same faith his word proclaim.
   Alleluia! Alleluia! Alleluia!

6. So shall God's will on earth be done,
   New lamps be lit, new tasks begun,
   And the whole Church at last be one.
   Alleluia! Alleluia! Alleluia!

Text: George Kennedy Allen Bell, 1883-1958, alt., © Oxford University Press
Tune: GELOBT SEI GOTT, 888 with alleluias; Melchior Vulpius, c.1560-1616

287 For All the Saints

1. For all the saints who from their la - bors rest, All
2. You were their rock, their for - tress and their might;
3. O may your sol - diers, faith - ful, true and bold,
7. But then there breaks a yet more glo - rious day: The
8. From earth's wide bounds, from o - cean's far - thest coast, Through

who by faith be - fore the world con - fessed, Your
You, Lord, their Cap - tain in their well-fought fight;
Fight as the saints who no - bly fought of old, And
saints tri - umph - ant rise in bright ar - ray; The
gates of pearl streams in the count-less host,

name, O Je - sus, be for ev - er blest.
You in the dark - ness drear, their one true light.
win with them, the vic - tor's crown of gold.
King of glo - ry pass - es on his way.
Sing - ing to Fa - ther, Son, and Ho - ly Ghost:

Al - le - lu - ia! Al - le - lu - ia!
Al - le - lu - ia! Al - le - lu - ia!
Al - le - lu - ia! Al - le - lu - ia!
Al - le - lu - ia! Al - le - lu - ia!
Al - le - lu - ia! Al - le - lu - ia!

4. O blest com - mun - ion, fam - i - ly di - vine!
5. And when the strife is fierce, the war - fare long,
6. The gold - en eve - ning bright - ens in the west;

We fee - bly strug - gle, they in glo - ry shine;
Steals on the ear the dis - tant tri - umph song,
Soon, soon to faith - ful war - riors comes their rest;

Yet   all   are   one   with - in   your   great   de - sign.
And   hearts   are   brave   a - gain, and   arms   are   strong.
Sweet   is   the   calm   of   par - a - dise   the   blest.

Al - le - lu - ia!   Al - le - lu - ia!
Al - le - lu - ia!   Al - le - lu - ia!
Al - le - lu - ia!   Al - le - lu - ia!

Text: William W. How, 1823-1897
Tune: SINE NOMINE, 10 10 10 with alleluias; Ralph Vaughan Williams, 1872-1958, © Oxford University Press

Come, Let Us Join Our Cheerful Songs 288

1. Come, let us join our cheer-ful songs With
2. "Wor-thy the lamb that died," they cry, "To
3. Je-sus is wor-thy to re-ceive All
4. All in cre-a-tion join in one To

an-gels round the throne; Ten thou-sand thou-sand
be ex-alt-ed thus"; "Wor-thy the lamb," our
praise and pow'r di-vine; And bless-ings more than
praise the sa-cred name Of God who reigns up-

are their tongues, But all their joys are one.
lips re-ply, "For he was slain for us."
we can give Be, Lord, for ev-er thine.
on the throne, And to a-dore the Lamb.

Text : Isaac Watts, 1674-1748, slightly adapt.
Tune : AZMON, 8 6 8 6; Carl M. Gläser, 1784-1829; harm. by Lowell Mason, 1792-1872

289 From Glory to Glory Advancing

1. From glo - ry to glo - ry ad - van - cing we praise you, O
2. Thanks- giv - ing, and glo - ry, and wor- ship, and bless- ing, and

Lord; Your name with the Fa - ther and Spir- it be ev - er a -
love, One heart and one song have the saints up - on earth and a -

dored. From strength un - to strength we go for - ward on
bove, O Lord, ev - er - more to your ser - vants your

Zi - on's high - way, To ap - pear be - fore God in the
pres - ence be nigh, Ev-er fit us by ser - vice on

cit - y of in - fi - nite day. earth for your ser - vice on high.

Text : Liturgy of St. James; tr. by Charles W. Humphreys, 1840-1921
Tune : ST. KEVERNE, 14 14 14 15; Craig Sellar Lang, 1892-1971, © Mrs. Craig S. Lang

290 How Firm a Foundation

1. How firm a foundation, O saints of the Lord,
Is laid for your faith in his excellent word!
What more can he say than to you he has said,
To you who for refuge to Jesus have fled?

2. "Fear not, I am with you, O be not dismayed,
For I am your God, and will still give you aid;
I'll strengthen you, help you, and cause you to stand,
Upheld by my righteous, omnipotent hand.

3. "When through the deep waters I call you to go,
The rivers of sorrow shall not overflow;
For I will be near you, your troubles to bless,
And sanctify to you your deepest distress.

4. "Those souls that on Jesus have leaned for repose,
I will not, I will not desert to their foes;
Those souls, though all hell should endeavor to shake,
I'll never, no never, no never, forsake."

Text : 2 Peter 1:4; Keen, Rippon's *A Selection of Hymns,* 1787, alt.
Tune : FOUNDATION, 11 11 11 11; American Folk Hymn

Lord God, We Give You Thanks 291

1. Lord God, we give you thanks for all your saints
2. In ev - 'ry word and deed they spoke of Christ,
3. Blest Trin - i - ty, may yours be end - less praise

Who sought the track - less foot-prints of your feet,
And in their life gave glo - ry to his name;
For all who lived so hum - bly in your sight:

Who took in - to their own a hand un - seen And
Their love was un - con-sumed, a burn - ing bush Of
Your ho - ly ones who walked dark ways in faith Now

heard a voice whose si - lence was com - plete.
which the Ho - ly Spir - it was the flame.
share the joy of your un - fail - ing light.

Text : *The Stanbrook Abbey Hymnal*, rev. ed., 1974, © Stanbrook Abbey Music
Tune : MORESTEAD, 10 10 10 10; Sydney Watson, b.1903, ©

292 Our Father, by Whose Servants

1. Our Fa-ther, by whose ser - vants Our house was built of old,
2. The change-ful years un - rest - ing Their si - lent course have sped,
3. They reap not where they la - bored; We reap what they have sown;
4. Be - fore us and be - side us, Still clasped in thy strong hand

Whose hand hath crowned her chil - dren With bless-ings man-i - fold,
New com-rades ev - er bring - ing In com-rades' steps to tread:
Our har-vest may be gath - ered By ag - es yet un - known.
A cloud un - seen of wit - ness, Our el - der com-rades stand:

For thine un-fail-ing mer - cies Far strewn a - long our way,
And some are long for-got - ten, Long spent their hopes and fears;
The days of old have blessed us With gifts be - yond all praise:
One fam-i - ly un - brok - en, We join, with one ac-claim,

With all who passed be - fore us, We praise thy Name to - day.
Safe rest they in thy keep - ing, Who chang-est not with years.
Our Fa-ther, make us faith - ful To serve the com - ing days.
One heart, one voice up - lift - ing, To glo - ri - fy thy Name.

Text: G.W. Briggs, slightly alt., © Oxford University Press
Tune: DANK SEI GOTT IN DER HÖHE, 76 76 D; Bartholomaeus Gesius, fl. 1605

The Father's Holy Ones, the Blest 293

1. The Fa-ther's ho - ly ones, the blest, Who drank the chal-ice of the Lord,
2. May all that splen-did com-pan - y, Whom Christ in glo - ry came to meet,

Have learned that bit-ter-ness is sweet And cour-age keen - er than the sword.
Help us on our un - ev - en road Made smooth-er by their pass-ing feet.

In dark-ness they were un - a - fraid, And kept a - light their liv - ing fire.
We praise you, Trin - i - ty in One, Sub-lime in maj-es - ty and might,

They now keep time-less days of joy Where God gives all their heart's de - sire.
Who reign for ev - er, Lord of all, in splen-dor and un - end-ing Light.

Text : *The Stanbrook Abbey Hymnal*, rev. ed., 1974, © Stanbrook Abbey Music
Tune : MERTHYR TYDFIL, LMD; Joseph Perry, 1870

294 Blessed Virgin Mother

1. Bless-ed Vir-gin Moth-er, daugh-ter of your Son,
2. When the Source of Hope sprang forth a-gainst De-spair,
3. You are lov-ing kind-ness, ev-er know our need;

High-est of all wom-en, hum-bler there is none.
And the God of Love was nour-ished by your care,
You are all com-pas-sion, glad-ly in-ter-cede,

When you bore the Sav-ior by di-vine de-cree,
Then the fire of grace did flour-ish and in-crease,
You are all per-fec-tion In the hu-man race,

You gave all cre-a-tion new no-bil-i-ty.
Spread-ing through the na-tions news of heav'n-ly peace.
Through your me-di-a-tion we can share God's grace.

Text : Based on the opening lines of the 33rd canto of Dante's *Paradiso*, Anthony G. Petti, 1932-1985, © 1971, Faber Music Ltd.
Tune : UNE VAINE CRAINTE, 11 11 11 11; French Nöel

Hear Our Prayer, O Gentle Mother   295

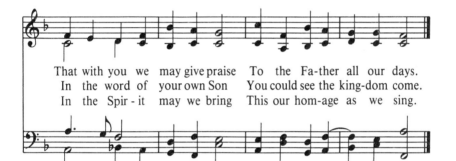

1. Hear our prayer, O gen-tle moth-er, Help us wor-ship as we gath-er
*2. Mir-ror of a true be-liev-er, Put-ting on the mind of Je-sus
3. Hear our prayer, most lov-ing Fa-ther, Through the vir-gin-born, our broth-er;

That with you we may give praise To the Fa-ther all our days.
In the word of your own Son You could see the king-dom come.
In the Spir-it may we bring This our hom-age as we sing.

* *This stanza may be replaced by an appropriate stanza taken from the following:*

January 1: Mary, Mother of God
Woman, raised above all nations,
  Chosen out of all creation,
Mary, you have brought to birth
  Jesus, Lord of all the earth.

March 25: Annunciation
Humbly you received the greeting
  Brought by Gabriel to your dwelling.
Though in darkness you believed,
  Through the Spirit you conceived.

May 31: Visitation
As your cousin comes to meet you,
  "Blest of women," so she greets you.
John who leaps within her womb
  Knows the Bridegroom will come soon.

August 15: Assumption
December 8: Immaculate Conception
Mary, virgin, sinless mother,
  Humble, pow'rful, full of wonder,
Help us have the calm to see
  What your Son calls us to be.

September 15: Our Lady of Sorrows
Mary, standing still and grieving
  As your Son in pain hung bleeding,
You have known within your heart
  All the torment of the dark.

Text: Ralph Wright, OSB, b.1938, © 1989, GIA Publications, Inc.
Tune: SOLLT ES GLEICH BISWEILEN SCHEINEN, 88 77; G. Ch. Störl, fl.1710

296 Mary, Powerful, Sinless Woman

1. Mar-y, pow'r-ful, sin-less wo-man,
2. Mar-y, search-ing in the tem-ple,
3. Mar-y, guest at Ca-na's wed-ding,
4. Mar-y, stand-ing on the hill-side,
5. Mar-y, wait-ing for the Spir-it,

Gen-tle moth-er of our
Search-ing for your child and
Car-ing moth-er of our
Griev-ing moth-er of our
Moth-er of our Lord and

God,   You con-ceived God's word in dark-ness And as
God,   For three days you failed to find him In the
God,   Tell-ing Je-sus wine is lack-ing That our
God,   Shar-ing in the pain of Je-sus As he
God,   Teach us peace and teach us free-dom In the

vir-gin bore his cross.
dark-ness of the cross.
joy may not be lost.   Mar-y, filled with
dies up-on the cross.
tri-umph of the cross.

prayer-ful won-der At the great-ness of your Son, You re-

veal the Fa-ther's glo-ry, Tell-ing all that he has done. Mar-y, moth-er of our Sav-ior, Moth-er of our Lord and God, You were called to be our moth-er By our broth-er from his cross.

Text: Ralph Wright, OSB, b.1938
Tune: SINLESS WOMAN, 8 7 8 7 with refrain; Margaret Daly
© 1989, GIA Publications, Inc.

297 Mary, Crowned with Living Light

1. Mar - y, crowned with liv - ing light, Tem - ple of the Lord,
2. Vir - gin - moth - er of our God, Lift us when we fall,

Place of peace and ho - li - ness, Shel - ter of the Word.
Who were named up - on the Cross Moth - er of us all.

Mys - ter - y of sin - less life In our fall - en race,
Fa - ther, Son and Ho - ly Ghost, Heav - en sings your praise;

Free from shad - ow, you re - flect Plen - i - tude of grace.
Mar - y mag - ni - fies your name Through e - ter - nal days.

Text : *The Stanbrook Abbey Hymnal*, rev. ed., 1974, © Stanbrook Abbey Music
Tune : GLORIFICATION, 75 75 D; Gossner's *Choralbuch*, Leipzig, 1832

Star of Sea and Ocean 298

1. Star of sea and o - cean, Gate - way
2. Wel - com - ing the A - ve, Ga - briel's
3. Loose the bonds that hold us Bound in
4. Show your - self our moth - er; He will
5. Gen - tlest of all vir - gins, That our

to God's ha - ven, Moth - er of our
sim - ple greet - ing, You have borne a
sin's own blind - ness That with eyes now
hear your plead - ing Whom your womb has
love be faith - ful Keep us from all

Mak - er, Hear our prayer, O Maid - en.
Sav - ior Far be - yond all dream - ing.
o - pened God's own light may guide us.
shel - tered And whose hand brings heal - ing.
e - vil, Gen - tle, strong, and grate - ful.

6. Guard us through life's dangers,
   Never turn and leave us.
   May our hope find harbor
   In the calm of Jesus.

7. Sing to God our Father
   Through the Son who saves us,
   Joyful in the Spirit,
   Everlasting praises.

Text: Ralph Wright, OSB, b.1938, © 1989, GIA Publications, Inc.
Tune: AVE MARIS STELLA, 6 6 6 6; Caspar Ett, d. 1847, *Cantica sacra*, Munich, 1840

299 Let All the World with Songs Rejoice

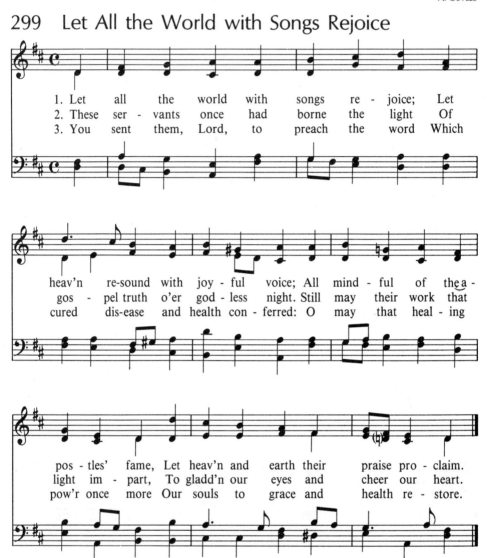

1. Let all the world with songs re - joice; Let heav'n re-sound with joy - ful voice; All mind - ful of the a - pos - tles' fame, Let heav'n and earth their praise pro - claim.

2. These ser - vants once had borne the light Of gos - pel truth o'er god - less night. Still may their work that light im - part, To gladd'n our eyes and cheer our heart.

3. You sent them, Lord, to preach the word Which cured dis-ease and health con - ferred: O may that heal - ing pow'r once more Our souls to grace and health re - store.

Text : *Exultet caelum laudibus,* Anonymous; Latin, 11th C.; tr. by Richard Mant, 1776-1848, *Ancient Hymms,* 1837, alt.
Tune : REX GLORIOSE MARTYRUM, LM; *Katholische Geistliche Gesänge,* Andernach, 1608

The Eternal Gifts of Christ the King 300

1. The e - ter - nal gifts of Christ the King, the a - pos - tles'
2. Their faith in Christ, the Lord, pre - vailed; Their hope, a
3. In them the Fa - ther's glo - ry shone, In them the

glo - ry, let us sing, And all with hearts of
light that nev - er failed; Their love a - blaze o'er
will of God the Son, In them ex - ults the

glad - ness, raise Due hymns of thank - ful love and praise.
path - ways trod To lead them to the e - ter - nal God.
Ho - ly Ghost, Through them re - joice the heav'n - ly host.

Text : *Aeterna Christi munera*, attr. to St. Ambrose of Milan, 340-387; tr. by John Mason Neale, 1818-1866, *Hymnal Noted*, 1852, alt.
Tune : THE AGINCOURT SONG, LM; 15th C. English Melody, adapt.; acc. by Russell Woolen, © 1980, ICEL, Inc.

301 Around the Throne, a Glorious Band

1. A - round the throne, a glo - rious band, The saints in count - less num - bers stand, Of ev - 'ry tongue, re - deemed to God, Ar - rayed in gar-ments washed in blood. Al - le - lu - ia!

2. Through trib - u - la - tion great they came; They bore the cross, de - spised the shame; From all their la - bors now they rest In God's e - ter - nal glo - ry blest. Al - le - lu - ia!

3. They see their Sav - ior face to face, And sing the tri - umphs of his grace; Each day and night they sing his praise, To him the loud thanks-giv - ing raise: Al - le - lu - ia!

4. "Wor - thy the Lamb, for sin - ners slain, Through end - less years to live and reign; You have re - deemed us by your blood, And made us kings and priests to God." Al - le - lu - ia!

5. O may we tread the sa - cred road That saints and ho - ly mar - tyrs trod; Wage to the end the glo - rious strife And win, like them, a crown of life. Al - le - lu - ia!

Text: Rowland Hill, 1744-1833, *A Collection of Psalms and Hymns,* 1782, alt.
Tune: ERSCHIENEN IST DER HERRLICH TAG (HERMANN), LM with alleluia; Nikolaus Hermann, c.1485-1561; arr. by Australian Hymn Book Committee, 1977

God Is My Strong Salvation 302

1. God is my strong sal - va - tion, What foe have I to fear?
   In dark-ness and temp - ta - tion My light, my help is near;
2. Though hosts en - camp a - round me, Firm to the fight I stand;
   What ter - ror can con-found me, With God at my right hand?
3. Place on the Lord re - li - ance, My soul with cour - age wait;
   God's truth my re - as - sur - ance When faint and des - o - late;
4. God's might my heart shall strength - en God's love my joy in - crease;
   Mer - cy my days shall length - en, the Lord will give me peace.

Text: Based on Psalm 27; James Montgomery, 1771-1854, *Songs of Zion*, 1822, alt.
Tune: CHRISTUS DER IST MEIN LEBEN, 7 6 7 6; Melchior Vulpius, c. 1560-1661, *Ein schön geistlich Gesangbuch*, Weimar, 1609

303 The Head That Once Was Crowned with Thorns

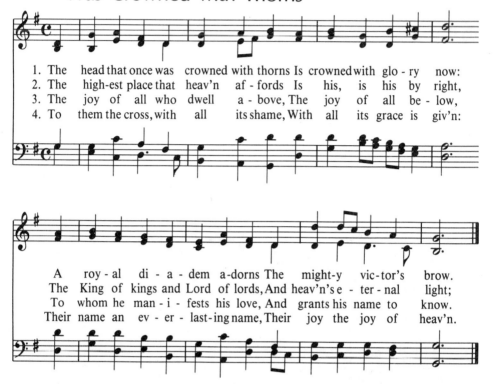

1. The head that once was crowned with thorns Is crowned with glo - ry now:
2. The high-est place that heav'n af - fords Is his, is his by right,
3. The joy of all who dwell a - bove, The joy of all be - low,
4. To them the cross, with all its shame, With all its grace is giv'n:

A roy-al di - a - dem a-dorns The might-y vic-tor's brow.
The King of kings and Lord of lords, And heav'n's e - ter - nal light;
To whom he man - i - fests his love, And grants his name to know.
Their name an ev - er - last-ing name, Their joy the joy of heav'n.

5. They suffer with their Lord below,
They reign with him above,
Their profit and their joy to know
The myst'ry of his love.

6. The cross he bore is life and health,
Though shame and death to him; ·
His people's hope, his people's wealth,
Their everlasting theme.

Text : T. Kelly, 1769-1854
Tune : ST. MAGNUS (NOTTINGHAM), CM; attr. to Jeremiah Clarke, 1659-1707

Let Us Sing Praises 304

1. Let us sing prais - es, praise the God who made us. Let us with
2. Strong was his wis-dom, strong were his con - vic - tions. Long would he
3. Proud - ly they scorned him, those who had not known him. Loud words of
4. Tor - tured and bro - ken for the truth he'd spo - ken, Love still un-
5. Praise to the Fa - ther of our gen - tle Mas - ter. Praise be to

glad - ness sing be - yond our sad - ness. Tell how this
pon - der God's own word with won - der, Till a deep
ha - tred for his rep - u - ta - tion. Lies and false
wav - 'ring in him still for - gave them. Na - ked in
Je - sus, whose love nev - er leaves us. Praise in the

slower

ser - vant stood the test of tor - ment, God's way of con - quest.
yearn - ing brought him his last jour - ney, God's way of con - quest.
wit - ness warped his work of jus - tice, God's way of con - quest.
dark - ness like his gen - tle Mas - ter, God's way of con - quest.
Spir - it, source of all our mer - it, God's way of con - quest.

Text: Ralph Wright, OSB, b.1938. © 1989, GIA Publications, Inc.
Tune: HEALING, 11 11 11 5; Douglas Mews, © 1981, ICEL

305A   We Praise You, Father

1. We praise you, Fa-ther, for your gen-tle might That
2. The ar - ro-gance of an - ger and of lust Bore
3. We praise the wit-ness of her ra-diant hope That
4. We praise you, Fa-ther, for your gen-tle might That

in this wom-an's life was so dis - played. She
down up - on her with its heav - y blade. She
held her through her dark-ness and her pain; Her
in this wom-an's life you have dis - played. We

calm - ly stood be - fore the rage of pride And
pa - tient - ly reached out to you in trust That
faith - ful - ness un - til the fi - nal stroke; She
praise you, Christ, who stood the rage of pride And

proved the great-ness of your pow'r to save.
you would raise her up be - yond the grave.
called the Bride-groom and the Bride-groom came.
in the Spir - it won the pow'r to save.

Text: Ralph Wright, OSB, b.1938
Tune: GENTLE MIGHT, 10 10 10 10; Margaret Daly
© 1989, GIA Publications, Inc.

We Praise You, Father 305B

1. We praise you, Fa-ther, for your gen-tle might That
2. The ar - ro-gance of an - ger and of lust Bore
3. We praise the wit-ness of their ra-diant hope That
4. We praise you, Fa-ther, for your gen-tle might That

in these wom-en's lives was so dis-played. They
down up - on them with its heav-y blade. They
held them through their dark-ness and their pain, Their
in these wom-en's lives you have dis-played. We

calm - ly stood be - fore the rage of pride And
pa - tient - ly reached out to you in trust That
faith-ful - ness un - til the fi - nal stroke; They
praise you, Christ, who stood the rage of pride And

proved the great - ness of your pow'r to save.
you would raise them up be - yond the grave.
called the Bride-groom and the Bride-groom came.
in the Spir - it won the pow'r to save.

Text: Ralph Wright, OSB, b.1938
Tune: GENTLE MIGHT, 10 10 10 10; Margaret Daly
© 1989, GIA Publications, Inc.

306 Father, We Thank You

1. Fa - ther, we thank you for this faith - ful wit - ness,
2. So now in cho - rus, giv - ing God the glo - ry,
3. Glo - ry and hon - or, praise and ad - o - ra - tion,

Whom through the ag - es all have held in hon - or, This day we
We sing his prais - es, fol-low in his foot - steps, That in his
To you we of - fer, Fa-ther, Son and Spir - it, May his ex -

praise you for his deeds of glo - ry With joy and glad - ness.
tri - umph we may be par - tak - ers Here and here- af - ter.
am - ple be a guide and mod - el For us to fol - low.

Text: Based on *Iste confessor*, 8th C., David F. Wright, OP, © 1989, GIA Publications, Inc.
Tune: HERR, DEINEN ZORN, 11 11 11 5; Johann Crüger, 1598-1662, © Oxford University Press

Praise the Glorious Light 307

1. Praise the glo-rious light of God-head   In so man-y   lives re-vealed,
2. Praise the shep-herds called to gov-ern,   Liv-ing hum-ble, pow'r-ful lives,
3. Praise the ser-vant   of the ser-vants   Bur-dened with the cares of each,
4. Praise the lead-ers   in their wis-dom   Faith-ful to the   liv-ing word,
5. Praise the Fa-ther, God Cre-a-tor,   In so man-y   lights re-vealed.

All the splen-dor of the spec-trum From   each sin-gle   pri-sm spilled,
Called to teach and called to wit-ness, With-out harsh-ness, with-out guile,
Tell-ing how the road is nar-row   That   will lead us   to the Feast,
Bring-ing from the gos-pel treas-ure Both   the new word and the old,
Praise the splen-dor of Christ Je-sus Through whom all has been ful-filled.

As the Art - ist through each per-son In new glo-ry   is ful-filled.
In the steps   of Christ the Shep-herd Glad   to go the   sec-ond mile.
Bring-ing words of joy   and com-fort, Leav-ing in his wake God's peace.
Har-bor-ing   a taste   of mys-t'ry Which their love of God has stirred.
Praise the Spir - it through whose pres-ence All our tu-mult may be stilled.

Text: Ralph Wright, OSB, b.1938, © 1989, GIA Publications, Inc.
Tune: FINNIAN, 8 7 8 7 8 7; Christopher Dearnley, b.1930, © Oxford University Press

308 Father, We Thank You

1. Fa - ther, we thank you for this faith - ful wit - ness
2. So now in cho - rus, giv - ing God the glo - ry,
3. Glo - ry and hon - or, praise and ad - o - ra - tion,

Whom you have giv - en ho - li - ness and wis - dom;
We sing his prais - es, tell - ing of his teach - ing,
To you we of - fer, Fa - ther, Son and Spir - it,

For this we praise you, source of light and know - ledge,
That in his tri - umph we may be par - tak - ers
Teach us to fol - low what in life he taught us,

Lord God al - might - y.
Here and here - af - ter.
Lord God al - might - y.

Text: David Wright, OP, © 1989, GIA Publications, Inc.
Tune: CHRISTE SANCTORUM 11 11 11 5; La Feilees *Methode du plain-chant*, 1872

Father, We Thank You 309

1. Fa - ther, we thank you for this faith-ful wit - ness
2. So now in cho - rus, giv - ing God the glo - ry,
3. Glo - ry and hon - or, praise and ad - o - ra - tion,

Whom you have giv - en ho - li - ness and wis - dom;
We sing her prais - es, tell - ing of her teach - ing,
To you we of - fer, Fa - ther, Son and Spir - it,

For this we praise you, source of light and know - ledge,
That in her tri - umph we may be par - tak - ers,
Teach us to fol - low what in life she taught us,

Lord God al - might - y.
Lord God al - might - y.
Lord God al - might - y.

Text: David Wright, OP, © 1989, GIA Publications, Inc.
Tune: ISTE CONFESSOR, 11 11 11 5; French Church Melody, *Poitiers Antiphoner*, 1746

310 O Raise Your Voices! Wake the World

1. O raise your voic - es! Wake the world! And let your
2. This ser - vant heard with - in his heart A call to
3. He gave his life to hear God's word And then pro -
4. He knew his weak - ness and his sin And God's great
5. O praise the Fa - ther, wake the world! And let the

song of praise be heard! For both in town and des - ert
leave his fam - 'ly hearth. He heard, he an-swered, left his
claim it to the world. He lis - tened, fast - ed, suf - fered,
mer - cy from with - in. In know-ing this and his own
Son's own praise be heard! And praise in town or des - ert

waste God's glo - ry finds a dwell - ing place.
home And gave a - way the goods he owned.
prayed And stood in dark - ness un - dis - mayed.
shame He learnt to reach and heal great pain.
waste The Spir - it glo - ri - fied in grace.

Text: Ralph Wright, OSB, b.1938, © 1989, GIA Publications, Inc.
Tune: WIR DANKEN DIR, LM; Nikolaus Hermann, fl. 1551, 1560

SECOND TUNE – 310

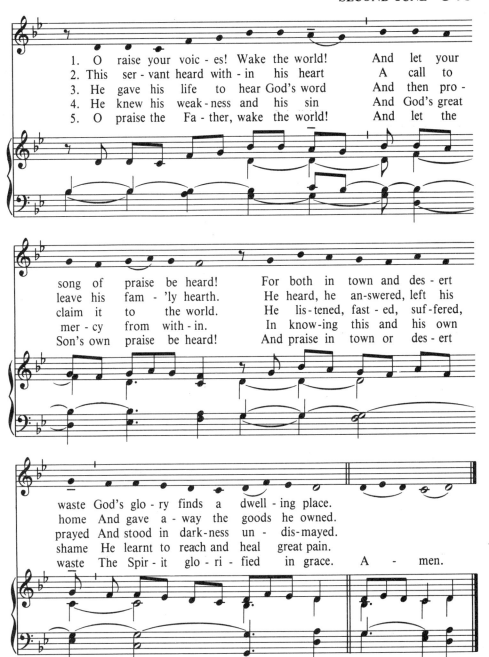

1. O raise your voic - es! Wake the world! And let your
2. This ser - vant heard with - in his heart A call to
3. He gave his life to hear God's word And then pro -
4. He knew his weak - ness and his sin And God's great
5. O praise the Fa - ther, wake the world! And let the

song of praise be heard! For both in town and des - ert
leave his fam - 'ly hearth. He heard, he an-swered, left his
claim it to the world. He lis - tened, fast - ed, suf-fered,
mer - cy from with - in. In know-ing this and his own
Son's own praise be heard! And praise in town or des - ert

waste God's glo - ry finds a dwell - ing place.
home And gave a - way the goods he owned.
prayed And stood in dark-ness un - dis-mayed.
shame He learnt to reach and heal great pain.
waste The Spir - it glo - ri - fied in grace. A - men.

Text: Ralph Wright, OSB, b.1938, © 1989, GIA Publications, Inc.
Tune: DEM HERRN, DER SEINER ZEUGEN DIENST, LM; Mode III; *Antiphonale zum Stundengebet*, © Vier-Türme-Verlag, Muensterschwarzach, 1979;
    acc. by Samuel Weber, OSB, b.1947, © 1987, Saint Meinrad Archabbey

311 Father, We Thank You

1. Fa - ther, we thank you for this faith - ful wit - ness
2. So now in cho - rus, giv - ing God the glo - ry,
3. Glo - ry and hon - or, praise and ad - o - ra - tion,

Whom through the ag - es all have held in hon - or;
We sing her prais - es, fol - low in her foot - steps,
To you we of - fer, Fa - ther, Son and Spir - it,

This day we praise you for her deeds of glo - ry
That in her tri - umph we may be par - tak - ers
May her ex - am - ple be a guide and mod - el

With joy and glad - ness.
Here and here - af - ter.
For us to fol - low.

Text: Based on *Iste confessor*, 8th C., David Wright, OP, © 1989, GIA Publications, Inc.
Tune: CHRISTE SANCTORUM, 11 11 11 5; *Paris Antiphoner*, 1681; harm. by Ralph Vaughan Williams, 1872-1958, © Oxford University Press

O Let Us Praise the Lord This Day   312

1. O let us praise the Lord this day And out of si - lence weave A
2. Then in the dark - ness of the night She stood with emp - ty hands And
3. Be - yond the dark - est hour of doubt She made your Word her home; The

song to hon - or one whose life Was might - y with God's deeds. She
pa - tient - ly be - lieved that you Through her would heal our wounds. She
storms of ar - ro - gance and strife Were stilled be - fore her calm. So

chose to seek the pearl of price, The treas - ure of the field. In
fed the hun - gry, clothed the poor, De - fend - ed the op - pressed; And
on this day we praise you, Lord, Good Fa - ther, ser - vant Son. O

giv - ing all to you she found Her emp - ti - ness re - vealed.
when the home - less had no roof, Re - ceived them as her guest.
in the Spir - it may this praise Keep us for ev - er one.

Text: Ralph Wright, OSB, b.1938, © 1989, GIA Publications, Inc.
Tune: MOZART, CMD; attr. to Wolfgang Amadeus Mozart, 1756-1791

313 We Praise You, Lord, with Joy This Day

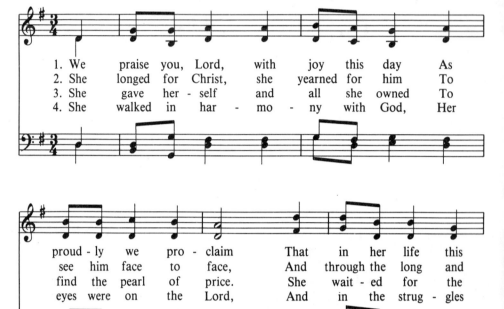

1. We praise you, Lord, with joy this day As
2. She longed for Christ, she yearned for him To
3. She gave her-self and all she owned To
4. She walked in har - mo - ny with God, Her

proud - ly we pro - claim That in her life this
see him face to face, And through the long and
find the pearl of price. She wait - ed for the
eyes were on the Lord, And in the strug - gles

wom - an's love Has glo - ri - fied your name.
pa - tient years She found in him her peace.
Bride-groom's call And lis - tened through the night.
of each day Her calm was in his word.

5. Her brothers and her sisters found
In her a mighty shield,
For in the fortress of her faith
They saw God's pow'r revealed.

6. O come and worship God this day,
The Father and the Son—
And in their Spirit know that joy
Which she now shares—O come!

Text: Ralph Wright, OSB, b.1938, © 1989, GIA Publications, Inc.
Tune: AZMON, 8 6 8 6; Carl M. Gläser, 1784-1829; harm. by Lowell Mason, 1792-1872

O Jesus, Lord, Increase Our Faith   314

1. O Je - sus, Lord, in - crease our faith, The
2. O give us trust in your great love That
3. Give us the com - fort of those tears You
4. O give us, Lord, a vi - brant hope That

faith that is e - ter - nal life. Re - lieve the bur - den
lives with pow'r be - yond the grave—A love un - like the
shed for Laz - a - rus your friend. Sus - tain us with your
sees be - yond the flow'rs that die. O help us, Lord, we

of our grief And lead our broth-er / sis - ter in - to light.
mead-ow flow'rs That bloom a while then quick - ly fade.
com - fort now Un - til our dark - ness has an end.
do be - lieve In your strong words, you do not lie.

5. O bring us quickly to that place
Where your own glory is revealed.
Then in full union we will know
The joy which still remains concealed.

6. O let us worship and adore
The Father and his risen Son.
For in the Spirit we may live
Through trial and torment ever one.

Text: Ralph Wright, OSB, b.1938, © 1989, GIA Publications, Inc.
Tune: WINDHAM, LM; Daniel Read, *The American Singing Book*, 1785

315A O Lord, You Died That All Might Live

1. O Lord, you died that all might live And rise to see the per - fect day. The full - ness of your mer - cy give To this our friend for whom we pray.

2. Lord, bless our friends who died in you, As you have giv - en him/her re - lease. En - liv - en him/her since he/she was true, And give him/her ev - er - last - ing peace.

3. In your green, pleas - ant pas - tures feed The sheep that you have sum - moned hence; And by the still, cool wa - ters lead Your flock in lov - ing prov - i - dence.

4. Di - rect us with your arm of might, That with our friends we may all come To dwell with - in your cit - y bright, Je - su - sa - lem, our heav'n - ly home.

O Lamb of God, Re - deem - er blest, Grant him/her e - ter - nal light and rest.

Text : Richard F. Littledale, 1833-1890, alt.
Tune : MELITA, LM, with refrain; John B. Dykes, 1823-1876

O Lord, You Died That All Might Live 315B

Plural Text

1. O Lord, you died that all might live And rise to see the
2. Lord, bless our friends who died in you, As you have giv - en
3. In your green, pleas - ant pas - tures feed The sheep that you have
4. Di - rect us with your arm of might, That with our friends we

per - fect day. The full - ness of your mer - cy give
them re - lease. En - liv - en them since they were true,
sum - moned hence; And by the still, cool wa - ters lead
may all come To dwell with - in your cit - y bright,

To these our friends for whom we pray.
And give them ev - er - last - ing peace. O Lamb of God,
Your flock in lov - ing prov - i - dence.
Je - ru - sa - lem, our heav'n - ly home.

Re - deem - er blest, Grant them e - ter - nal light and rest.

Text; Richard F. Littledale, 1833-1890, alt.
Tune: MELITA, LM, with refrain; John B. Dykes, 1823-1876

316 We Offer Prayer in Sorrow, Lord

1. We of - fer prayer in sor - row, Lord, As - sist our frail be -
2. O com - fort us, we do be - lieve But find the way so
3. Re - ceive in - to your dwell - ing place All those whose lives have
4. We praise you, Fa - ther, Lord of Light, We praise you through our

liev - ing. Make strong in us those pow'r - ful words To Mar - tha in her
dark - ened. We miss the one(s) we do not see, The pain of loss is
end - ed. For - give their sins and give that peace For which they were in -
sad - ness. We praise you, ris - en Je - sus Christ, Who tri - umphed o - ver

griev - ing: "Your broth - er, though now dead, will rise, For those who trust me
sharp - ened. O come with com - fort, gen - tle Word, Be close to us, for
tend - ed. You died, O Lord, that they might live. Have mer - cy; in your
dark - ness. We praise you, Spir - it of them both. O come with glad - ness,

will not die." O hear these words of plead - ing.
in you, Lord, We find our own de - part - ed.
love for - give, For - give where they of - fend - ed.
give us hope, And mit - i - gate death's harsh - ness.

Text: Ralph Wright, OSB, b.1938, © 1989, GIA Publications, Inc.
Tune: ICH STEH' AN DEINER KRIPPE; *Orgelchoralbuch zum envangelischen, 1966*

Hymns by Ralph Wright, O.S.B.
Original versions, prior to textual alterations made by author in keeping with criteria established by committee for HYMNAL FOR THE HOURS.

#5.	O GRACIOUS MAKER OF THE STARS	
	2:3	You came as man to touch our wounds
	3:3	...Bridegroom leaves
	3:4	You left your Mother's virgin womb.
	4:4	The God who comes to set man free.
	6:2	To God the Father and his Son
	6:3	Who comes as man that we may be
	6:4	Within his Spirit ever one

#20.   MY BURDEN IS LIGHT
1:5   the burden of seeing that all men are given
2:5   The burden of being new hope to our brothers
3:1   Come, Lord Jesus, and gaze on your brothers

#62.   JESUS CALLS US OUT OF DARKNESS
1:1-2   God has called us out of darkness
        into his own wondrous light
1:7-8   Calling God himself your Father
        in the love he has outpoured

Verse 2.   Omitted
           From the moment when he forms us
           in the womb, until we die,
           we are his eternal children
           with a destiny on high.
           May we live by this great vision,
           may we share this gift of sight,
           may we serve beyond the darkness
           all who hunger for the light.

#92.   THE REGAL DARK MYSTERIOUS CROSS
1:3-4   The wood on which our God was stretched
        As man against the sky

#142.   CREATING SPIRIT, MIGHTY LORD
        Creating Spirit, mighty Lord,
        Find home within our heart and mind,
        With warmth and power and gentleness
        In grace refashion all mankind

#157.   O BLESSED LIGHT
1:2   O source of deepest unity,
1:4   Bring light and peace lest hope should die.

#215.   THE MYSTERY OF THE HIDDEN PLAN
2:1   .. killed his only Son
2:4   and in his love forgave
3:1   ...his Holy Spirit

#262.   COME RAISE YOUR VOICES, PRAISE THE LORD,
        PARTS I and II
        Original is one complete hymn involving the first verse,
        the doxology and six verses in between.

#270.   A TAX-COLLECTOR, SCORNED BY ALL
        The original hymn consisted of four verses without a
        doxology. Original order of verses:
        PART I: verses 1,2; PART II: versus 2,1.

        PART II: EVENING
        1:2   To trumpet forth his name

#272.   COME RAISE A SONG OF JOY THIS DAY
        PART I: MORNING
        1:3   the man whose gospel has revealed
        2:1   In simple words he told the world

        PART II: EVENING
        verse 1: same as above (MORNING)
        2:1   He told of one... Used when all verses are sung
                together

        The original hymn consists of five verses without a
        doxology.
        PART I: verses 1,2,3; PART II: verses 2,3.

#277.   WE SING OF THAT DISCIPLE
        Original hymn consisted of seven verses without the
        doxology.
        PART I: verses 1,2,3; PART II: verses 2,3,4; PART I:
        verse 4.

#281.   O JERUSALEM, THE BLESSED
        4:2   or the anvil of men's hate
        5:1   May all glory, praise and honor
                Be to him who reigns on high

#298.   STAR OF SEA AND OCEAN
        1:2   gateway to man's haven
        2:2   of God's simple greeting

#310.   O RAISE YOUR VOICES!
        1:4   God's glory shines upon man's face

318   Acknowledgments

HYMNAL FOR THE HOURS

The publisher gratefully acknowledges the following holders of copyright whose permission has been granted for the inclusion of material in this book. Every effort has been made to determine the ownership of all tunes, texts and harmonizations used in this edition and to make proper arrangements for their use. The publisher regrets any error or oversight which may have occurred and will readily make proper acknowledgment in future editions if such omission is made known. Acknowledgments are stated in accordance with the requirements of the individual copyright holder.

2 Harm: From *Resource Collection of Hymns and Service Music for the Liturgy,* © 1981, International Committee on English in the Liturgy, Inc. All rights reserved.

4 Music: © 1981, The Order of St. Benedict, Inc., Collegeville, Minnesota 56321 from *Swayed Pines Song Book.* Published by The Liturgical Press, Collegeville, MN 56321

5 Trans: © 1989, GIA Publications, Inc. Acc: From *Resource Collection of Hymns and Service Music for the Liturgy,* © 1981, International Committee on English in the Liturgy, Inc. All rights reserved.

6 Text: © 1989, GIA Publications, Inc.

7 Music: Setting © 1978, *Lutheran Book of Worship*

8 Text: © Mrs. M. E. Peacey by permission of Mrs. M. I. Hancock, London. Harm: From *BBC Hymnbook,* © Oxford University Press, London

9 Harm: © 1975, GIA Publications, Inc.

11 Text: Adaptation © 1971, Faber Music Limited. Reprinted from the *New Catholic Hymnal* by permission of Faber Music Limited.

12 Text: © Emmanuel College, University of Toronto

13 Text and Music: © 1969, by permission of Concordia Publishing House

15 Harm: © 1975, GIA Publications, Inc.

16 Text: © 1974, Stanbrook Abbey Music, Worcester, England. Acc 1: © 1989, GIA Publications, Inc. Music 2: © 1987, Saint Meinrad Archabbey

17 Text: By permission of St. Joseph's Abbey, Spencer, MA. All rights reserved. Harm: © *Catholic Liturgy Book*

20 Text: © 1978, Daughters of St. Paul, 50 St. Paul Avenue, Jamaica Plain, MA 02130. Music: © 1989, GIA Publications, Inc.

22 Text: © 1982, Charles P. Price

23 Text: Revision © 1989, GIA Publications, Inc.

24 Text: © 1970, McCrimmon Publishing Co. Ltd., Essex, England

25 Trans: © 1982, Hope Publishing Company, Carol Stream, IL 60188. All rights reserved. Used by permission.

26 Harm: From *Resource Collection of Hymns and Service Music for the Liturgy,* © 1981, International Committee on English in the Liturgy, Inc. All rights reserved.

27 Harm: © John Ainslie

29 Text: © 1955, World Library Publications, Inc. Used with permission. Music: Setting © 1969, by permission of Concordia Publishing House.

30 Text: © 1969, James Quinn, SJ. Reprinted by permission of Geoffrey Chapman, a division of Cassell Publishers Limited, Artillery House, Artillery Row, London 1RT.

31 Trans: © 1989, GIA Publications, Inc. Music 1: Copyright renewal © 1969 assigned to United Church Press, New York, NY, and used by permission of the publisher from *The Hymnal* (Evangelical and Reformed Church). Music 2: © 1987, Saint Meinrad Archabbey

32 Text: © 1989, GIA Publications, Inc. Music: © 1971, Faber Music Limited. Reprinted from the *New Catholic Hymnal* by permission of Faber Music Limited.

33 Text: Vs. 3-4, © 1982, James Waring McCrady, Sewanee, TN

34 Text: © 1971, Faber Music Limited. Reprinted from the *New Catholic Hymnal* by permission of Faber Music Limited. Music: © Oxford University Press, London

35 Acc: From *Resource Collection of Hymns and Service Music for the Liturgy,* © 1981, International Committee on English in the Liturgy, Inc. All rights reserved.

37 Text: © 1989, GIA Publications, Inc. Music: © 1989, Hope Publishing Company, Carol Stream, IL 60188. All rights reserved. Used by permission.

38 Text: © 1978, *Lutheran Book of Worship.* Music 2: © 1987, Saint Meinrad Archabbey

39 Acc 2: © 1987, Saint Meinrad Archabbey

40 Text: Revision © 1989, GIA Publications, Inc. Music: From *BBC Hymn Book,* © Oxford University Press, London

42 Text and Acc: From *Resource Collection of Hymns and Service Music for the Liturgy,* © 1981, International Committee on English in the Liturgy, Inc. All rights reserved.

43 Text: © 1978, *Lutheran Book of Worship*

44 Acc 1: © 1985, GIA Publications, Inc. Arr 2: 1984, Bruce Neswick

47 Text and Music: © Oxford University Press, London

48 Text and Music: © 1964, World Library Publications, Inc. Used with permission.

50 Harm: © 1984, Thomas Foster

51 Harm: © 1978, *Lutheran Book of Worship*

55 Text: Adaptation © 1971, Faber Music Limited. Reprinted from the *New Catholic Hymnal* by permission of Faber Music Limited.

56 Text and Music 1: © 1989, GIA Publications, Inc.

57 Text: Adaptation © 1989, GIA Publications, Inc.

60 Text: © 1989, GIA Publications, Inc. Music 2: © 1987, Saint Meinrad Archabbey

61 Text: © 1984, Hope Publishing Company, Carol Stream, IL 60188. All rights reserved. Used by permission.

62 Text: © 1989, GIA Publications, Inc. Music: © 1980, Austin Rennick, OSB

63 Text and Music: From *Resource Collection of Hymns and Service Music for the Liturgy,* © 1981, International Committee on English in the Liturgy, Inc. All rights reserved.

64 Text: Adaptation © 1971, Faber Music Limited. Reprinted from the *New Catholic Hymnal* by permission of Faber Music Limited.

66 Text and Music: © 1989, GIA Publications, Inc.

67 Text: © 1974, Stanbrook Abbey Music, Worcester, England. Acc: © 1989, GIA Publications, Inc.

68 Acc 2: © 1987, Saint Meinrad Archabbey

69 Text: © 1989, GIA Publications, Inc.

71 Trans and Acc 1: © 1989, GIA Publications, Inc.

72 Trans: © Oxford University Press, London

74 Text: © Mrs. Esmé D.E. Bird

75 Text: © 1974, Stanbrook Abbey Music, Worcester, England. Acc 2: © 1987, Saint Meinrad Archabbey

76 Text: © 1989, GIA Publications, Inc. Music 1: © 1976, The Panel of Monastic Musicians — Liturgy in Community. Harm 2: © 1943, 1971, 1981, Church Pension Fund

77 Music: From the *Australian Hymn Book*

78 Trans: © Peter J. Scagnelli

79 Text: © 1982, Thomas H. Cain

80 Acc 2: © 1987, Saint Meinrad Archabbey

83 Text: © 1969, James Quinn, SJ. Reprinted by permission of Geoffrey Chapman, a division of Cassell Publishers Limited, Artillery House, Artillery Row, London SW1P 1RT.

84 Text: © 1969, David Edge, Edinburgh, Scotland. Music: © 1989, Hope Publishing Company, Carol Stream, IL 60188. All rights reserved. Used by permission.

85 Text: © 1972, *Praise the Lord.* Harm 1: © 1984, Thomas Foster. Acc 2: © 1987, Saint Meinrad Archabbey

86 Text: © J. Donald P. Hughes. Acc 2: © 1987, Saint Meinrad Archabbey

87 Trans: © 1989, GIA Publications, Inc. Melody: © Trustees of Priknash Abbey. Acc: © Br. Ashenden

Acknowledgments/*continued*

88 Trans: © 1989, GIA Publications, Inc. Acc 2: © 1987, Saint Meinrad Archabbey.

90 Music: © John Ireland Trust, 35 St. Mary's Mansions, London, W2 1SQ England

91 Text: © 1974, Stanbrook Abbey Music, Worcester, England. Music 2: © 1987, Saint Meinrad Archabbey.

92 Trans : © 1989, GIA Publications, Inc. Music: © Austin Rennick, OSB

93 Text: St. 2 © 1961, World Library Publications, Inc. Used with permission.

94 Trans: © 1989, GIA Publications, Inc. Music: Setting © 1967, by permission of Concordia Publishing House

95 Music: First published in *Cantate Domino* (full music edition 1980). © World Council of Churches Publications, Geneva, Switzerland. Used with permission.

96 Text and Music: From *New Hymns for the Lectionary,* © 1985, Oxford University Press, Inc., New York

97 Text: © 1971, Faber Music Limited. Reprinted from the *New Catholic Hymnal* by permission of Faber Music Limited. Music 1: © 1941, H. W. Gray Co., Inc. Renewed 1969, H. W. Gray Co., Inc. Assigned to Belwin-Mills Publishing Corporation, c/o Belwin, Inc., Miami, FL 33014. All rights reserved. Used by permission.

98 Harm: © 1985, Church Pension Fund

100 Text: © 1989, GIA Publications, Inc. Harm: © 1985, Church Pension Fund

101 Text: © Peter J. Scagnelli

102 Acc. 2: From *Resource Collection of Hymns and Service Music for the Liturgy,* © 1981, International Committee on English in the Liturgy, Inc. All rights reserved.

104 Trans: © 1978, *Lutheran Book of Worship.* Harm: From *Songs of Praise,* © Oxford University Press, London.

105 Text: © 1989, GIA Publications, Inc.

107 Text: © 1939, Burns and Oates. Harm: © 1978, Church Pension Fund

108 Trans and Music 2: © 1989, GIA Publications, Inc.

109 Harm: From *Songs of Praise,* © Oxford University Press, London

111 Text: © 1969, James Quinn, SJ. Reprinted by permission of Geoffrey Chapman, a division of Cassell Publishers Limited, Artillery House, Artillery Row, London SW1P 1RT. Tune: © Geoffrey Chapman

112 Text: © Hamish Swanston. Music: 1971, Faber Music Limited. Reprinted from the *New Catholic Hymnal* by permission of Faber Music Limited.

114 Text and Music 1: From the *Oxford Book of Carols,* © Oxford University Press, Oxford. Harm 2: © 1978, Church Pension Fund

115 Trans: St. 1,3,5 from *Bach's Four-Part Chorales,* © Oxford University Press, London.

116 Music 2: © 1987, Saint Meinrad Archabbey

117 Trans: © Peter J. Scagnelli

118 Text: © 1970, World Library Publications, Inc. Used with permission. Harm: From the *English Hymnal,* © Oxford University Press

119 Harm: © 1972, C.C.C.

121 Text: St. 3 translation © 1989, GIA Publications, Inc.

122 Harm: From *English Hymnal,* © Oxford University Press, London

123 Text: Adaptation © 1971, Faber Music Limited. Reprinted from the *New Catholic Hymnal* by permission of Faber Music Limited. Music: © Kenneth D. Smith

124 Text: © 1958; renewed 1986, Hope Publishing Company, Carol Stream, IL 60188. All rights reserved. Used by permission. Harm 1: © 1958, from *The Pilgrim Hymnal,* used by permission of The Pilgrim Press, New York, NY. Harm 2: Setting © 1969, by permission of Concordia Publishing House

125 Text: © Oxford University Press, London. Melody: © Vier-Türme-Verlag, Münsterschwarzach, Federal Republic of Germany. Harm: © 1987, Saint Meinrad Archabbey

126 Trans: © 1958, *Service Book and Hymnal,* Augsburg/Fortress Publishers

127 Trans: © 1971, Faber Music Limited. Reprinted from the *New Catholic Hymnal* by permission of Faber Music Limited.

129 Text: © 1989, GIA Publications, Inc. Arr 1: © 1965, Abingdon Press. From *The Book of Hymns* (#426) Music 2: © 1987, Saint Meinrad Archabbey

130 Text: Adaptation © 1971, Faber Music Limited. Reprinted from the *New Catholic Hymnal* by permission of Faber Music Limited.

132 Text: © 1974, Stanbrook Abbey Music, Worcester, England. Acc 2: © 1987, Saint Meinrad Archabbey

133 Harm: Setting © 1969, by permission of Concordia Publishing House

136 Trans: © 1978, *Lutheran Book of Worship.* Harm: From the *English Hymnal,* © Oxford University Press, London

137 Music: © Oxford University Press, London

138 Trans: © 1989, GIA Publications, Inc. Harm: © Executors of G. H. Knight

139 Text: © 1969, James Quinn, SJ. Reprinted by permission of Geoffrey Chapman, a division of Cassell Publishers Limited, Artillery House, Artillery Row, London SW1P 1RT.

140 Text: St. 1-3 Adaptation © 1971, Faber Music Limited. Reprinted from the *New Catholic Hymnal* by permission of Faber Music Limited. St. 4 © 1989, GIA Publications, Inc. Music: From the *English Hymnal,* © Oxford University Press, London

141 Text: © 1974, Stanbrook Abbey Music, Worcester, England.

142 Trans and Music: © 1989, GIA Publications, Inc.

144 Trans and Music: © 1971, Faber Music Limited. Reprinted from the *New Catholic Hymnal* by permission of Faber Music Limited.

145 Trans: © 1989, John Webster Grant. Music: © 1975, GIA Publication, Inc.

147 Text: © James Quinn, SJ

148 Trans: © 1989, GIA Publications, Inc. Melody: From the *English Hymnal,* © Oxford University Press, London. Harm: © 1978, *Lutheran Book of Worship*

149 Trans: © 1989, GIA Publications, Inc. Acc: © 1987, Saint Meinrad Archabbey

150 Trans: © Abbey of Gethsemani. Acc 2: © 1987, Saint Meinrad Archabbey

151 Trans: © 1989, GIA Publications, Inc. Harm 1: © Evang. Gesangbuch- und Choralbuchverlag, Stuttgart, Federal Republic of Germany. Acc 2: © 1987, Saint Meinrad Archabbey

152 Trans: © 1989, GIA Publications, Inc. Harm: Setting © 1969, by permission of Concordia Publishing House

153 Trans: © 1989, GIA Publications, Inc.

154 Trans: © 1989, GIA Publications, Inc. Acc 2: © 1987, Saint Meinrad Archabbey

155 Translation of this hymn by Rev. Roger Schoenbechler, OSB, taken from *The Book of Prayer,* © 1975 by The Order of St. Benedict, Inc., Collegeville, Minnesota 56321. Published by The Liturgical Press, Collegeville, Minnesota 56321.

156 Trans: © 1989, GIA Publications, Inc. Harm: © 1978, *Lutheran Book of Worship*

157 Trans: © 1989, GIA Publications, Inc. Harm: © 1971, Stanley L. Osborne

158 Text: © St. Joseph's Abbey, Spencer, MA. All rights reserved.

160 Text: © 1969, James Quinn, SJ. Reprinted by permission of Geoffrey Chapman, a division of Cassell Publishers Limited, Artillery House, Artillery Row, London SW1P 1RT. Harm: From *Revised Church Hymnary 1927,* © Oxford University Press, London

161 Text: © 1982, Anne K. LeCroy Music: © 1985, GIA Publications, Inc.

162 Text: © 1969, James Quinn, SJ. Reprinted by permission of Geoffrey Chapman, a division of Cassell Publishers Limited, Artillery House, Artillery Row, London SW1P 1RT.

164 Melody and Harm: From the *English Hymnal,* © Oxford University Press, London

166 Text: Paraphrase © St. Joseph's Abbey, Spencer, MA. All rights reserve. Acc 2: © 1987, Saint Meinrad Archabbey

167 Trans: Adaptation © 1989, GIA Publications, Inc. Music: © Oxford University Press

168 Harm: © 1978, *Lutheran Book of Worship*

170 Trans: © William G. Storey. Acc: © 1975, GIA Publications, Inc.

172 Trans and Music: © 1971, Faber Music Limited. Reprinted from the *New Catholic Hymnal* by permission of Faber Music Limited.

173 Music: 1977, Praise Publications, Whittier, CA

175 Trans: © 1989, GIA Publications, Inc. Acc 1: From *Resource Collection of Hymns and Service Music for the Liturgy,* © 1981, International Committee on English in the Liturgy, Inc. All rights reserved. Acc 2: © 1987, Saint Meinrad Archabbey

Acknowledgments/*continued*

176 Harm: From the *English Hymnal,* © Oxford University Press, London
178 Acc: © 1987, Saint Meinrad Archabbey
180 Text and Music: From *New Hymns for the Lectionary,* © 1985, Oxford University Press, Inc., New York
182 Text: © 1989, GIA Publications, Inc.
183 Text: © 1989, GIA Publications, Inc.
184 Text: © 1974, Stanbrook Abbey Music, Worcester, England. Acc 2: © 1987, Saint Meinrad Archabbey
186 Harm: From *English Praise,* © Oxford University Press, London
187 Text: © Emmanuel College, University of Toronto. Harm: © David Kingsley
188 Acc 2: © 1987, Saint Meinrad Archabbey
189 Text: Adaptation © 1989, GIA Publications, Inc.
191 Trans: © Abbey of Gethsemani. Music 2: © Saint Meinrad Archabbey
192 Music: © 1983, GIA Publications, Inc.
195 Text: © T. & T. Clark, Edinburgh, Scotland. Acc: © 1987, Saint Meinrad Archabbey
197 Text: Mrs. J. Tyrell, Goldalning, Surrey, England. Harm: © 1985, Hope Publishing Company, Carol Stream, IL 60188. All rights reserved. Used by permission.
198 Acc: From *Resource Collection of Hymns and Service Music for the Liturgy,* © 1981, International Committee on English in the Liturgy, Inc. All rights reserved.
199 Text: © 1982, Hope Publishing Company, Carol Stream, IL 60188. All rights reserved. Used by permission.
200 Text: © 1974, Stanbrook Abbey Music, Worcester, England. Music: © 1989, GIA Publications, Inc.
202 Text: © 1989, GIA Publications, Inc. Music: © Irish Institute of Pastoral Liturgy
204 Text: © 1989, GIA Publications, Inc. Music 1: Adaptation © 1971, Faber Music Limited. Reprinted from the *New Catholic Hymnal* by permission of Faber Music Limited. Music 2: © 1987, Saint Meinrad Archabbey
205 Text: © 1969, James Quinn, SJ. Reprinted by permission of Geoffrey Chapman, a division of Cassell Publishers Limited, Artillery House, Artillery Row, London SW1P 1RT. Harm: From *Enlarged Songs of Praise,* © Oxford University Press, London
206 Text: © 1969, by permission of Concordia Publishing House
209 Text: © 1974, Stanbrook Abbey Music, Worcester, England.
210 Text: © 1974, Stanbrook Abbey Music, Worcester, England.
211 Text: © 1959. Renewal 1987 by The Hymn Society of America, Texas Christian University, Ft. Worth, TX 76129. All rights reserved. Used by permission.
212 Text: © 1974, Stanbrook Abbey Music, Worcester, England.
215 Text: © 1989, GIA Publications, Inc.
217 Text: © Oxford University Press, London. Music: © 1989, Hope Publishing Company, Carol Stream, IL 60188. All rights reserved. Used by permission.
218 Harm: © From the *English Hymnal,* © Oxford University Press, London
221 Acc 2: © 1987, Saint Meinrad Archabbey
222 Text: © 1989, GIA Publications, Inc. Melody: © Trustees of Prinknash Abbey. Acc: © Br. Ashenden
223 Trans: © 1989, GIA Publications, Inc.
224 Harm: From the *English Hymnal,* © Oxford University Press, London
225 Trans: © 1989, GIA Publications, Inc. Melody: © Trustees of Prinknash Abbey. Acc: © Br. Ashenden
226 Text: From *Enlarged Songs of Praise,* © Oxford University Press, London. Harm: © 1964, Abingdon Press. From *The Book of Hymns* (#256)
227 Text: St. 1-2, from *The Hymnal 1982,* © 1985, Church Pension Fund; St. 3, © James Waring McCrady, Sewanee, TN. Acc: © 1984, Gerard Farrell, OSB, Princeton, NJ
228 Trans: © Malling Abbey, West Malling, Kent, England. Melody: © Trustees of Prinknash Abbey. Acc: © Br. Ashenden
229 Text: © 1970, The Lutheran World Federation, Geneva, Switzerland. Harm: Setting © 1978, *Lutheran Book of Worship*
231 **Harm:** © 1985, Hope Publishing Company, Carol Stream, IL 60188. All rights reserved. Used by permission.
232 Trans: © 1989, GIA Publications, Inc. Music: © Ampleforth Abbey Trustees

233 Trans: © 1989, GIA Publications, Inc.
234 Text: © 1982, Hope Publishing Company, Carol Stream, IL 60188. All rights reserved. Used by permission.
235 Music: © Oxford University Press, London
236 Music: From the *English Hymnal,* © Oxford University Press, London
237 Text: St. 1-4, from *The Hymnal 1982,* © 1985, Church Pension Fund; St. 5, © Anne K. LeCroy, Johnson City, TN. Acc: © 1984, Richard P. Solly, Furlong, PA
239 Trans: © 1989, GIA Publications, Inc. Harm: © 1976, Hinshaw Music, Inc.
240 Text: © 1974, Stanbrook Abbey Music, Worcester, England. Harm: Setting © 1969, by permission of Concordia Publishing House
241 Music: © 1971, Faber Music Limited. Reprinted from the *New Catholic Hymnal* by permission of Faber Music Limited.
242 Text: © 1971, Faber Music Limited. Reprinted from the *New Catholic Hymnal* by permission of Faber Music Limited. Music: © Herbert Howells
243 Text: © Malling Abbey, West Malling, Kent, England. Harm: © Redmund Shaw
244 Text: © 1974, Stanbrook Abbey Music, Worcester, England.
245 Text and Music: © Oxford University Press, London
246 Text: © Christian Conference of Asia. Melody: © Silliman Music Foundation Inc. Arr: © L. F. Bartlett
247 Text: © 1989, GIA Publications, Inc. Melody: © Vier-Türme-Verlag, Münsterschwartzach, Federal Republic of Germany. Acc: © 1987, Saint Meinrad Archabbey
248 Trans: © 1959, 1977 by The Order of St. Benedict, Inc., Collegeville, Minnesota 56321. Published by The Liturgical Press, Collegeville, Minnesota 56321. Harm: © 1958, by Willis Music Co.
249 Acc 1: © 1975, GIA Publications, Inc.
250 Trans: © 1989, GIA Publications, Inc.
251 Harm: © Oxford University Press, London
252 Trans: © 1989, GIA Publications, Inc. Music: © 1985, Hope Publishing Company, Carol Stream, IL 60188. All rights reserved. Used by permission.
254 Trans and Music: © 1989, GIA Publications, Inc.
255 Text: © 1980, Gracia Grindal, St. Paul, MN. Music: © 1984, M. Lee Suitor, Melville, NY
256 Text: © 1989, GIA Publications, Inc.
257 Text: © Abbey of Gethsemani
260 Text: © 1989, GIA Publications, Inc.
261 Text: © 1989, GIA Publications, Inc.
262 Text: © 1989, GIA Publications, Inc. Music: © 1981, by The Order of St. Benedict, Inc., Collegeville, Minnesota 56321 from *Swayed Pines Song Book.* Published by The Liturgical Press, Collegeville, Minnesota 56321
264 Trans: © 1989, GIA Publications, Inc. Music: © 1989, Hope Publishing Company, Carol Stream, IL 60188. All rights reserved. Used by permission.
265 Text: © 1980, Hope Publishing Company, Carol Stream, IL 60188. All rights reserved. Used by permission. Music: © Boekencentrum BV, The Hague, The Netherlands
266 Trans: © 1989, GIA Publications, Inc.
267 Text: © Search Press, Ltd.
268 Text and Music: © 1974, Hope Publishing Company, Carol Stream, IL 60188. All rights reserved. Used by permission.
270 Text: © 1989, GIA Publications, Inc. Music: © 1958, The Pilgrim Press, New York, NY, and used by permission.
271 Trans: © 1989, GIA Publications, Inc.
272 © 1989, GIA Publications, Inc. Harm 1: Oxford University Press, London
273 Text: © 1969, James Quinn, SJ. Reprinted by permission of Geoffrey Chapman, a division of Cassell Publishers Limited, Artillery House, Artillery Row, London SW1P 1RT.
274 Trans and Music: © 1989, GIA Publications, Inc.
275 Music: © Oxford University Press, London
277 Text: © 1989, GIA Publications, Inc.
278 Text: © Oxford University Press, London. Music: © 1983, Wilbur Held
279 Text: Revision © 1989, GIA Publications, Inc.

Acknowledgments/*continued*

280 Text: © 1989, GIA Publications, Inc. Music: © 1981, by The Order of St. Benedict, Inc., Collegeville, Minnesota 56321 from *Swayed Pines Song Book*. Published by The Liturgical Press, Collegeville, Minnesota 56321

281 Text and Music: © 1989, GIA Publications, Inc.

283 Trans: © 1989, GIA Publications, Inc.

284 Text: © 1982, Church Pension Fund. Music 1: © Oxford University Press, London. Harm 2: © Oxford University Press, London

285 Text: Adaptation © 1971, Faber Music Limited. Reprinted from the *New Catholic Hymnal* by permission of Faber Music Limited.

286 Text: © Oxford University Press, London

287 Tune: © Oxford University Press, London

289 Music: © Mrs. Craig S. Lang, Polzeath, North Cornwall, England

291 Text: © 1974, Stanbrook Abbey Music, Worcester, England. Music: © Sydney Watson

292 Text: From *Songs of Praise*, © Oxford University Press

293 Text: © 1974, Stanbrook Abbey Music, Worcester, England.

294 Text: © 1971, Faber Music Limited. Reprinted from the *New Catholic Hymnal* by permission of Faber Music Limited.

295 Text: © 1989, GIA Publications, Inc.

296 Text and Music: © 1989, GIA Publications, Inc.

297 Text: © 1974, Stanbrook Abbey Music, Worcester, England.

298 Text: © 1989, GIA Publications, Inc.

300 Acc: From *Resource Collection of Hymns and Service Music for the Liturgy*, © 1981, International Committee on English in the Liturgy, Inc. All rights reserved.

301 Music: From the *Australian Hymn Book*

304 Text: © 1989, GIA Publications, Inc. Music: From *Resource Collection of Hymns and Service Music for the Liturgy*, © 1981, International Committee on English in the Liturgy, Inc. All rights reserved.

305 Text and Music: © 1989, GIA Publications, Inc.

306 Text: © 1989, GIA Publications, Inc. Music: Oxford University Press, London

307 Text: © 1989, GIA Publications, Inc. Music: © Oxford University Press, London

308 Text: © 1989, GIA Publications, Inc.

309 Text: © 1989, GIA Publications, Inc.

310 Text: © 1989, GIA Publications, Inc. Melody 2: © Vier-Türme-Verlag, Münsterschwartzach, Federal Republic of Germany. Acc 2: © 1987, Saint Meinrad Archabbey

311 Text: © 1989, GIA Publications, Inc. Harm: © Oxford University Press, London.

312 Text: © 1989, GIA Publications, Inc.

313 Text: © 1989, GIA Publications, Inc.

314 Text: © 1989, GIA Publications, Inc.

316 Text: © 1989, GIA Publications, Inc.

Liturgical Index   319

Liturgical Index/*continued*

Liturgical Index/*continued*

Liturgical Index/*continued*

Index of Composers, Authors and Sources   320

Index of Composers, Authors and Sources/*continued*

Index of Composers, Authors and Sources/*continued*

Metrical Index of Tunes   321

Metrical Index of Tunes/*continued*

Metrical Index of Tunes/*continued*

322 Index of Tunes

Index of Tunes/*continued*

323   Index of First Lines and Common Titles

Index of First Lines and Common Titles/*continued*

Index of First Lines and Common Titles/*continued*